SACRED STONES

CELTIC CROSSES
and Their Timeless Call
for Soul Growth, Community,
& Connection with Nature

ANAMCHARA BOOKS
Vestal, New York 13850
www.AnamcharaBooks.com

Scripture quotations throughout this book are from the New Revised Standard Version Updated Edition (NRSVue). Copyright © 2021 National Council of Churches of Christ in the United States of America. Used by permission. All rights reserved worldwide.

Throughout this book, the publisher has replaced LORD with "Yahweh" wherever the original Hebrew word in scripture was YHWH, the proper name by which Divinity identified God-Self to Moses in the Book of Exodus. Because the name was considered too sacred to be spoken, YWHH or "Yahweh" was replaced with "Lord" in the Hebrew scriptures, a tradition that Christian translators continued. Bible scholars suggest the name has a range of literal meanings, including Life-Giver, Creator, the Ever-Living One, the I Am, Being, the One Who Brings into Being, the One Who Is Ever-Coming into Manifestation, and the One Who Is. Using this original sacred word is a wonderful way to move away from the patriarchal implications of "Lord."

Illustration and interior design by Micaela Grace.

Print ISBN: 978-1-62524-923-4
eBook ISBN: 978-1-62524-924-1

SACRED STONES

CELTIC CROSSES
and Their Timeless Call
for Soul Growth, Community,
& Connection with Nature

KENNETH MCINTOSH

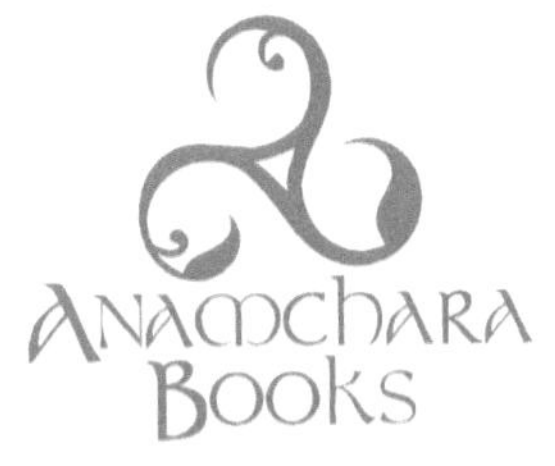

CONTENTS

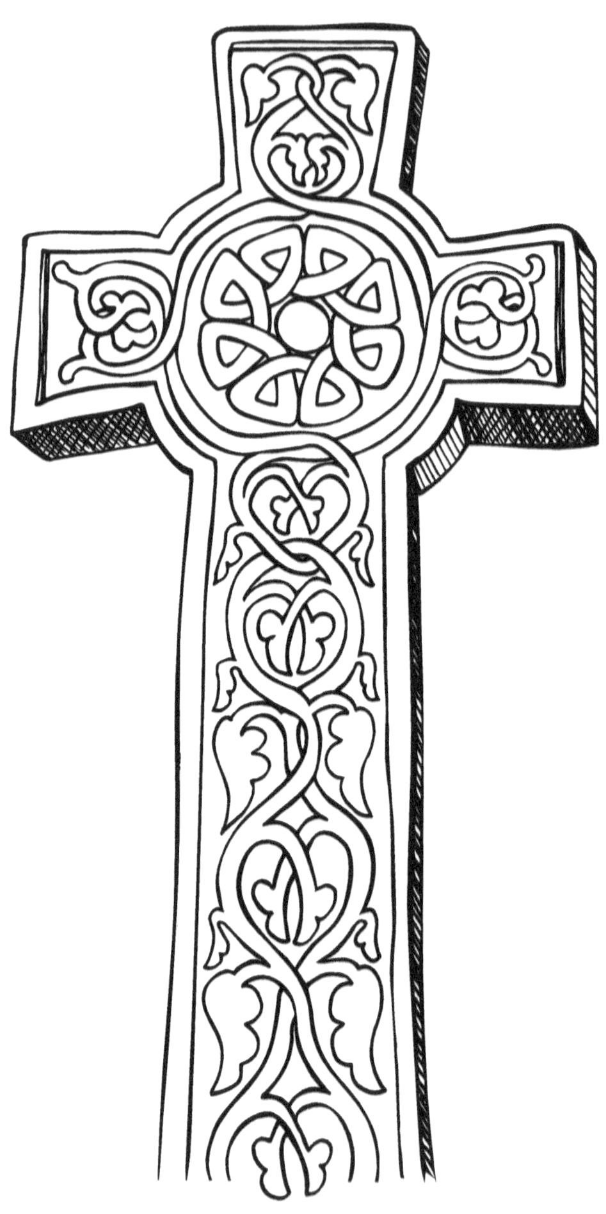

Drawing is based on the Keil Cross at Morvern.

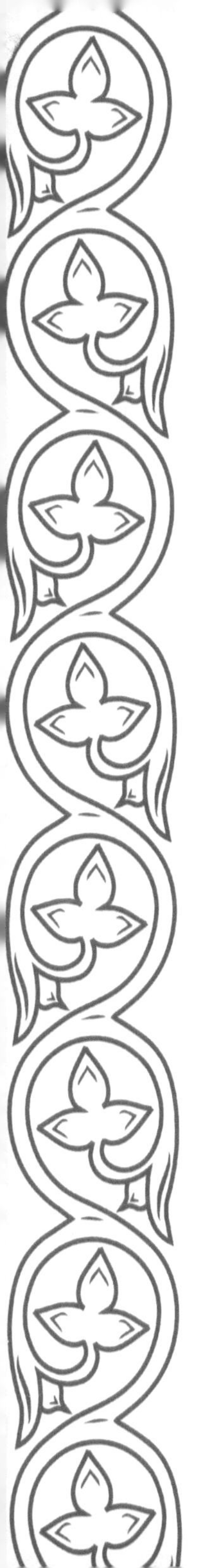

Beginning
and Welcome

*(some important things
to know about this book)*

"**H**ey! Cool! I have a cross like that!"

Strolling in a New York greenspace, I came upon a busker strumming a worn guitar, dressed all in black, his head crowned with a stovepipe hat. He grinned and pointed at a wheel cross on a necklace over his chest. It was indeed a likeness of the same Celtic cross that I wore.

I wasn't surprised by this busker's enthusiasm for his pendant; the symbol of the Celtic cross is ubiquitous. From the Council of Argyll and Bute (a Scottish district) to the vigilante movie *Boondock Saints*, from the official logo of the Presbyterian Church USA to the logo for a kilt maker, the wheeled cross has become an all-around symbol of . . . well . . . lots of things. A tattoo shop I saw recently advertises a Celtic cross tattoo design as a "pagan, druid, goth, metal, wicca cross." How's that for covering all the bases?

The popularity of the Celtic cross is obvious. And yet, of the thousands of people who wear some form of this emblem, most have little understanding of the cross's actual history or meaning. Even the most obvious question—*Why do these crosses have a ring around the center?*—defies easy explanation. If you search the internet, you'll find various answers, as well as much "information" about the Celtic cross, most of which is spurious.

Since childhood, I've owned a wall plaque of an ancient Irish cross, and I've often pondered its meaning. The first time I came into the presence of a medieval high cross, my heart leapt to see the familiar image in its "natural setting."

At the time, my wife and I were in Lochaline on the Morvern Peninsula of Scotland, waiting for the ferry to cross over to Mull and then on to the fabled island of Iona. A sign near the car park pointed to nearby Kiel Church, founded by Saint Columba, so we dashed up to have a look at the site. In the churchyard, on a promontory looking out over the ocean, stood the Keil Cross. The grey stone, half again my height, was weathered and lichen-covered. Delicate vine designs with a star pattern decorated the center, and two serpents coiled on its base.

That cross grabbed a little bit of my soul. I realized then and there that these ancient stone monuments hold messages for us today. Those messages would take years to unfold in my mind, however.

Over many subsequent trips, I've gathered photos and knowledge of the ancient stone crosses. I believe I've now answered some of the questions they pose—and found more questions still unanswered. In all this travel and research, I've become still more convinced that these ancient crosses have meaning to share.

MEDIEVAL SACRED ART

Back in the Early Middle Ages, people took for granted that sacred art would communicate to its onlookers. You might be thinking, *Well, of course. Sacred art still communicates messages to viewers,* but you might be surprised to learn how literally medieval folk understood the concept of artwork communication. Wendy A. Stein, a researcher at the Cloisters, Metropolitan Museum of Art in New York City, says, "*Art in the Middle Ages had agency*; as a conduit to the sacred person represented, it was deemed able not only to listen to a supplicant's prayers but also to win battles and cure illnesses. As a stand-in for its prototype in heaven, *an image . . . would be treated as a person in its own right.*"[1]

That may be a bit of a mental stretch for some of us in the twenty-first century, but let's look at Stein's words more closely: If the ancient crosses do indeed convey messages, *who* speaks through them? Who is the messenger? We can consider three possibilities.

First, of course, is *the artist.* No one will argue that a painter, sculptor, filmmaker, or composer desires to convey ideas to their audiences. The individuals who fashioned the high crosses surely intended to convey messages to all people who would gaze at their work in the future.

The cross artists (often a small team working together) also intended their work to impart messages representative of their *faith communities.* Art scholars have documented various clues that indicate how rulers, monastery leaders, and honored teachers provided input into these messages.

While both these are valid ways to understand the messenger behind Celtic crosses, I choose to believe in something even larger. (Feel free to disagree with me. You'll still benefit from reading this book.) This third belief is what impelled me to labor for eighteen months writing this book. I believe the living Spirit of the Universal Christ still speaks through these objects that human hands formed.

People of the Early Middle Ages, across the expanse of Christendom, placed representations of the cross "on a level with the Holy Scriptures . . . as one of the forms of revelation and knowledge of God. . . . Each is the reflection of a higher world, each the Symbol of *the Spirit contained within them*, each transmits teaching and expresses the grace given to the life of the church."[2] Revelations imparted by ancient Celtic crosses speak with Christ's compassionate voice, imparting healing, encouragement, joy, and God's heartfelt affection. They assist the process of our transformation into the Divine nature.[3]

SOME DEFINITIONS

With that said, before we dive in further, I want to explain a few of the terms used in this book, beginning with the word *Celtic*. Centuries before the time of Christ, the ancient Greeks encountered tribes in Europe they called *Keltoi*. Thousands of years later, eighteenth-century antiquarians revived the term *Celtic* to refer to people living in Brittany, Cornwall, Ireland, the Isle of Man, Scotland, and Wales (and some lists add Galicia, Spain, as a seventh Celtic nation). The inhabitants of these Celtic regions share related ancestral languages. While modern-day scholars debate the usefulness of the term *Celtic*, it persists in common usage (usually surrounded by a magical haze that does little to define the term except imply that it belongs in the same category as mythical images such as dragons and unicorns).

In this book, when I speak of *Celtic crosses*, I'm referring to those constructed during the Early Middle Ages (between 400 and 1100) in the Celtic nations, as defined in the paragraph above. These stone crosses usually have a circle around the cross, often with carved patterns adorning their surfaces. I also use the terms *circle cross*, *wheel cross*, and *encircled cross*.

READING THIS BOOK

Long before the faith of Christ reached their lands, Celtic people loved the number three, carving triskeles (three-headed swirls) on Stone-Age monuments. Likewise, each chapter of this book follows a *three-fold pattern*: First, the chapter opens with an "Encounter" section that offers a narrative, either my lived experience or a fictional vignette. "Deepening" comes next, consisting of historical or artistic information. Finally, the "Application" section of each chapter shares some thoughts and spiritual practices for your personal transformation. You may read the chapters in any order.

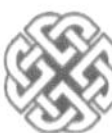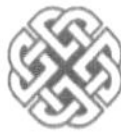

When the street musician showed me his cross, I smiled back and asked him, "What does it mean to you?"

He told me, "It's like the stuff I'm into."

Apparently, that was the Goth metal music scene. I chatted with him for a few minutes and put a donation in the open guitar case.

I expect the Celtic cross might also connect with "stuff you're into." Whether that is Celtic mythology, the history of the Isles, family heritage, or following the Christ-way, something in this work will interest you. People drawn to the Celtic forms of Christian faith and practice may find an even richer boon: I believe a survey of the ancient high crosses, paying heed to the communications hidden in their forms, can yield a complete guide to the whole domain of Celtic Christian spirituality.

In any case, I hope that reading this book will not only bring you pleasure and knowledge but also something more valuable—wisdom and the warming of your heart.

CARMINA GADELICA[4]

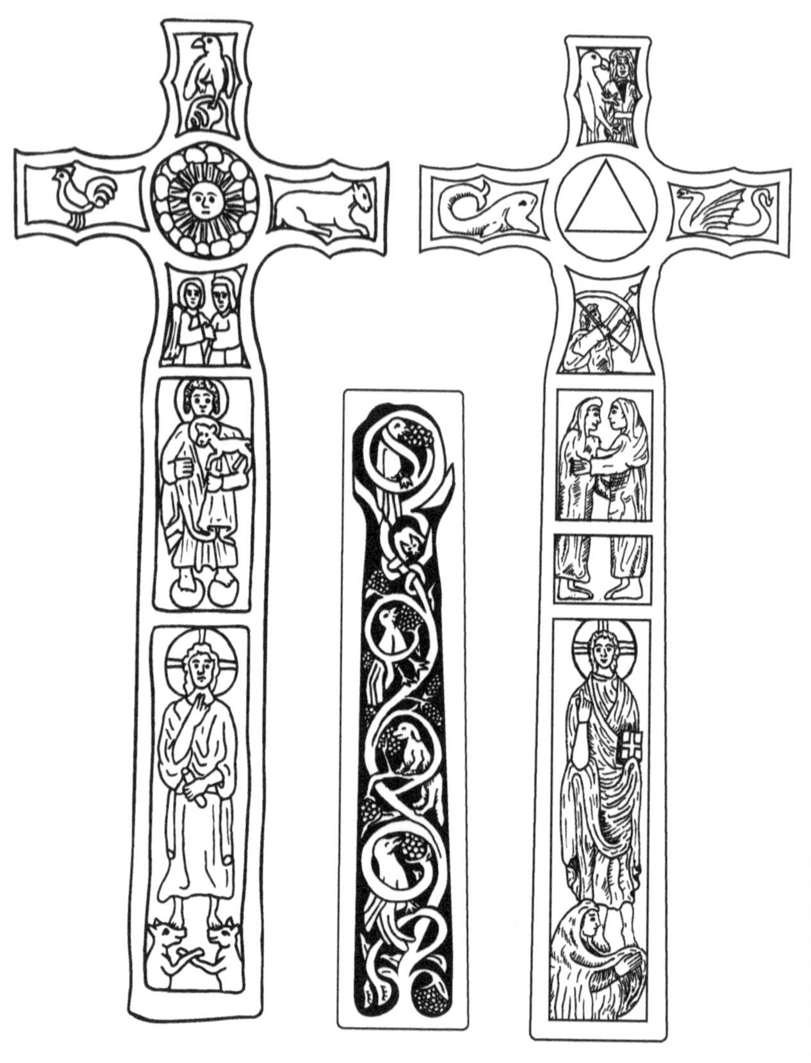

*The Ruthwell Cross is an impressive example of
early medieval Celtic and Anglo-Saxon art.*

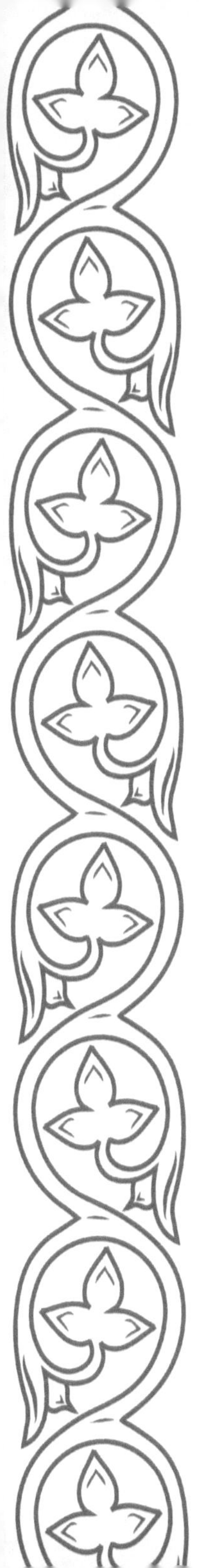

CHAPTER 1

The Still-Speaking Rood

Then shall the trees of the forest
sing for joy before Yahweh.

1 CHRONICLES 16:33

I nevertheless beheld sorrowing the Savior's tree
until I heard it utter words, begin to speak.

THE DREAM OF THE ROOD[5]

ENCOUNTER

1642: Ruthwell, Scotland

"I won't do it, I cannot. It is blasphemy dressed up as piety."

As the Reverend Gavin Young spoke, his hand shook, making the awful letter it held tremble as well. Unconsciously, his other hand pulled at his clerical collar as if it were choking him. He stood in the nave of his church and gazed up at what he knew was the most important monument of early Christianity in Scotland or England. "For five centuries it's stood protected here in our kirk! What madness has gripped these men?"

His wife Jeannie, standing beside him, put a comforting hand on his back and gently pulled the letter from his grasp. She read aloud:

Reverend Young,

It has come to the attention of this assembly, by the testimony of reliable and devout men, that the popish travesty stands still in the centre of Ruthwell Kirk. Ye know well the unanimous decision of this holy assembly, declared now two years past, that idolatrous monuments, made by false and popish hands, bearing images of Christ, Mary, or saints departed, must be cast down, demolished, and destroyed. As ye have failed to cleanse the House of God in your parish of these defilements, we are of holy necessity forced to act. Soon we shall send a venerable and sober emissary, who will expect to see the idol cast down and destroyed. If any remnant remains standing in the holy place, we will know ye to be unsuited for the sacred ordination to which ye have been called.

"Ah, Gavin, what will you do?" Jeannie asked.

"I'll not let them in, I'll bar the door."

"Nay, my love." She took a moment to think and then said, "You cannot defy all the weighty men of the assembly in Aberdeen. They will only appoint a new minister to this parish, and that one will do their bidding. And what then would we do? Our storehouse is empty, and you have no other skills. What would become of us?"

Reverend Young sank to his knees and put his head in his hands. Jeannie spoke sooth, but doing this thing was unthinkable.

How could it be that the presbytery elders saw only heresy on the sides of the great cross? Over the years of his ministry, Young had caressed the intricate vine patterns and ancient runes while dreaming of the earliest Christ-followers in this land who performed this miracle of artwork and masonry. The cross itself preached; it told the stories of the Gospels to people who lacked the ability to read God's Word for themselves. In the time of the Crusades, local workers had built this church to protect the great cross. Young knew in his heart that over the centuries, as eyes gazed upward at the ancient rood, their hearts had likewise lifted in adoration of Christ.

"There may be a way," Jeannie whispered, crouching beside him, "to see that all is not lost."

He turned to her, his eyebrows raised. "What are you plotting, my dear?"

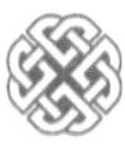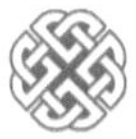

The following week, the Ruthwell congregation met many times. None of the meetings were formally announced, but members came together in small gatherings at the manse or in their cottages. Finally, farmers and laborers brought their tools to the church, and workers hastily erected a wooden scaffolding around the great stone cross.

A week after the arrival of the dolorous letter, the good minister again stood within the sacred building, his wife at his side, along with his children and a small representation of the congregation. Brawny men with heavy hammers in their hands stood on the scaffolding beside the arms of the cross.

A call came down from the towering framework: "We are ready, Reverend."

The minister hesitated. His wife squeezed his hand to reassure him.

"Very well, Mister McKenzie, now be sure that your hammers and chisels go straight to those chalk marks I showed you. And when you hear the stone of the crossbars start to creak, be ready with the hoist so they come down gently."

"Aye, Reverend, we know our task!"

The sharp sound of hammer blows echoed from the walls of the nave.

 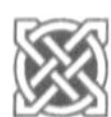 

Three weeks later, the messenger from Aberdeen arrived. He wore a black jacket and hat, like the city man he was. In an expressionless tone, he demanded entry into the church. Young walked him into the building and pointed to the stones and dirt that covered the hole where the cross had once stood.

"Honored sir, here"—the reverend produced a satchel of folded leather and opened it so the messenger could see the paper inside—"is a document notarized by a dozen honest men of this village, each sworn with their hand on Holy Scripture and in the presence of a judge, who declare that the ancient stone crucifix has been broken, cast down, and buried, to no more cause trouble for God's people in this place."

The messenger read the letter, glanced at the signatures, and looked for a long minute at the clumped earth in the church. "Very well, Reverend Young, the assembly of learned and devout men thanks you." And with that, he departed.

The minister walked slowly back to the manse, removed his boots at the entrance, and sat at the little table beside the inglenook. Jeannie set before him a dram of their best whisky, which she kept back in a cupboard for special occasions.

"It's all done then, Gavin?"

"Aye."

"You told him the cross is broken, cast down, and duly buried from sight, as the dour men have demanded?"

He nodded.

"And you spoke nothing but God's own truth, for you did by the letter what they asked." She ran a hand through his hair, and a sly smile crossed her lips. "But ye did not tell that man how you marked out the lines for the cross's disassembly, so that each section would carefully be preserved?"

"I did not."

"And you did not tell him how carefully each bit of the rood was lowered to the ground, so the ancient stone be not crumbled?"

He chuckled and shook his head.

"So he knows not that each bit is wrapped and covered and buried carefully, and all this recorded in a letter with instructions for the minister after you, so the cross may be reassembled in a more sensible age?"

"Please, let it be so," her husband whispered, "in the time of God's choosing,"

March 2012: Ruthwell, Scotland

"Hey! Stop! Turn around!" I cried.

My wife was driving the little Vauxhall we'd rented, and we were headed to see the town of Dumfries. From the corner of my eye, I had just caught sight of a sign: RUTHWELL CROSS. I had read about this cross, but I hadn't realized it would be right on our route.

We turned around and parked beside an old church. Raspy cries from rooks in a nearby tree echoed among the lichen-covered gravestones that lay in the grass around the church. Would the church be open?

It was! We stepped into the sanctuary, alone except for the ancient cross itself, which was a palpable and formidable presence. It was bigger than I had imagined it would be—three times my six-foot height—and more beautiful than pictures had portrayed.

Reading a conveniently placed booklet, we identified the themes portrayed in separate panels on the sides of the great stone edifice: On one face of the cross, we saw Jesus' crucifixion, then a scene of him healing, then Mary Magdalene washing the Savior's feet; on the other face were Egyptian saints Paul and Anthony, as well as Jesus glorified with book and halo. On the narrower sides of the cross were tanglewoods of vines and birds.

DEEPENING

The Dream of the Rood

While the artwork on the Ruthwell Cross is impressive, there is something even more unique about this particular high cross: Runic letters cover the frames around the sculptures. The words inscribed there are an excerpt from the long Anglo-Saxon poem *The Dream of the Rood*, similar in age to the more famous tale of *Beowulf.* The inscription makes the Ruthwell Cross literally a message from the past.

The Dream of the Rood recounts the story of a talking cross (*rood* was the Old English word for the instrument of Jesus' death). This living cross speaks of its previous life as a tree and recounts how the Romans felled it to serve as the site of Christ's sacrifice. The words inscribed on the Ruthwell Cross tell how "the young hero that was God almighty ascended the wretched gallows." The rood then describes how it shared the same suffering as the crucified Savior: Evil men "pierced me with dark nails, mocked us both together." After Jesus' body was removed from the rood, then he "rested there awhile, weary after the great war." Men buried the cross, but later, it rose up from its grave to be honored as a "great beacon" of hope.

The story told by the talking rood—how, like Christ, it died, lay buried, then rose—seems amazingly appropriate for the Ruthwell Cross itself. Although my account is fictional, in 1642, when the Church of Scotland ordered the destruction of the "popish" cross, the minister of the church was in fact so reluctant to destroy it that he dismantled it, then buried the cross in portions.[6] Centuries later, one of his successors exhumed the cross, reassembled it, and placed it in the center of a newly constructed church home. The story of the shamed and reglorified Ruthwell Cross brings to mind Jesus' words to his detractors in the Gospel of Luke: Despite human attempts to silence the Good News, the stones themselves will shout Christ's message of love.[7]

Standing in the Ruthwell Church, I felt a sense of vibrancy and timelessness as I gazed at the cross. In defiance of the grey skies outside the kirk, in defiance of time and human attempts to destroy it, this rood still spoke, proclaiming the resilience of faith and love.

Messages in Stone

Oliver Crilly, Irish priest and scholar, describes one of the ancient stone crosses as "an icon which persists in the landscape of faith, like a gateway leading to the rich traditions of the early Irish Church."[8] I have had similar impressions throughout the Celtic nations. In addition to the Ruthwell Cross, the great and revered crosses of Iona Abbey, the Cross of the Scriptures in Clonmacnoise, Ireland, and many others seemed to speak to me, as if they yearned to share life-affirming truths.

The ancient crosses hold within them mysteries and revelations; locked within their mineral core are expressions of "the manifold wisdom of God."[9] John Scotus Eriugena—a renowned ninth-century Irish theologian—wrote that each passage of the Bible holds innumerable meanings, like the multicolored splendors of a peacock's tail feathers[10]—and just as Anglo-Celtic Christians celebrated the immensity of meaning in each portion of the Bible, they also expressed many levels of meaning in their stone crosses. These crosses still embody layers of truth for today.

Does it seem incredible that a cross, an inert object, should speak? To us jaded modern folk, the idea of a talking cross may seem as laughable—and unlikely—as Jesus' face appearing on a tortilla. Yet over the long span of Christian history, the communicating cross made sense to people of faith.

Jesus' original followers had a deep sense of bafflement regarding the way their master died. The Romans intended the cross to both torture and humiliate the one crucified—so how could the One exalted to sit at God's right hand die so horribly? Eventually, Jesus' followers came to understand that "in Christ, God was reconciling the world to himself."[11] Over the next two thousand years, Christians would continue to work out exactly *how* the crucifixion accomplished this great redemption, but all agreed that it *did*. They enshrined a Roman torture device as the nexus point of humanity's deliverance.

The grisly reality of crucifixion was still a real experience in the Roman Empire during the first, second, and third centuries,[12] which is most likely why depictions of the cross do not appear in Christian art until several centuries after Christ's death and resurrection. However, we find the idea of the talking cross in the second-century apocryphal writing called *The Gospel of Peter*. This early-Christian document tells how on the morning of Christ's resurrection, two angels lifted an enormous cross extending from the empty tomb up into heaven. A voice from heaven cries out, "Have you preached to those who sleep?" and the cross itself replies, "Yes!" (See chapter 10 of this book to discover the meaning of this question and its answer.) Centuries later, Irish sculptors depicted this story of the talking cross on their stone crosses.[13]

Saint Francis's Talking Cross

In the twenty-first century, Assisi, Italy, still seems imbued with the sanctity and sacredness of its most famous citizen. Ochre-tinted stone dwellings from the twelfth and thirteenth centuries lean over winding narrow streets, much as they did in Francis's time (1182–1226). The places of his birth, baptism, and childhood home can still be seen today. Franciscan friars and Sisters of Saint Clare walk about the city, singing God's praises in its churches. Known as "the most perfect imitation of Christ," Francis himself continues to influence Christians around the world who care for the poor, for peace, and for the environment.

One of the most famous tales of a talking cross concerns Francis of Assisi. The church of Santa Chiara is a tall and stately edifice, with a smaller nave that stands beside the larger main sanctuary, sheltering the cross that spoke to Francis and changed the course of Western history.

A Franciscan priest explains how a talking cross brought about Francis's spiritual conversion:

> The San Damiano cross . . . hung in the abandoned chapel near Assisi. While still in his early 20s and seeking his place in the world, Francis of Assisi was praying before this cross when he heard the voice of God commanding him to "rebuild my church." All Franciscans cherish this cross as the symbol of their mission from God.[14]

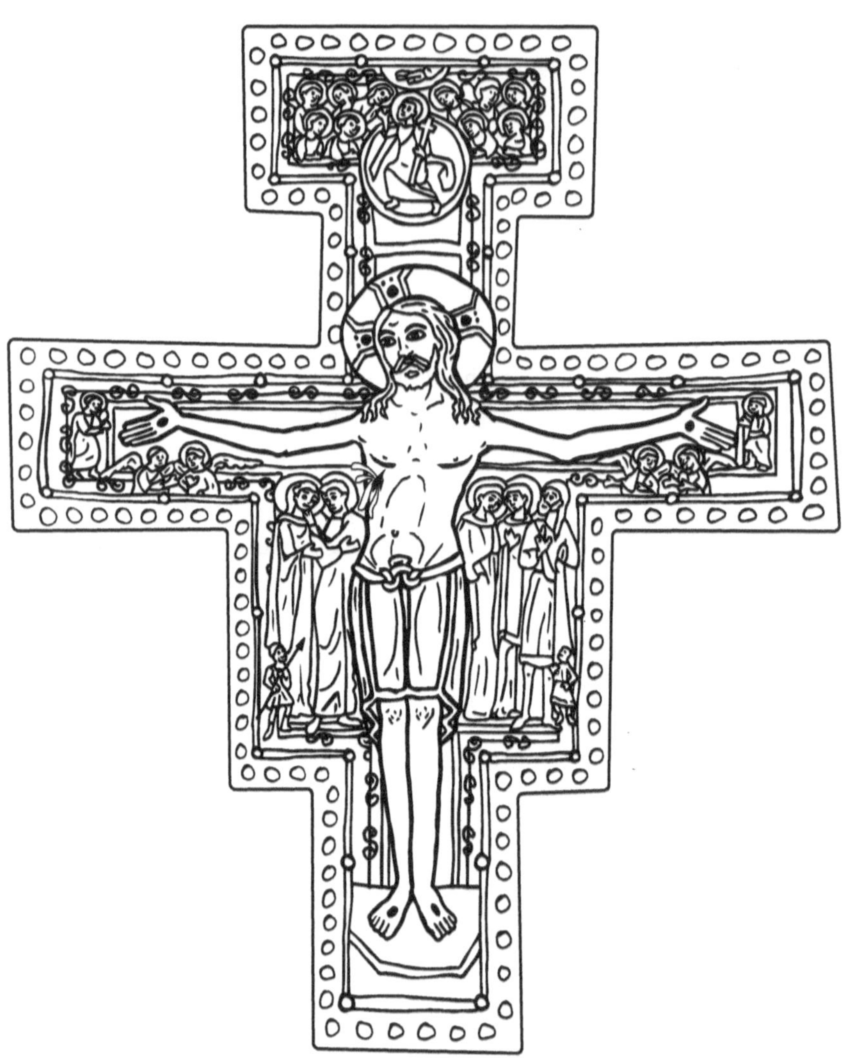

*Saint Francis of Assisi heard
the San Damiano Crucifix speak to him,
calling him to rebuild God's church.*

After Saint Clare's death and entombment, the San Damiano cross was moved to its present location in Santa Chiara.

When I visited Santa Chiara, as I waited for Sisters of St. Clair to sing Compline, I sat gazing at the very cross that spoke to Francis. Softening my gaze a little (beholding the cross as much with my heart as with my ocular vision), the form of Christ seemed to take on three-dimensional form. As Christ's eyes gazed into mine, I felt a deep tenderness. Unlike Francis, I received no audible command—and yet this ancient piece of wood, so carefully rendered by Byzantine artists of the Early Middle Ages, still communicated Christ's compassion to my soul.

Icons

Any cross can serve as an *icon*. As Wendy Stein of the Metropolitan Museum of Art explains, in the Middle Ages, "An object depicting a sacred scene had an active role in religious practice . . . to connect the worshiper to heaven."[15] Iconic objects are vessels of God's power, means of Divine grace. Christians in the Orthodox Church see icons as "windows" that enable worshipers to enter, via contemplation, the realm of God, the saints, and the angels. As such, they can inspire, guide, protect, or heal people in their immediate presence. They are instruments of God's work on Earth.

To use a popular spiritual expression, each icon is a "thin place" where the curtain between visible and invisible realms draws

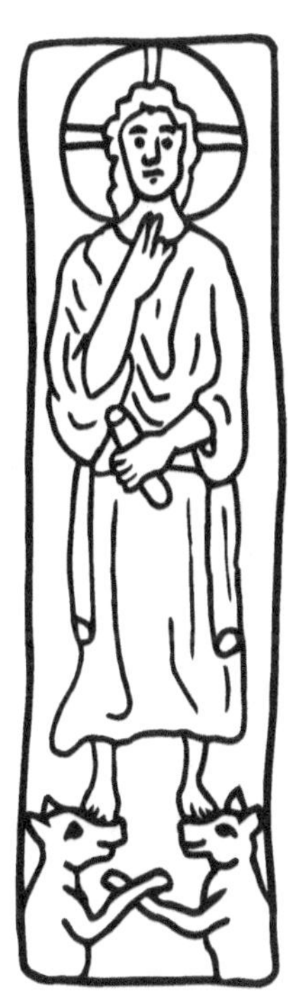

The Ruthwell Cross sculpture of Christ treading on wild beasts is also a common motif in Eastern and Continental icons created around the same time.

back. Such art, in the words of Irish artist Patrick Pye, "does not tell us what to believe, it tells us what it feels like to believe."[16]

If you are of Orthodox or Roman Catholic faith, this might make easy sense for you. There may be holy icons in the churches where you worship, and sacred objects such as a rosary or a home shrine may have been part of your devotional life since childhood. The power of sacred objects is an instinctive part of your faith.

For Protestant readers, however, or those unfamiliar with the Christian faith, attributing holy power to inanimate objects may be a more challenging concept to wrap your head around. Still, the investment of agency into physical objects seems an instinctive part of human thinking; spiritual practices inevitably lean toward embodiment of some kind. Today's "spiritual but not religious" practitioners, for example, affirm the healing powers of incense, crystals, dream catchers, and other ritual objects. Devotees of twenty-first-century mythic worlds—such as the Star Wars or Marvel Comics universe—also collect likenesses of the power-objects of their legends (from light sabers to Thor's hammer).

As the existential challenges to humanity mount, so does the importance of God's union with the material world. Franciscan Father Richard Rohr, in his widely read book *The Universal Christ*, brings together the scriptures of the Christian faith, the emerging discoveries of physics, and the perennial wisdom of spiritual traditions to explain how "everything visible, without exception, is the outpouring of God."[17]

Spiritual masters of the Early Middle Ages and of our own time agree that God can be discerned in objects, so shouldn't this be especially true of the cross, Christianity's symbol for the very heart of God's love for humankind?

The "Voice" of Celtic Crosses

The ancient high crosses are a unique development in the history of sacred objects. Throughout the Celtic nations and the British Isles, over the course of five centuries, artists erected hundreds of stone crosses, many of which endure today. These crosses were part of the larger belief in the power of sacred icons, yet they make their own unique contributions. They speak more loudly, more strongly, and from a greater height than other holy vessels.

The stone crosses remind us of what the psalmist declares about the heavens:

> Day to day pours forth speech, and night to night declares knowledge. There is no speech, nor are there words; their voice is not heard; yet their voice goes out through all the earth, and their words to the end of the world.[18]

Many times, I have experienced this "voice" that "declares knowledge" without audible words. Because it is the still-speaking voice of Christ—the Word, the Divine Logos—it comes to us not merely for our growth in knowledge; as the Bible says, "Knowledge puffs up, but love builds up."[19] The ancient crosses convey meaning for us to experience for ourselves, to *live*, for as the apostle Paul reminds us, "the only thing that counts is faith working through love."[20]

APPLICATIONS FOR TODAY

Paying Attention

In the well-preserved monastery of Saint Kevin, in Glendalough Ireland, Marsha and I watched a Dublin tour bus disembark. We heard the tour guide say, "Okay, this was an ancient monastery.

Be back on the bus in fifteen minutes." And back the tourists came after only a few minutes. I suspect they had gained nothing more than a few quick photos and a stop at the loo. By contrast, Marsha and I spent two days around that sacred enclosure (which includes medieval high crosses), drinking it all in. Even then, mere days seemed too little time to absorb the meaning of the site.

If we wish to learn the meaning of the Celtic cross, we need to pay attention. *Looking* at an object is not the same as *seeing* it. When we see anything deeply, we focus our attention, our energy, on that object. In our interactions with other humans, we know if we are actually *seeing* them or merely casting a distracted glance their way. When we look at people with loving attention, they are more likely to reciprocate by revealing more of themselves, enriching both parties in a mutually trusting relationship. The time-honored stone monuments respond the same way to loving attention. If we look long and hard at one, focusing on it, it will gradually reveal its treasures.

A Cross That Speaks to You

As you read this book and see the many illustrations, I invite you to select a cross and commit to a relationship with that. Ideally, you should visit it in person, but your goal is to see *beyond* the object—or, to put it another way, your perception of a physical cross can give you access to spiritual truths.

If you happen to live near one of the ancient Celtic crosses, either in a churchyard, outdoor enclosure, or in a museum, then you are fortunate indeed. Your practice of cross-gazing may involve simply slipping on your waterproof and wellies for a stroll. When you visit, be sure to protect and honor these time-touched survivors from the past; don't handle the stone surface and respect the space around the cross.

For those of us living outside of Cornwall, Wales, Ireland, Scotland, or Northern England, forming a relationship with a cross may require a bit more creativity. The internet has multiple images of the ancient crosses, though, and books have glossy photographs of them. (These unfortunately tend to be expensive—but that is why public libraries exist.)

Artistic reproductions of many high crosses, done in clay, bronze, or plastic compounds, are also available online. Small-workshop artists produce many of these, and you will bless them with your purchase. You can then incorporate the cross into your own home devotional space.

YOUR PERSONAL CROSS

Are you more intrigued by crosses from your own culture— or from another culture? What speaks most clearly to your heart and mind—a turquoise-embellished yucca wood cross from the Southwestern United States or an intricate Ethiopian bronze-cast cross? A cross of blue-glazed Portuguese porcelain or a brightly painted cross from Central America? Perhaps an olive wood cross from Jerusalem? If you can find an affordable version, consider installing it in your home where you can form a daily relationship with it. (And if the actual cross isn't available, find a high-quality photograph to frame and post on a wall.)

Outside the Anglo-Celtic nations, many beautiful examples of Victorian or modern Celtic crosses also stand in cemeteries, churchyards, and church buildings. For example, in Flagstaff, Arizona, the Episcopal Church of the Epiphany has an extraordinary Celtic cross wrought in iron overlooking the church's equally delightful labyrinth; in Mount Hope Cemetery in Rochester, New York, an elaborate and well-executed stone memorial cross stands over a grave. You might find that these more modern crosses also have a "voice"!

And you don't need to limit yourself to a Celtic wheel-shaped cross. The so-called Celtic crosses of the Early Middle Ages actually combined motifs from Africa, the Middle East, the Mediterranean, Eastern Europe, Italy, and Scandinavia with the region's indigenous motifs; they were global-fusion artworks. If you research the crosses created in these regions, you may find one that "speaks" to you.

USING A CROSS AS A CONTEMPLATION OBJECT

Either sit in the physical presence of a cross, hold a replica, or gaze at a picture of it. Focusing on the cross will help you drift into contemplation; notice its color, composition, material, geometry, patterns, portrayals, symbolism, and history. Sit still with it the way you'd sit in the quiet presence of a friend. Be willing to hear anything it has to say to you—and be equally willing to simply sit in silence.

Can you hear the voice of love speaking to you from the cross?

With the appearance of a particular cross in your mind's eye, regard it as a portal. Christ himself awaits you on the other side, longing for your company.

The cross carries the voice of the Divine, the One who intimately formed you in the womb, who has walked beside you throughout your life, feeling your joys and hurts—the One who asks for nothing except the joy of your affection.

> *The cross of Christ at my sitting.*
> *The cross of Christ at my lying.*
> *The cross of Christ all my strength,*
> *until we reach the King of heaven.*
> *The cross of Christ over my community.*
> *The cross of Christ over my church.*
> *Until the day I die,*
> *before returning to the earth,*
> *I shall trace on myself*
> *the cross of Christ upon this face.*
> THE LORICA OF MUGRON[21]

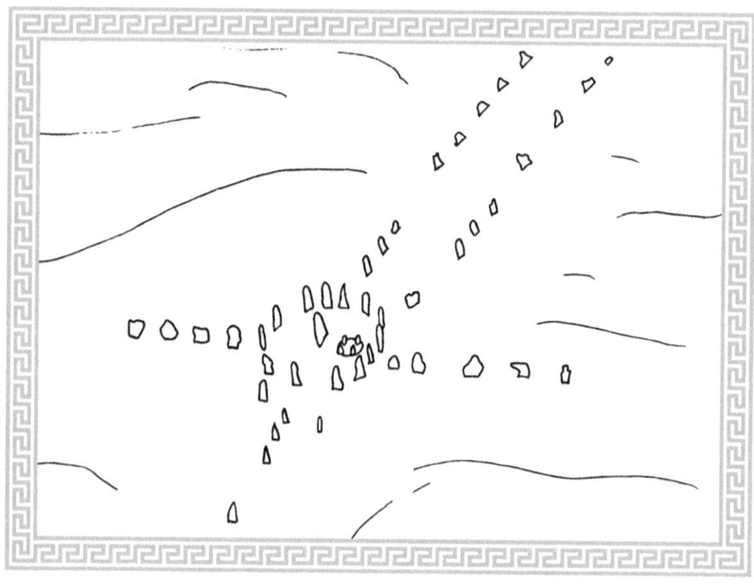

From the air, the cross shape of the Callanish stone circle is clearly visible.

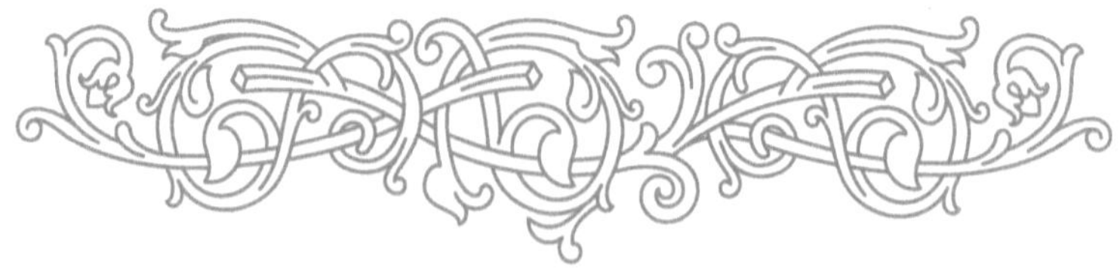

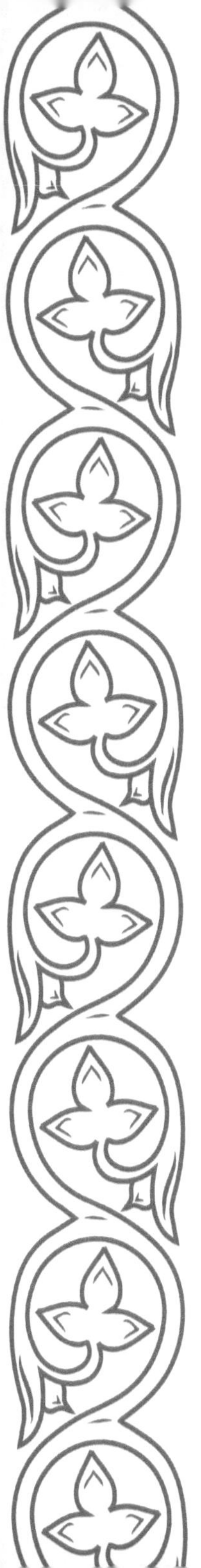

CHAPTER 2

The Stones Cry Out

Some of the Pharisees in the crowd said to him,
"Teacher, order your disciples to stop."
He answered, "I tell you, if these were silent,
the stones would shout out."

LUKE 19:39–40

I bind unto myself today the stable earth . . .
the old eternal rocks.

FROM A LORICA PRAYER OFTEN
ATTRIBUTED TO SAINT PATRICK

ENCOUNTER

In the time now known as 2,800 BCE:
On the island now known as Lewis, in
the Outer Hebrides of Scotland

Master Stone-Wielder Altann clenched his fists. The future prosperity of all the tribes on the island relied on a successful outcome to this day's work. The erection of the Skystone would be evidence of the Celestial Powers' favor upon the land, but if it shattered, that would surely betoken their curse.

Men grunted, struggling under the weight of the ropes, and swore oaths under their breath. Teams of oxen strained forward. They were putting too much pressure on the scaffolding; Altann could see the leather cords starting to pull loose from the elm pylons. "Whoa!" he shouted. "Crew on the seaward ropes, slow down!"

For the greater part of the past three temperate seasons, they had hewn the Skystone, three times the height of a human, from the rock surface around it. The workers knew the holy importance of their work, and their desire to renew the land drove them onward, even as their hands numbed and muscles tore. They pounded the unyielding stone into the shape ordained by their priests, for the forests were dying, and the crops stunted. The energy of the Sky World had to be drawn down into the Earth for the soil to pour forth abundance again. No effort was too great to achieve this sacred union.

After the stone workers completed their work at the quarry, teams of oxen had pulled the stone over log rollers on its journey to its permanent setting. Now, atop a promontory overlooking the East Inlet from the sea, the great slab was poised in its upward course, suspended between land and sky, halfway upright. Never had anyone attempted such a great feat of balanced forces: the muscles of men and beasts, the strength of tightly braided flax ropes and cords made from hide, and the log scaffolding made from just the right combination of soft and hard woods. Each element had to be counterforced just so. If a man slipped, if a cord broke, if the bed of stones at the monolith's base should give way, then the Skystone would crash into pieces.

"Great Sun, Luminous Moon, Bright Stars, and Deep Waters, bless us with favor," chanted the chief priest Narlor, on his knees beside Altann. Stag horns and a golden circlet bedecked the holy man's head, eagle feathers covered his shoulders, and woad darkened his face. To

Altann and the other villagers, Narlor seemed more than human; he was the voice of the elements.

Now, every man, woman, and child from all the clans on the isle had gathered around to see this wonder put in place. "Make that lead ox pull harder!" Altann's voice boomed. "The stone is leaning westward. It has to straighten before it drops into position."

And then . . . this was the moment. The crowd hushed; everyone held their breath as the monolith aimed upward, straightened, and then, with an earth-shaking boom, slammed down into the pit that would hold it upright.

"Let go of the ropes," Altann commanded. The cords slackened, fell away—and the Skystone pointed straight up toward the heavens, immovable as the hills.

"The Sky Lords and Sea Powers favor us!" the high priest exclaimed. At his words, a troop of musicians began pounding on hide drums and blowing horns, while the women of the gathered clans broke out in ululations. Altann felt his wife's gleeful embrace as he stared up at the point where the Skystone seemed to touch the Sun.

This was the proudest moment of his life; countless days of hard work and skillful management had paid off. Together, he and his men had erected something never before seen. Yet he knew this was only the beginning.

Altann knew that someday—generations hence—his descendants would complete a great circle of tall stones around the Skystone. Then four processional rows, also on a grand scale, would mark the progress and reversals of the celestial bodies. The powers of earth, water, and sky would join into a grand cosmic dance. The elements' blessings would flow onto the isle, ensuring full bellies and fruitful loins.

Altann returned his wife's embrace as he smiled down at their small daughter. Surely, he was the most fortunate of mortals, having begun the great work of uniting Heaven and Earth in this place.

DEEPENING

Neolithic Monuments

Callanish (also spelled *Calanais*) on the Isle of Lewis, part of the Outer Hebrides Islands in the North of Scotland, has been called the "Stonehenge of the North," and it may be the oldest stone monument in the British Isles. Its configuration is unique. Aubrey Burl, the twentieth century's foremost scholar of prehistoric stone monuments, explains: "Three rows of stones and an avenue lead up to the ring *like the arms of a buckled Celtic cross.*"[22] The circle-cross layout can be hard to discern from the ground level; I've spoken to people who visited the site in person and didn't recognize the shape. But seen from the sky, the image of a Celtic cross is clear.

What did that encircled cruciform design mean to the Stone Age people who constructed the vast pattern almost 5,000 years ago? Their purpose remains uncertain. These cyclopean structures were thousands of years old before any form of writing arrived on these islands.

Over the centuries, scholars and storytellers have applied successive waves of interpretation to the henges and stone circles. At first, people thought them to be the work of wizards, giants turned into stone. In Victorian times, scholars believed them to be the work of druids. More recent research, however, proved them to be much older than the druids. Twentieth-century archeologists found that the stones have complex alignments with the motions of the Sun, Moon, and constellations, resulting in the current belief that they are prehistoric observatories.

But will future research reveal that these great stones have still other meanings? Given the inability of scholars to achieve lasting consensus on the purposes of prehistoric monuments in general, we have even less hope of guessing what the Callanish cross-shaped monument meant to its architects.

Yet we cannot help but ponder its meaning. Recent scholarship emphasizes the connection of ancient stone monuments within larger sacred landscapes, so the cross-shaped configuration of the monument could have been designed to align with the stars; they might also have created a line-of-sight to neighboring landscape features, serving as guideposts for processional walkways.

Archetypal Significance

In the twentieth century, Carl Jung defined archetypes as thought patterns built into the collective subconscious of humanity. These patterns translate into shared symbols around the globe.

The cross design of Callanish and other pre-Christian objects may reflect these global symbolic meanings. Indigenous cultures on every continent saw sacred power in a circle's form. The features that give and sustain life—the Sun, the Moon, the womb—all come in rounded form. Circular tents, huts, and enclosures were easy to design and build, and they were strong for shelter, defense, and enclosing livestock. In various times and places, people have seen a circle as a symbol of completion, wholeness, timelessness, eternity, and unity.

Cultures scattered across the globe have divided the circle into quarters representing the four directions or the four basic elements (air, earth, water, fire). The number four is also archetypal, embraced by many diverse societies throughout history. The Buddha, for example, shaped his insights into the Four Noble Truths. For the ancient Jews, the unutterable Divine name is the Tetragrammaton (four-letter name). Christians thought it appropriate that there also be four Gospels.

The combination of the cross (with its four points) enclosed within a circle combines two elements of great symbolic importance. Carl Jung believed the basic form of the Celtic cross was an archetypal shape. The circle cross, he wrote, has an "extraordinary universality," "a never-failing mystical power, one may call it psychic, which again and again expresses a primordial psychic fact."[23]

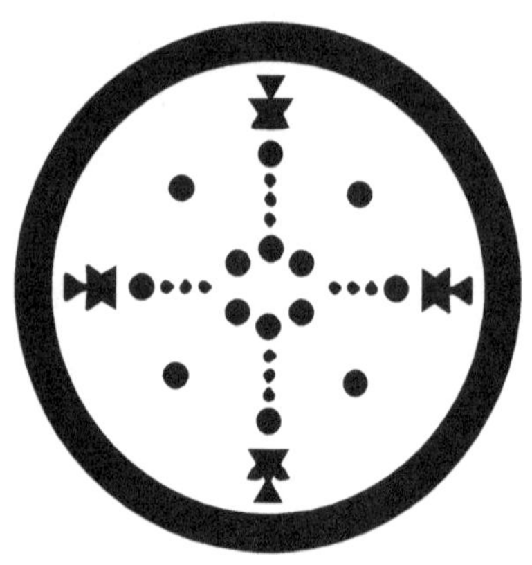

The Indigenous Medicine Wheel reflects the same spiritual understanding of the power of a circle as the circle cross and the Kongo cosmogram.

Although Jung believed the cross was a cross-cultural symbol, he believed that from a Christian perspective, the cross points to Christ's individuation and wholeness. For each of us, it represents the path of submission to our personal destiny, the expression of our true "Self," which Jung believed is the expression of the Divine within each individual.

Jung described the circle cross—like that seen in Indigenous medicine wheels and the African cosmogram, as well as the Celtic cross—as the "squaring of the circle," which, he said, "is one of the many archetypal motifs which form the basic patterns of our dreams and fantasies. . . . Indeed, it could even be called the archetype of wholeness."[24]

Why Crosses of Stone?

Thousands of years after the time of the megalith builders, a new crop of stone monuments sprang up from the soil of the Celtic nations: the stone high crosses. Like the older standing stones, the high crosses are also cloaked in mystery. What caused Christ-followers in these lands to fashion the cross—an object made originally from wood—into stone? Why are there so many of them? And why were they built on such a massive scale?

Personally, I believe the enduring legacy of the megaliths inspired the creators of the high crosses. Medieval people grew up beside these timeless pillars. Like us, they felt a sense of sacred power attached to these stones. Perhaps they thought: *If our ancestors built these magnificent altars to unknown Gods, shouldn't we render our God's most important symbol in equally impressive stone monuments?*

People in the Early Middle Ages also encountered stone memorials in the scriptures. In the first book of the Bible, after the patriarch Jacob has a life-changing vision of angels ascending and descending, he takes the stone on which he slept, anoints it with oil, and creates a marker called *Beth El.*[25] Later in the Hebrew scriptures, the prophet Samuel erects a large stone and names it Ebenezer, meaning "the stone of help."[26] God also commands the Hebrew people to worship God on altars of unhewn stone.[27]

Beyond those reasons, ancient stone monuments also have three features that speak to the imagination and the soul. The first is *shape.* Some standing stones seem to be natural in shape, formed by the forces of Nature, while others are clearly sculpted. Perhaps some stones already possessed a desired shape naturally, and others needed the help of human hands. In either case, the shape apparently mattered. In the West Kennet Processional way at Avebury, Wiltshire, for instance, the stones have alternating shapes: one squat and round, the next vertical and pointy, then another rounded, and so on. These are thought to be male and female symbols.[28]

Ancient stone works' second meaningful feature is the *arrangement* of the stones in relation to one another and to natural landmarks surrounding them. The most common arrangement of standing stones is in circles, sometimes set within earthen banks called *henges*, but not all megaliths are circular. In the Merrivale Prehistoric Settlement, in Dartmoor, Devon, for example, upright stones stand in long parallel rows, creating a sort of trackway (the purpose of which is unknown; perhaps, it marked the route for ritual processions).

Visitors to ancient megaliths also respond to a third feature: the *mineral composition* of the stones themselves. The bluestones in the Stonehenge circle, the most ancient part of the monument, are positioned between the outer and inner rings of larger sarsen stones. Builders brought the bluestones 150 miles from their quarry in Preseli, West Wales, an arduous feat for prehistoric people that demonstrates the value of the raw material. According to one archeological hypothesis, "the bluestone group . . represents not simply a collection of building materials, but the components of an existing stone circle that stood in Wales before being uprooted and brought to Stonehenge."[29]

What is so special about this kind of rock? As the name implies, it has a bluish tint due to the mineral content in the dolerite (sandstone). The medieval scholar Geoffrey of Monmouth, who claimed the wizard Merlin was responsible for Stonehenge, said water that poured over the stones gained healing qualities.[30] More recent scholars have suggested that the bluestone circle was actually constructed for musical purposes: If you strike Preseli bluestones with another stone, they reverberate like a gong or a drum.

Spiritual Geology

As a boy in France late in the nineteenth century, Pierre Teilhard de Chardin's most prized possession was a collection of small stones and pebbles he'd found in the forest around his home. As he grew a little older and realized the impermanence of human life, he turned to stones as a source of stability. In his search for a permanent reality, Auvergne, the region of France where he grew up, offered him a rainbow of stones to study—amethyst, citrine, and chalcedony, as well as fossils and volcanic rocks—sparking a lifelong passion for stone.

This passion was the doorway that led Teilhard into the deeper, spiritual layers of reality. He grew up to be a renowned geologist and paleontologist, as well as a Jesuit priest and theologian. His engagement with geology, he said, constantly broadened his interior life. For him, stone was not a lifeless substance but rather, a pathway for spiritual exploration. "There is a communion with God through the earth," he wrote.[31] Throughout his life, he turned to the Earth's "pages of stone" as a source of wisdom and transformation from which, he said, "emerges a vast and luminous picture."[32]

Teilhard was not the first to find a new understanding of God through geology. In the eighteenth century, Thomas Erskine studied the formation of rocks and realized: "We are evidently in the middle of a process [like that which forms stone], and the slowness of God's process in the material world prepares us . . . to trust that [the One] who takes untold ages for the formation of a bit of old red sandstone" is not limited to the span of our mortal life. Based on his understanding of stone, Erskine believed death was not the end of salvation but the continuation of a process.[33]

I believe Teilhard's sense of "communion with God through the earth" also began to work in my life through my childhood fascination with fossils. That once-living, -moving creatures had been metamorphosized into solid stone seemed a miraculous thing.

When I was nine, on a family vacation to Canada, my father insisted we go to an abandoned quarry site to look for fossils. Just as we pulled into the dirt parking lot, a steady rain began to fall, but my father was undaunted. My mother decided to stay warm in the car. I had a rain poncho, so I began walking with my father. Unfortunately, the downpour was quickly turning the ground underfoot into mud, and my shoes had inadequate traction. My dad suggested I step onto a large rock that would keep my feet out of the muck. I could wait for him there while he trudged on.

Not too long after, he returned.

"Did you find any fossils?" I asked.

He shook his head, and I was disappointed.

But then, he looked more closely at the stone where I was standing. "Kenneth!" he declared. "I believe you are right on top a prize fossil! This trip is not for naught."

I stared in amazement at the rock I was perched on. It was much larger than my child-sized shoes, wider than my shoulders, and circular. I noticed lines, shining with rainwater, radiating from the center outward. I was standing on a giant fossil sea sponge!

More than a half-century later, that sponge-turned-to-rock is still the largest fossil I have ever found—and I still have it. I've moved it with me to all the places I've lived, all around the country. It is currently on the breezeway of the manse we occupy, just beside the door, and visitors often remark on how "alive" this stone appears to be, even though hundreds of millions of years have passed since the creature's life in the ocean.

This early fascination with fossils gave me a sense of deep time, time more vast than I had ever previously imagined. Fossils also remind me that ever since the Earth's birth, the planet keeps changing. Teilhard's "pages of stone" reveal the evolution of flora and fauna, as well as the ongoing transformation of the Earth's surface. Today, as an adult, I can still scarcely take in the wonder. Stones were my gateway to a new sense of my own place in the vast oneness of life.

Having a spiritual affinity for stones, however, might raise some Christians' eyebrows. After all, gems, crystals, and other specially selected stones are the stock-in-trade of New Age spirituality. Giving stone spiritual qualities may, at first glance, seem akin to worshipping "created things rather than the Creator" (a practice the apostle Paul warns against[34]).

Yet the scriptures bear witness to the beneficial aspects of stones, gems, and minerals. God, says the psalmist, is a "rock" of strength for humanity.[35] Hebrew scriptures describe in detail the high priest's garment adorned with onyx gemstones[36] and his breastplate studded with carnelian, chrysolite, emerald, turquoise, a sapphire, moonstone, jacinth, agate, amethyst, beryl, onyx, and jasper.[37] (Doesn't this garment sound like the top shelf in a modern-day crystal shop?) Two mysterious stones—the Urim and Thummim—also revealed God's will for the people.[38] In the Book of Job, God promises: "You shall be in league with the stones of the field"[39]; we might dismiss this as merely poetic language, but the implication here is that we can develop relationships with stones—spending time with them, listening to them, looking at them, learning from them.

In the Gospels, Jesus likens himself to a monolithic cornerstone[40] and says the rocks will proclaim him.[41] Describing his Jewish ancestors, the apostle Paul writes: "They drank from the spiritual rock that followed them, and the rock was Christ."[42] John's Apocalypse, the final book in the Christian scriptures, uses rocks and gems to symbolize the life to come: "To everyone who conquers I will give . . . a white stone, and on the white stone is written a new name that no one knows except the one who receives it."[43] The heavenly Jerusalem appears to John "like a very rare jewel, like jasper, clear as crystal,"[44] its gates "adorned with every jewel": jasper, sapphire, agate, emerald, onyx, carnelian, chrysolite, beryl, topaz, chrysoprase, jacinth, and amethyst.[45]

Given the lovingly detailed listings of gems and crystals in the books of the Bible, I believe stones and minerals have spiritual purposes. Could it be that in the distant past, the Creator also sought connection with people by touching their hearts via prehistoric stone monuments? And is it possible that in the twenty-first century, God is reaching out to show Divine beauty and goodness through crystals and rocks, in order to beckon people who have been turned off by the abuses of some Christian churches? The Christian scriptures say people come to God through Christ[46]—and the apostle Paul says the rock in the Hebrew Bible is Christ.[47]

Theologians, philosophers, and even scientists have long pondered the sacred attributes of stones. The ancient mythological Greek philosopher, Hermes Trismegistus, speaks of a marvelous Stone, "which . . . leads from darkness into light, from this desert wilderness to a secure habitation, and from poverty and straits to a free and ample fortune."[48] In the 1600s, the British mystical poet Thomas Traherne writes that every stone has "a tongue," for "the Earth did undertake the office of a priest."[49] Two centuries later, Gustav Mahler, an Austrian composer, says the "mystical force" that "every created thing, even the very stones, feels with absolute certainty as the center of its being" is the "force of love."[50] In the nineteenth century, Nicola Tesla, the famous scientist and researcher, writes: "In a crystal we have clear evidence of the existence of a formative life principle, and though we cannot understand the life of a crystal, it is nonetheless a living being."[51] And in the early twentieth century, Austrian psychologist Carl Jung writes:

Many people cannot refrain from picking up stones of a slightly unusual color or shape and keeping them, . . . without knowing why they do. It is as if the stone held a mystery in it that fascinates them. . . . [People] have collected stones since the beginning of time and have apparently assumed that certain ones were the containers of the spirit of the life-force with all its mystery. . . . The stone symbolized something permanent that can never be lost or dissolved, something eternal that some have compared to the mystical experience of God within one's own soul.[52]

Today, well-respected theologians and spiritual teachers still speak of the spiritual "voice" that issues from stones. Popular spiritual teacher Eckhart Tolle says:

Even a stone . . . could show you the way back to God, to the Source, to yourself. When you look at it or hold it . . . a sense of awe, of wonder, arises within you. Its essence silently communicates itself to you and reflects your own essence back to you.[53]

Steven Charleston, a retired Episcopal bishop who unites Indigenous wisdom with Christian theology, writes:

The nature of God, the essence of God, the love of God have touched all things, for nothing exists that is outside of God. For this reason, many native traditions speak of the stones of the Earth as our oldest relatives in a spiritual sense. Stones have known the mind of God for a very long time, from a time before time. Therefore, Native people pay attention to stones, to rocks and mountains and canyons because these first elements embody the ancient will of God in creation.[54]

In most Indigenous languages, a stone is not referred to as an "it" but with a pronoun that indicates that stones are animate, spirit-filled in their own way.

Christian author Barbara Taylor Brown describes stones as grieving the crucifixion:

> When that Word fell silent on Golgotha . . . the earth shook with grief. Rocks made the only sound they could, splitting open with small explosions that were their best version of tears. . . . The whole inanimate world leapt in to fill that silence.[55]

Another popular twenty-first-century spiritual teacher, Franciscan priest Richard Rohr, tells the story of a small boy who asks his rabbi how he can love God, when God is invisible. The rabbi answers,

> Start with a stone. Try to love a stone. Try to be present to the most simple and basic thing in reality so you can see its goodness and beauty. Then let that goodness and beauty come into you. Let it speak to you. Start with a stone.[56]

Christian psychologist M. Scott Peck describes his pilgrimage through the British Isles exploring the ancient stone circles and their spiritual meaning. He concludes this study by saying:

> Although I suspect the megalithic people worshiped certain stones . . . I am certain that they also worshiped *through* them. One reason for my certainty is that such would be typical of much human religious behavior. I am referring to icons, objects . . . that are symbols of God.

Peck says that the builders of the ancient stone monuments "would have thought that something of God was within the stone but also known that God was much greater than the stone itself."[57]

Spiritual folk are not the only ones "listening" to stones. After French geologists Arnold Rheshar and Pierre Escollet studied rock specimens from around the world, they concluded that stones have some kind of vital activity, though a very slow one; they possess a form of life, the geologists claimed, perhaps even consciousness.[58] And if that seems like utter nonsense to you, consider these words written from the scientific perspective of quantum physics:

> How can we say with certainty that rocks, and even mountain ranges, do not react also as living organisms, but with a reaction time so slow that to catch it with time-lapse photography would require millennia between exposures! Of course, there is no way to prove this, but there is no way of disproving it either.[59]

Ilia Delio, a Franciscan sister who specializes in evolution, physics, neuroscience, and the import of these fields for theology, does not dismiss such claims. She writes:

> To the modern mind, the idea that rocks . . . have consciousness seems incredible. Yet, if we follow the implications of the observer universe down to the smallest level, then we must engage the notion that consciousness must be part of inanimate matter.[60]

APPLICATIONS FOR TODAY

A Sit Stone

Humans have always found that some stones make convenient chairs. When I lived in Flagstaff, Arizona, I frequently visited a stone I dubbed Aslan's Throne. It became my place to pray, and I had some intense spiritual experiences while there. (You can read about one of these in my earlier book, *Water from an Ancient Well*.)

If you've ever read any books by Madeleine L'Engle, you may remember her "stargazing stone." She included the stone in many of her fiction books, but it was a real stone, a glacial boulder in her backyard. That stone, L'Engle wrote in her nonfiction, was the place where her spirituality had deepened and expanded. Much like my Aslan's Throne, the stargazing stone was her place to listen: to the Sun, to the sky, to the stars, to the wind. Seated on ancient stone, looking up at the vast glitter of stars, she felt she was a part of something ageless and alive, something that connects the universe and makes it one.

HOW OLD ARE YOU?

Consider this question:

How old are you?

At first, you might answer with the years since your birth; you might even include the months and days of your recorded life. Years, months, days are merely human measurements, though, and applying them to yourself may be misleading. The truth is more complex.

How old are you?

This time, as you think about the question, feel your skin. As an adult, your epidermis renews itself about every 28 days. The "you" that others see and that you can feel is only a month old!

How old are you?

Consider now the reality that your body is composed of 55 to 60 percent water. That water mostly dates back to the time when the Earth cooled, about 4.5 billion years ago. This means that more than half of you is over 4 billion years old. Dinosaurs may have once sipped the same water molecules that are now inside your body.

How old are you?

Each time you think about this question, you're using the 100 billion neurons contained within the sphere of your cranium. Whenever you have a thought, those billions of neurons transmit tiny charges made possible by trace elements of gold. Yes, you are golden! And that gold—which enables you to be sentient—came from stars that exploded about 10 billion years ago.[61]

How old are you?

You—like all life—are carbon-based; your body is built from minuscule chains of carbon atoms. Scientists theorize that at the moment of singularity known as the Big Bang, all the constituents of reality, including carbon, blipped into the newborn universe. This means that the atoms in your body date you at 13.7 billion years!

In the Divine, you live and move and have your being. You are made of star stuff and God stuff, formed of the Eternal One, infinite in time and in dimensions. So—

How old are you?

Visiting the Megaliths

Many people testify to the heightened sense of holy reality they encounter at megalithic sites. If you live near the prehistoric monuments of Europe or the British Isles, you are probably already accustomed to spending time in these places, soaking in the mood, the emotions, and the thoughts they convey to you as the lighting and weather shift around you. If you're from North America, however, and you're planning a trip across the pond, consider adding one or more of these megaliths to your tour schedule.

Neolithic or Bronze Age stone circles are usually part of larger sacred landscapes that include other megalithic monuments, earthen formations, or notable natural features. Traversing the routes between associated megaliths, you can retrace pilgrimage routes that are thousands of years old (far more ancient than the Canterbury Pilgrim Trail or Camino de Santiago).

The Avebury stone circle and henge in Wiltshire, England, encompasses a small village and pub. You can walk freely among the immense stones of the circle, touch them, and seat yourself in the "chair" in one of the larger stones (watch out for sheep droppings). This immense circle connects to a long processional path flanked by standing stones. On a hillside to your left, you'll see another stone circle in the distance. Continuing straight, you'll pass Silbury Hill—the largest human-made structure from prehistoric England—and then, across a road and into a field, you will come to the West Kennet long barrow, an ancient stone burial chamber extending into an earthen mound. People conjecture that the stones and earthwork of this entire sacred landscape portray an immense serpent. The whole complex takes about a day of leisurely hiking.

The Merrivale Prehistoric Complex in Dartmoor, England, includes parallel stone rows, a circle and menhir, numerous round prehistoric hut foundations, a prehistoric cistern, and a medieval waymark cross, all within the easy distance of an afternoon stroll. (You'll also encounter friendly ponies!)

Visitors at the most famous megalithic site—Stonehenge—usually spend time at the visitor center or strolling around the site itself with a guided audio tour. A mapped-out walking tour also encompasses several nearby neolithic sites. Woodhenge is just two miles from Stonehenge, and by walking from one to the other, you will experience the link between these two sites; their builders understood them as intrinsically connected parts of one sacred reality.

"Thin places" are not restricted to any particular cultural or geographic setting. While the term *thin place* is associated with Celtic spirituality, the idea of liminal-and-holy places is found globally in Indigenous cultures. The Americas have many natural places, including rock formations, where the people of the First Nations discern the presence of the sacred. Many tribes believe each stone possesses its own spirit or essence, which acts as an intermediary between the physical and spiritual realms, offering humans guidance, healing, and spiritual insights. I try to avoid these natural shrines and prayer spots, however, since they are still sacred to my Native neighbors; I don't want to appropriate their customs or intrude on the privacy of their ceremonies.[62] But Earth is full of "thin places." There's more than enough to go around.

GO ON A FIELD TRIP

Take time to hike or drive to natural areas around your home. Discover your own sacred stones.

Gathering Stones

If you can't always bring yourself to the stones, you can bring the stones to your home (observing, of course, legal, and environmental considerations). As noted previously by Carl Jung, "Many people cannot refrain from picking up stones . . . and keeping them." I am one such person. In environments as varied as the sun-scorched Sonoran Desert and the wave-soaked pebble beaches of Lake Michigan, I have found such "stones of slightly unusual color and shape," which now sit on a shelf in my home. On other occasions, I have chosen common-looking stones because they are located at very special sites: I have such stones from Columba's Bay on Holy Island Iona.

A tray in our home's hallway holds a special treasure: a tiny vial filled with "Cuthbert's beads." These are crinoid fossils, which form tiny rings smaller than the diameter of a little finger, that I found at Cuthbert's Beach on the Holy Island of Lindisfarne. They are doubly precious because Ray Simpson, a doyen of Celtic wisdom, helped me find them.

I've also found unusual stones on the beach in front of Saint Ninian's cave in Whithorn, Dumfries, and Galloway, Scotland. The cave is the hermit site of one of the first missionaries to the Picts in Scotland; ten crosses are carved into the cave wall, and eighteen finely carved medieval

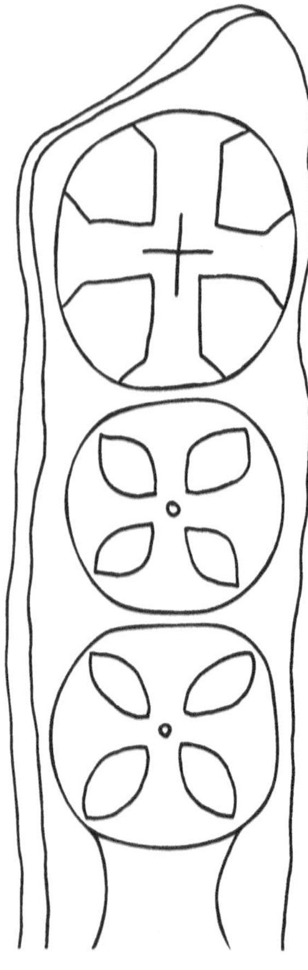

A pillar slab bearing these carvings was originally built into a wall at St. Ninian's Cave.

crosses, now displayed within the Whithorn Priory Museum, were found in the cave. In what to me seems an act of Providence, the ocean-worn stones in front of the cave have intersecting straight lines of crystal embedded in a darker matrix, forming vivid white crosses.

Take a moment to consider:

- What stones are special to me?

- How has God spoken to me through stones?

Take some time to journal your answers.

For Indigenous people, the selection and discovery of sacred stones is also a sacred act. Many Native Americans believe the stones choose their owners, rather than the other way around; when the right stone is found, it will call out to the individual. Ellyn Sanna, the managing editor of Anamchara Books, wears a small "hag stone" (a stone with a natural hole in it) on a chain around her neck; she found the stone when she was a four-year-old (a gift from God, she believed at the time), and today, she says, the stone still speaks to her about her sense of her identity as God's beloved.

Stones also can signify powerful prayers. Personally, I've found that small, smooth stones are especially suited to use as "prayer stones," carried in a pocket as tactile reminders for intercession or adoration. Stones can also be used in more ceremonial ways to represent prayer within a group of people. At my church, one of our Sunday school teachers has a pile of stones from a nearby creek in her middle school classroom. During class, each teen selects a stone, holds it, prays about a concern in their life (and some of their concerns are dire), and then places the stone in a container. Each week, the container—with all the prayer stones in it—goes next to the adult midweek Bible study, where the older members of the church hold the stones and pray for our teens.

Instinctively, human beings have always used stones as physical touchpoints for letting go of fears and anxieties. "Worry stones," often sold in crystal shops, have a long history that stretches back at least as far as the ancient Celts; archeologists tell us that the Ancient Greeks and the Indigenous peoples of North America and Tibet also used stones in the same way. (They were usually called palm stones or finger stones.) Modern-day psychologists say a small, smooth stone, pleasing to the touch, can be a tactile tool for coping with emotional anxiety; as a person holds the stone in their hand, they are brought back to the present moment, reassured by the stone's familiar constancy, and distracted from their worries.

According to the Merriam-Webster online dictionary, the word *touchstone*, which once referred to a stone used to test the purity of gold, is now considered to mean " a simple test of the authenticity or value of something intangible." Something as simple as a pebble in our pocket can be a touchstone that speaks to us about what is most authentic in our lives, reminding us of "something intangible"—a memory, a prayer, the very presence of God.

A Pocket Stone's Uses

- Something to do with your hands as a distraction from boredom or worrisome thoughts.

- A reminder of a loved one who is no longer with you, allowing you, in some sense, to carry that person with you wherever you go.

- A meditation or prayer object; just as a mantra can be an audible cue for meditation, a stone can be a tactile cue to quiet and focus your mind.

- A relaxation tool before bed; turning the stone over between your fingers can help lull your mind and body.

- A reminder to keep your cool—or stand up for yourself—during challenging interactions with other people; holding the stone in your hand while you speak and listen can help your interactions be more intentional and mindful.

- A symbolic carrier of prayer: either a reminder to pray for a particular person or a reminder that a particular person is praying for you.

- A sacred object that represents the Divine, the living Stone.[63]

O God,

who shot forth this entire glorious unfolding Universe,

who coalesced and cooled matter into rocks and minerals,

who formed from the elements our God-image selves,

we praise you for your servants, the rocks and stones.

They are our companions on the way,

whispering of deep time,

offering us their solidity,

anchors for our wave-swept life,

surfaces we touch as we touch you,

and signs of your Son, the Cornerstone of redemption.

Bless to us each stone, each boulder, each craggy surface,

O Rock of Our Salvation.

Amen

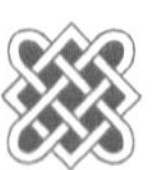

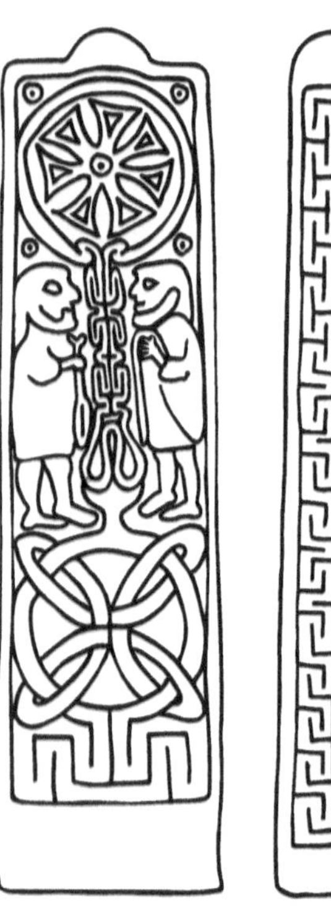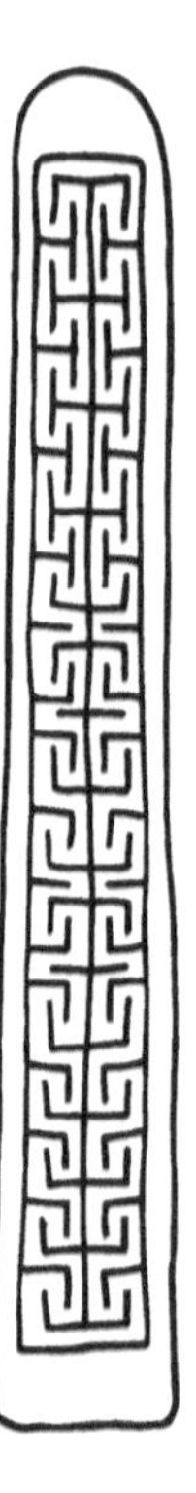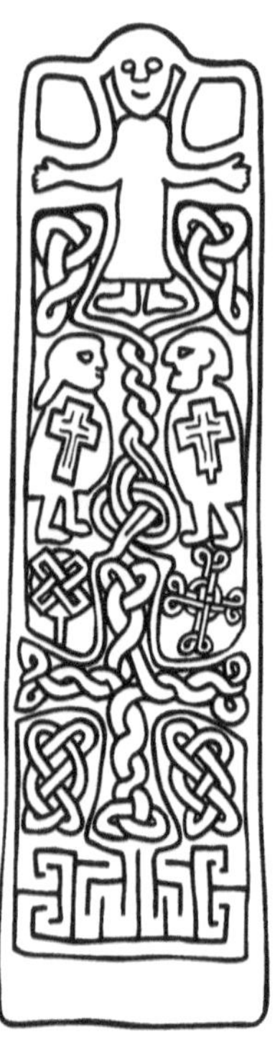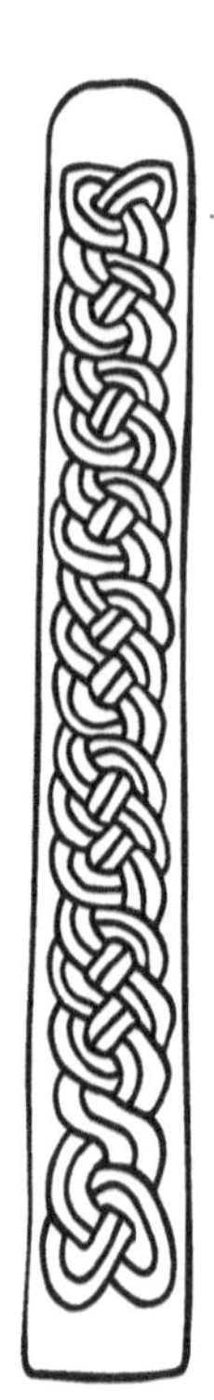

These drawings show the designs on the four sides of
the "Marigold Stone" in County Donegal, Ireland.

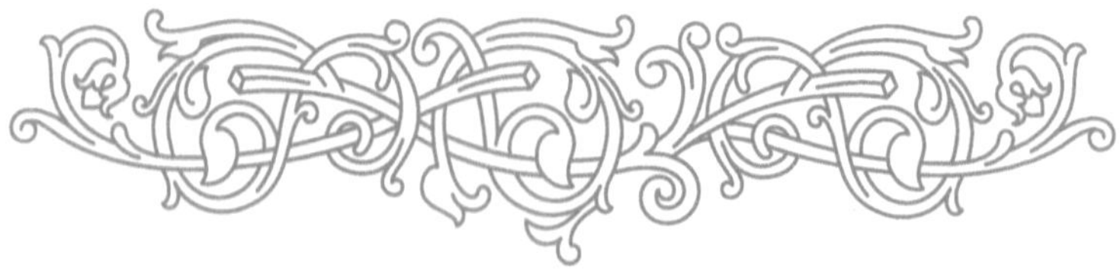

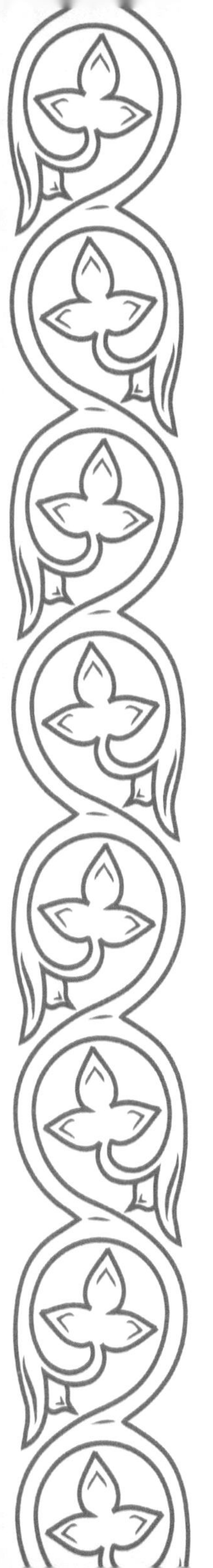

CHAPTER 3

Bright Heaven's Sun

Praise Yahweh!
Praise Yahweh from the heavens;
praise him in the heights!
Praise him, sun and moon
praise him, all you shining stars!
Let them praise the name of Yahweh,
for he commanded and they were created.

PSALM 148:1–5
(ABRIDGED)

High King of heaven, my victory won,
May I reach heaven's joys, O bright heaven's sun,
Heart of my own heart, whatever befall,
Still be my vision, O ruler of all.

"BE THOU MY VISION"
(TRADITIONAL IRISH HYMN
DATING FROM THE EARLY MIDDLE AGES)

ENCOUNTER

June 21, 2015, 2:30 AM, Orkney, Scotland

We had traveled so very far to be part of the summer solstice celebration on the Island of Orkney. Was rain now going to ruin our plans?

Earlier that morning, I woke up to the sound of rain pounding hard on the roof. When I opened my eyes, I saw a river of rainwater pouring over the plexiglass skylight above my hotel bed.

With my wife, my cousin, and her husband, I had come to Orkney to be part of the solstice celebration held at the stone ring of Brodgar. This holy day is known as *Alban Hefin*, which means "the Light of the Shore" or "the Light of Summer." You may think the meanings of *shore* and *summer* are quite far from each other, but both words refer to times and places when the light shines brightest. "The Light of the Shore" also signifies that the seashore is where the three realms of earth, sea, and sky meet, an intersection that forms a thin place.[64]

If we had been traveling in the south of England, we could have joined the throng at the world-famous Stonehenge solstice celebration. Since our route lay to the north, we planned to join the celebration at the Ring of Brodgar, known in folklore as the Temple of the Sun due to its alignment with the midsummer sunrise. While Stonehenge's size makes it unique among megalithic monuments, Brodgar also has its own powerful atmosphere. The modern-day setting of Stonehenge, with the nearby roadway and massive tourist center, seems distanced from its intended connection with the natural world. Brodgar, however, perched on a raised henge that borders the ocean, feels like a truly timeless thin place where land, sky, sea, and Sun all interweave.

Sunrise this solstice morning was less than an hour away, and a group of Scottish Pagans had plans for a sacred ceremony—but the rain was fierce. It was pitch dark and cold outside, and it looked like a waterfall was dumping over us.

I groaned. "It's useless," I told Marsha. "No solstice celebration this morning. Let's go back to bed."

But just then, my cousin Nancy and her husband John knocked on the door. "Let's go! It's almost time."

"No!" I groaned. "Go back to sleep."

But they insisted, and so we kitted up with warm sweaters, rain jackets, boots, and umbrellas. We slowly drove our rental car through the descending sheets of water to the stone circle.

And—just as we pulled into the car park—the rain slackened, then simply stopped, as if someone had just turned off a faucet. A good number of other vehicles were pulling in with us. The celebration was a go after all.

The clouds overhead were grey and thick, and yet the whole expanse was lit by an eerie phosphorescence. The great stones stood in majestic rows, outlined against the sky. Dozens of people had joined us, speaking in hushed whispers or walking in silence. I noticed a variety of accents: French, Australian, American, Canadian, as well as British and Scottish.

The crowd fell silent then, attuned with the greater silence of the sky and water about us. As a man and woman began the ceremony, I felt as if the Earth and elements were hushed and listening with us. The officiants invoked a sacred circle, honoring Nature's forces and recalling the timeless continuity of people gathered on this same occasion at this ancient place. At one point, the male officiant pointed to a narrow spot between stones and said, "At this moment the Sun is arising at this mark, as it has for five thousand years. We can't see it this morning because of the clouds, so imagine it right there."

After that, came a handfasting; participants then recited poems and shared sweetcakes and mead. When it was over and the circle of people had disbanded, the rain recommenced, as if someone had turned it back on with a faucet.

We drove back to our hotel in a downpour and slept for a few more hours before waking again in time to worship with the congregation in the much more recently built (twelfth-century) stone monument of Saint Magnus's Cathedral. As I joined in the prayer and song, I was thankful the day had begun, despite the foul weather, in accordance with a tradition that endures from my Stone-Age ancestors. Together, enclosed by ancient sacred stones, we had honored the Sun, who gives life to the Earth.

DEEPENING

Megalithic Sun Temples

When humans first began to articulate spiritual beliefs, they regarded the Sun as an expression of cosmic benevolence. Light, warmth, and the fertility of plants all came from this singular source. While the length of its daily rule varied, it could be depended on like no other force. Many prehistoric people regarded it as a deity; later, spiritual people regarded it as the effulgence of the invisible Creator.

Ancient architects shaped the earliest large-scale stone works to celebrate the Sun. Megalithic monuments at Stonehenge and Avebury, the Callanish stone circle-and-cross in the Hebrides, the Ring of Brodgar in the Orkneys, and a great many lesser-known megalithic structures all display solar alignments. Then, with the coming of Christianity, the high crosses continued to celebrate our nearest star.

One of the most impressive and finely wrought neolithic monuments is the Newgrange Stone-Age tomb in the Boyne Valley of County Meath, Ireland. The Newgrange mound is 279 feet in diameter and more than 40 feet high. A chambered passageway leads into the heart

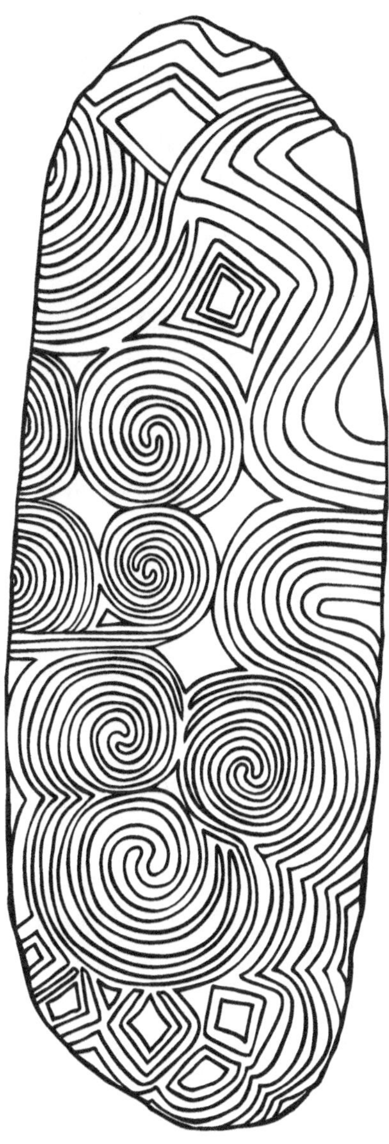

At first glance, the spirals carved on stone at Newgrange may look typically "Celtic," but actually, they predate the Celts by some 2,500 years.

of the mound, supporting tons of dirt and stone, with no water leakage, for over five millennia. Archeologists estimate that more than three hundred people together labored more than thirty years to move the 200,000 tons of material that built the monument.[65]

After most of the edifice was completed, its builders carefully hewed and placed a set of stones at the entrance of the tomb to perfectly align with the light of the winter solstice. On that one occasion, a beam of light moves along the entirety of the passageway and floods the interior chamber with radiance. It took an extraordinary amount of thinking, surveying, and skill to create this effect—and then, from the moment the Neolithic builders finished the stone lightbox that sealed the passageway, only the interred dead saw the annual dazzling light display within the tomb. Nowadays, however, more than 200,000 tourists visit Newgrange each year, and hundreds vie for the privilege of being inside the tomb on that magical moment of the winter solstice.

We cannot say what the Newgrange solstice passage meant to its original builders. In Celtic mythology, Newgrange was known as *An Brug*—the "mansion" or "dwelling place" of the *Tuatha De Danann* (Ireland's faerie folk, an ancient race who inhabited the Other World).[66] But these beliefs existed thousands of years after the tomb mound was finished, and they belonged to an entirely different culture from that of the Newgrange builders. Today, archeologists conjecture that the creators of Newgrange may have believed the sunlight would rejuvenate the dead and guide them into the next life.[67] Beyond a doubt, the Sun held paramount spiritual significance for the prehistoric Irish people.

Other artistic carvings and objects also attest to this, both in Stone-Age Ireland and in the neighboring islands. According to Swiss scholar Jakob Streit, "The sun symbols belong to the oldest of all symbols that [humans] have carved. . . . Their god was not our physical sun. The sun for them was the eye and the raiment of the divine . . . a visibly creating being which revealed itself to [humanity] in mythical form as an all-embracing essence of light."[68]

An example of Ireland's prehistoric Sun art is the central carved stone in the tumulus of Slieve na Caillighe, northwest of Dublin in County Meath. This stone has eleven solar symbols carved into it; some rays point out in straight lines like a child's depiction of the Sun, others have rays shaped like flower petals, some are simple orbs, and some are shaped like an equal-armed cross. Streit writes: "Unmistakably these symbols in the tumulus demonstrate the worship of the light of the world."[69]

The Nebra Sky Disk, a centerpiece in the British Museum's 2022 "World of Stonehenge" display, also testifies to the Sun's significance to spiritual life in the megalithic era. This artifact is shaped like a dish about a foot wide, with a gold sun and moon, along with thirty-two smaller gold stars that include identifiable constellations, inlaid into its bronze face. Though the disk was found in Germany, the gold and the tin used to alloy the bronze face originated in Cornwall. It is considered the world's oldest representation of a specific astronomical phenomenon, coordinating both lunar and solar calendars.[70]

Solar Symbolism

The Hebrew scriptures tell us that God made the Sun; the Sun is not itself God. In the beginning, in the Book of Genesis, God sets the Sun as a light in the sky.[71] Later, the psalmist compares the Sun to a bridegroom leaping forth from his tent to "declare the glory of God."[72]

At the same time, both the Hebrew and Christian scriptures employ the Sun as a symbol of God's activity in the world. For the Prophet Isaiah, the Sun signified Divine favor: "Then your light shall break forth like the dawn, and your healing shall spring up quickly; your vindicator shall go before you, the glory of Yahweh shall be your rear guard."[73] In the Gospels, when Christ declares himself "the light of the world," it is hard not to think of the Sun.[74] His mission was to show the limitlessness of Divine kindness, for God causes the "sun to rise on the evil and the good."[75]

The Sun and the Son

Early Christians continued this interpretation of the Sun as a reflection of the greater Son. "Life is offered to everyone; the whole world is filled with glory," writes Hippolytus of Rome in the second century, comparing the Sun's universal light to the life of Christ. He goes on to say: "A heavenly light more brilliant than all others sheds its radiance everywhere, and he who was begotten before the morning star and all the stars of heaven, Christ, mighty and immortal, shines upon all creatures more brightly than the sun."[76] In the third century, church father Archelaus refers to "the true Sun, who is our Saviour."[77] Another church father from the same century, Cyprian, bishop of Carthage, also calls Christ "the true sun."[78] A century later, Saint Ambrose of Milan was still using the same metaphor connecting Christ and the Sun: "Throw wide the gate of your heart, stand before the sun of the everlasting light that shines *upon everyone*."[79]

Burial images indicate this was not merely a theological concept, pondered by intellectuals and church leaders, but an idea that also existed at the grassroots level. A third-century funeral mosaic discovered in a mausoleum beneath the Vatican, for example, portrays Christ as Apollo—Sol, a haloed sun god carrying an orb and driving a horse-drawn chariot. Other images from the mausoleum (of a fisherman, Jonah, and the Good Shepherd) confirm that this image was intended to represent Jesus, however. In the mosaic, he rides his sun chariot through tendrils of grapevines.

The connection between the Son and the Sun continued into the Middle Ages and beyond. Desiderius Erasmus, the seventeenth-century theologian and philosopher, writes:

O Thou, who art the true Sun of the world, evermore rising, and never going down; who, by Thy most wholesome appearing and sight dost nourish, and make joyful all things.[80]

Some critics of Christianity have gone so far as to dismiss Christ as "only" a solar god. French scholar Charles Francois Dupuis, for example, claims, "Christ has all the characteristics of the God Sun in his birth, or in his incarnation in the womb of a virgin, and that this birth arrives just at the same moment, when the ancients celebrated that of the Sun . . . he has also the characteristics of the God Sun in his resurrection."[81] For Dupuis, this is evidence that both the historical and cosmic Jesus can be dismissed as a primitive form of Sun worship.

He concludes: "The pretended history of a God, born of a Virgin at the winter solstice, who resuscitates at Easter or at the equinox of spring, after having descended into hell; of a God, who has twelve apostles in his train [representative of the Zodiac], . . . a God-conqueror of the Prince of Darkness, who restores to mankind the dominion of Light, and who redeems the evils of Nature—is merely a solar fable."

This criticism of Christianity goes all the way back to the early church, when theologians such as Tertullian, Pope Leo the Great, and Saint Augustine took pains to repudiate such attacks by outlining how their faith differed from Sun worship.[82] In the sixteenth century, theologian Paracelsus explains: "There is an earthly sun, which is the cause of all heat. . . . There is an Eternal Sun, which is the source of all wisdom, and those whose spiritual senses have awakened to life will see that sun."[83] Nearly three centuries later, William Blake, the visionary poet, gives a similar defense: When he sees the Sun rise, he writes, he does not "see a round disc of fire" but rather a glimpse into Heaven, where the heavenly host are praising Christ.[84] As Northrop Frye points out, "the Hallelujah-Chorus perception of the sun makes it a far more real sun," and critics who would have it otherwise are looking at things backward. Christ cannot be reduced to "merely" the Sun—but the Sun, when seen through spiritual eyes, can become a window through which we see a larger Reality.[85]

In June of 2023, my wife Marsha and I walked the Camino de Santiago Frances pilgrimage across Spain; when we reached the traditional destination of Santiago de Compostela, we felt the itch to walk further, so we continued hiking to Finisterre, which means "the end of the world." For many people, reaching the point where Finisterre drops into the ocean is the ultimate end of their Camino pilgrimage. Marsha and I would continue our trek for another couple of days, but for now, as the Sun sank, we lingered in this remote place.

An ancient Roman text records that a Celtic temple devoted to the setting Sun once stood in Finisterre.[86] Its exact location is uncertain, but some historians link that temple with a Christian hermit's cell attached to the site centuries later. Saint Guillerme (*William* in English), who built the hermit's cell, was an early medieval Christian contemplative who sought to emulate the Egyptian Desert Fathers—as did many of the saints in Ireland and the British Isles at the same time. The saint built his chapel and living quarters on the side of an enormous stone ridge with a cave underneath.

The setting Sun aligned with the peak of the stone ridge. I sensed this was a thin place, imbued with wonder and devotion, a temple first of the Sun—and then of the Son.

Solar Signs in Celtic Spirituality

Ancient Pagan Celts, before the arrival of Christianity, considered Ogma, their Sun god, to be the Divine Word—what the Greeks called the Logos—and so, when they heard of Jesus, the Celts easily made the connection between Son and Sun. An ancient Irish prayer refers to Christ as "King of the fierce Sun,"[87] and in Saint Patrick's autobiography, he tells of a crisis in which he experienced Christ in the light from the Sun. He felt weighted down with supernatural heaviness, he writes, but then—

> I saw the sun rise in the sky and while I called out "Helia, Helia" with all my strength, behold the sun's splendor fell on me and dispelled immediately all the heaviness from upon me. And I believe that Christ, my Lord, assisted me.[88]

Other early medieval Celts also saw Christ in the Sun. The well-known ancient Irish hymn "Be Thou My Vision" refers to Christ with this phrase: "May I reach heaven's joys, O bright heaven's sun."

This connection between Divinity and the Sun persisted in Celtic Christianity. In the sixteenth century, the Welsh poet Sion Mowddwy wrote:

> *Fair sun, with enduring and beautiful light,*
> *Having thy course from Paradise,*
> *By the Name of God dost thou quietly*
> *Illumine all around the globe;*
> *Thou art the light of heaven, worthy fosterer,*
> *Light of the world, clear knowledge.*[89]

Then, in the late nineteenth century and early twentieth, when Carmichael collected prayers from ordinary people across Scotland, he recorded the belief that on Easter morning, the rising Sun literally dances, in joyful celebration of the Resurrection. Author Geoffrey Moorhouse argues that statements such as these indicate "the sun is not a metaphor or image of Christ, but a medium through which Christ shines."[90]

Solar Symbols on Celtic Crosses

Amid the great puddles of ink spilt to explain the symbolism of ancient Celtic crosses, only one primary document—to the best of my knowledge—explicitly explains the meaning of the encircled cross symbol. John Scotus Eriugena, an exiled Irish philosopher who was arguably the most influential Christian theologian of the ninth century, writes, "Behold the orb" [referring to the circle on the Celtic cross] *"which shines with the rays of the sun."*[91] (I will unpack this more fully in chapter 12.)

The lack of literary references, however, does not disprove that people alive at the time the great crosses were erected connected them with the Sun; a connection so obvious may not have required much discussion at the time. Ancient monument builders carved and situated the Irish high crosses to harmonize with the Sun's daily movement across the sky. Professor Eamonn Ó Carragain suggests that stoneworkers fabricated and placed the crosses in early medieval monasteries to function in a way "not dissimilar to sundial-pillars."[92]

Furthermore, the makers of the great Irish stone crosses of the ninth and tenth centuries carved detailed scenes from scripture and early Christian legends, placed on each cross in such a way that as the Sun moved on its daily course, each panel would be illumined (or fade into shadow) in a daily progression that highlighted the meaning of each panel. If you were looking at the cross at Moone, County Kildare, at sunrise, for example, you would see the panel with the creation of Adam and Eve lit by the first of the Sun's rays. If you were so attentive as to remain watching throughout the day, you would see the cross's panels lighting in turn, according to the chronology of the same narratives from the beginning of the Hebrew scriptures to the end of the Christian.[93]

Some of the crosses' artwork also points to the solar association. The Marigold Stone in Carndonagh, County Donegal, Ireland, a large slab with crosses carved in bas-relief, displays an image on its west side that gives the Marigold Stone its name: a cross topped with a circle in which are seven petal-like rays. While "marigold" serves as a handy descriptor, more scholarly writers indicate this cross depicts either the Sun or a flabellum, two symbols that are closely connected.

A flabellum is a ritual fan, a pole topped with a circle of feathers, that was originally said to represent the hand of Divinity—and, as Lawrence Parmly Brown informs us:

The mythic concept of the sun on or near the horizon as one of the hands of the solar or cosmic god is of great antiquity and wide distribution, having been naturally suggested by the resemblance of wide-spread human fingers to the fan-shaped or finger-like radiations of the solar flabellum (fan) often observable in the clouds at sunrise and sunset.[94]

Brown also states that the Egyptian gods, especially Osiris, are pictured holding a "winnowing fan"—a flagellum—in their lifted hands, which Brown compares to the Gospels' description of Jesus coming "with his fan"[95]; although modern English Bibles usually use the term *winnowing fork,* both the King James Version and the original Greek indicate Jesus is, in fact, holding a flabellum.

The flabellum as a ceremonial object representing the Sun first originated in the courts of the Egyptian pharaohs.[96] From there, it passed into the rites of the Egyptian Coptic church, and then to the early Celtic Christians. We see the Egyptian influence in the Book of Kells, which portrays flabellum on several of its pages.[97] Saint Columba was said to have had a flabellum that was venerated as a relic for hundreds of years after his death.[98] Although the solar connection was forgotten (replaced by the need to shoo flies away from the Eucharist), flabella are still used today in Roman Catholic and Eastern Orthodox church processions. Their use in ancient Celtic Christianity, however, indicates yet another connection between the Sun and the Son.

Other crosses in Ireland and the British Isles also portray the double symbolism of Christ and the Sun. In Wales, the Margham Cartwheel Stone Cross is likely the Sun with its extending rays, rather than the wheel of a cart as its name indicates. Ancient Scottish crosses in Whithorn, topped with prominent discs pierced in turn by smaller discs, also seem to be obvious solar symbols.

Walking the Camino, trekking through Basque country in the Pyrenees Mountains, I noticed in several settings—museums, church-yards, and public monuments—the Basque wheel crosses called

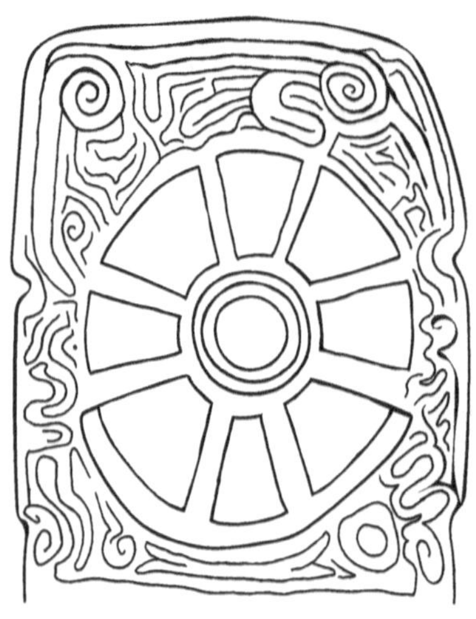

The Margham Cross in Wales bears a solar design.

Hilarri. The ones that I saw ranged from the Early Middle Ages to the High Middle Ages in their antiquity, but the pattern appears as early as 100 BCE; the ancient stoneworkers likely intended their monuments to symbolize the Sun.[99] This is apparent because many of the medieval Hilarri have a typical wheel cross pattern atop the shaft on one side, and the backside of the same stone wheel depicts the Sun with rays projecting from its side.

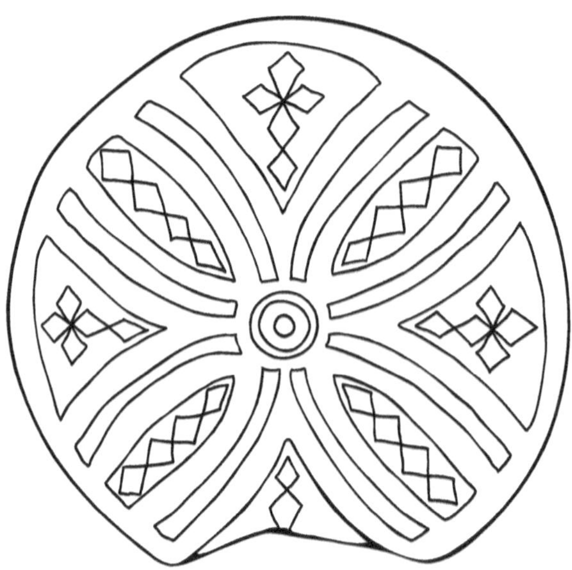

An example of a Basque Hillari, from St. Jean Pied de Port, France. "Hilarri" means "dead stone," and their design—disc-shaped heads facing the rising sun atop a wedge-shaped support stone—belong to an old tradition found throughout Mediterranean Europe and North Africa. Today, they are mostly found in Basque Country.

It's tempting to see a connection between these Hilarri and the wheel crosses that are the most common icon of Celtic spirituality. Although scholars have found no evidence of a connection, the artistic forms are almost identical. Both the Basque and the Irish were skilled seafarers, from the Iron Age until now, and as they traveled back and forth, they would have inevitably shared cultural and artistic ideas. Reverence for the Sun—the giver of all light and life on our world—is a common element of perennial spiritual wisdom.

APPLICATIONS FOR TODAY

Sunshine for the Soul

In the twenty-first century, we are less dependent on elemental forces. Air conditioning in the summer and heating in the winter enable those of us who are so privileged to ignore the vicissitudes of our environment. Yet even indoors, in a "controlled" environment, we cannot ignore the Sun's power over our lives. For many years, both past and present, I have lived in Upstate New York, in one of the most overcast parts of the country. Every winter, depression afflicts me, necessitating St. John's wort, a good therapist, and—indispensably—a "sun lamp" to dispel the ill humors of the darkness. Even in our technologically savvy era, the soul still relies upon Sol.

Ironically, we take some of the finest things in life for granted, especially when they are reliable. The Sun has asserted its influence on every moment of our lives, from the gravitational pull that keeps Earth on its steady looping motion to the warmth that establishes the perimeters of our survival. This is what makes the Sun such an overarching and archetypal spiritual symbol: God's love is like the Sun, governing the existence of all things; shedding warmth and energy upon us all, without exception; blessing and cheering us up, from conception to eternal reunion.

When do you most vividly experience the Sun? Watching the sunrise dispel night's shadows? Observing a blazing sunset as the light sinks beneath an ocean or lake? Skiing over snow that glitters like diamonds in the sunlight—or sunbathing on a beach? Have any of these moments contained a spiritual element? Have you, like Saint Patrick, ever heard the Divine voice speaking through the sunshine?

Solar-Powered Medieval Art

For more than thirteen hundred years, Christ-followers have worshiped in chapels and cathedrals with stained-glass windows. Stained glass seems especially suited to contemplation of our Creator, since the medium combines the work of human efforts (the window itself) and the unpredictable and unescapable influence of God's daily participation (as the Sun's effulgence vivifies the work of human hands).

STAINED-GLASS CONTEMPLATION

Spend some time simply looking at a stained-glass window. This could be in a church or chapel, but it might also be in your own home, a circle of stained glass that you've hung in a window. Notice that the glass changes perceptibly as clouds come and go in the sky and the angle of the Sun's light changes. Not only does the glass change, but at the same time, the prism filtered through the glass also changes. I find that half-closing my eyes while facing a stained-glass window enhances the state of consciousness attained through contemplative prayer or meditation.

Sun-Circled Prayers

A traditional Celtic Christian form of prayer is the caim prayer (*caim* is Gaelic for "circle"). This ancient Celtic practice brings God's boundless power for spiritual protection into the consciousness of the person praying. The elemental form of the rounded Sun (along with the elemental form of the Moon and the swelling of a pregnant woman's belly) assured Indigenous people of a powerful benevolence surrounding their lives, and the caim prayer is a way of expressing this primal sense of wholeness in a full-body manner.

The circle prayer is not unique to the Gaelic people. Jewish records describe a second-century holy man named "Honi the circle drawer." According to a rabbi, "Honi was known for his ability to pray successfully for rain in times of drought, while standing in the middle of a circle he had drawn on the ground."[100] The mystic-trance practice of the Mevlevi Sufis also consists of circling dance motions, which is why they are sometimes called "whirling dervishes."

HOW TO PRAY A CAIM

First, draw a circle around yourself, either mentally or with a gesture (such as pointing your forefinger in a 360-degree circle around your body or spinning around on your feet). You can then make up the words for your own circling prayer using the formula of "within" and "without." For example:

Keep fear without. Keep peace within.

Keep sadness without. Keep joy within.

Keep hatred without. Keep love within.

Caim prayers are a way of praying with your body and word to affirm the loving reality of Bright Heaven's Sun, who embraces your being.

I suspect some of my ancestors thought of the circle prayer the same way modern science fiction presents the forcefield, as a magic shield-bubble to keep the person safe from any physical harm. When I engage in this form of prayer, I do imagine a protective orb around me—but it isn't magic; rather, it is the surrounding energy of God's affection for me in Christ, giving me the courage, tenacity, and compassion I need to surmount any challenge. I find this concept in a portion of the Lorica prayer attributed to Saint Patrick[101]:

Christ be with me, Christ within me, Christ behind me,
Christ before me, Christ beside me, Christ to win me,
to comfort me and restore me, Christ beneath me,
Christ above me, Christ in the hearts of all that love me.

A DIVINE HUG

Here's another way to think of a caim prayer: a big hug from Abba God. Imagine the Divine presence embracing you as an ideal parent hugs their most precious child, with the parent receiving even more joy in the embrace than the child receives comfort. God loves you like that! God cherishes you as if you were their only begotten child.

At the heart of Celtic spirituality is the here-and-now-ness of God. Unfortunately, "the cares of this world" and "the desire of other things" too often choke our experience of God's presence (see Mark 4:19). We need tangible reminders—and the Sun is humanity's most common, omnipresent, and beneficent reminder.

Do not neglect this powerful representative of the Divine! Instead of taking the Sun for granted, notice its warmth—and imagine it's the touch of Divine love. See Divinity in the sunlight. Let the Sun's daily cycle serve the function of prayer beads, reminding you to honor the sacred in each moment of the day.

Many of the traditional Scottish Highland prayers collected in the *Carmina Gadelica* were used to sanctify the various actions performed during the changing sunlight of ordinary days. It even includes a prayer to say while washing your face!

> *I wash my face in the sun,*
> *In the nine rays of the sun,*
> *As Mary washed her Son*
> *In the rich fermented milk.*[102]

Consider making the Sun your prayer companion with a small, personal ritual. A few possibilities include:

- When you first open your eyes, greet each day's new light—using your own words—affirming that Divinity fills your life, gives you life, and brings warmth and beauty to your world. Your prayer could be something as simple as "Let your light shine on me today."

- At noon, when the Sun is highest in the sky, silently say a two- or three-word prayer, such as "Let me shine," "Shine on me," or "Light me up."

- As the Sun sets and the day grows dark, release yourself and all that has concerned you during the day into God's hands. You might say, "I trust you," "I give it to you," or "Thank you."

A practice that takes up less than a minute of your day can give you more awareness of God's presence throughout the rest of your day.

As the Sun rises, Light Giver,
Let your light shine on me.
Destroy the darkness about me,
Scatter the darkness before me,
Disperse the darkness behind me,
Dispel the darkness within me.
Let your light shine on me. . . .
The warmth of your Presence,
The brightness of your love,
The radiance of your joy,
The shining of your hope.

ADAPTED FROM DAVID ADAM,
POWER LINES: CELTIC PRAYERS ABOUT WORK

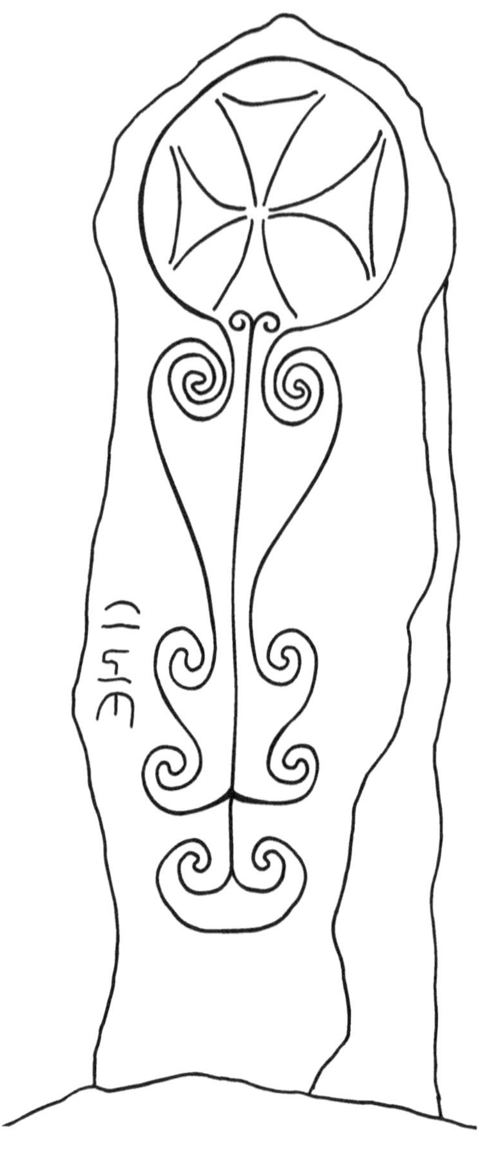

Archeological excavations in County Kerry, Ireland, in the 1970s revealed a monastic site that was probably built in the sixth century. Scattered around the site are a number of cross slabs and pillar stones, including this inscribed pillar stone decorated with a Greek cross within a circle with pendant spiral designs. The stone stands at 1.65 meters high and just over half a meter wide.

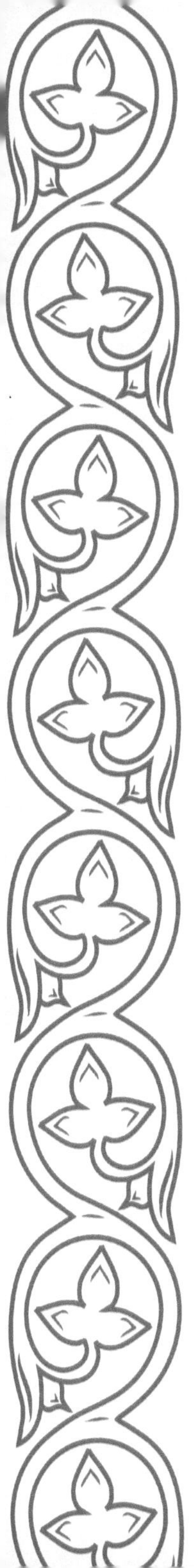

CHAPTER 4

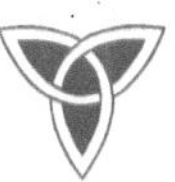

From Jerusalem to the Celtic Nations

May I never boast of anything
except the cross of our Lord Jesus Christ.

GALATIANS 6:14

The Prophet Hosea says:
"Those who were not my people
I will call 'my people'
. . . they will be called 'sons of the living God.'"
. . . Such indeed is the case in Ireland
where they . . . are now called "the sons of God."

SAINT PATRICK[103]

ENCOUNTER

June 2015 and July 2019:
Kildonan, Sutherland, Scotland

Some historical objects jump out at us, demanding we recognize the presence of the past. Cathedrals, for example, are hard to miss, with their spires overshadowing their surrounding landscapes. Other artifacts have remained in place for more than a thousand years, testifying to important events, but they are sometimes difficult to find. And some ancient stone crosses have a beautiful significance even though they are hard to locate and may at first glance seem rough and forgettable.

The cross of Saint Donan is one such overlooked monument. An image from my childhood led me to this cross, making it particularly important to me. I would not have found it, though, without the help of family members over two successive trips to the Scottish Highland.

My mother, a devoted researcher of our family genealogy, had uncovered the fact that some of her ancestors came to America from a place called Helmsdale, in Sutherland, Scotland; hence, I grew up looking at a nice color photograph of Helmsdale. My parents never went there, but it was fixed in my mind as the "old country."

My cousin took up my mother's research and expanded it, and then, in June 2015, my wife and I joined my cousin and her husband on a trip to our Scottish roots. While we were there, my cousin spent time with a genealogist at a museum in Helmsdale who suggested we visit the Kildonan Kirk to better understand our ancestors. We took his advice and made the pleasant drive about twenty minutes inland from Helmsdale, through highland hills, past trout-filled rushing streams, and into the valley of Kildonan with its small but unmissable church.

In the church's choir balcony was an exhibit explaining that the church is named after Saint Donan, a companion of Saint Columba, who traveled across the width of Scotland and first preached the gospel at the same site in 650. (The existing church building, however, only dates from 1786.) The exhibit mentioned a nearby cross-marked stone from Donan's time, but to my disappointment, I never located the stone during that visit.

Four years later, however, my wife and I had the good fortune to return to Kildonan, this time with my sister for company, and on this second trip, I found better directions to Saint Donan's cross-marked boulder. These directions said the boulder was about the height of a person and located "to the north of the manse." That put us in the general vicinity, but we still couldn't find the stone. Again, I was disappointed.

We were driving away, when my sister looked behind us and saw a large stone upright in a bracken-covered field. "Could that be it?" she asked.

We turned around, parked, and then trekked across a gorse-covered hill. Nettles tore at our ankles and arms, and thanks to steaming sheep droppings and many hard-to-see holes, we proceeded cautiously. Nature seemed determined to make our search more challenging.

Sometimes, things can be close by yet hard to find. We were well and truly frustrated—and then my sister exclaimed, "Kenneth, this is it!" We had walked by the stone several times, but it was covered so thoroughly with lichen that we'd missed the cross carved onto its surface.

This standing stone is so unimpressive and so devoid of any plaque or signage, that it is not only easy to overlook; it is downright difficult to find! Despite that, the effort we'd invested in the search made us value this encounter. For me, that weathered and ignored stone forms a Celtic knot that weaves together the faith of an ancient saint with my nineteenth-century ancestors and with the faith that informs my life today.

The earliest Celtic saints worshipped with wooden crosses more often than stone. Some of these may have been of impressive size or shape, but we don't know anything about them. Wood is perishable, and they have all perished. Fortunately, some of these ancient Gaels spent extra effort shaping the cross in stone, so concrete testimonies of their devotion remain in our own time.

DEEPENING

Many ancient Celtic crosses are lines cut onto preexisting standing stones. We don't know who carved these simple expressions of faith; were they monks or priests or laypeople overflowing with love for Christ? All we know for sure is that sometime in the sixth or seventh centuries, the image of a Roman torture device, signifying Jesus of Nazareth who was executed upon it, was transmitted to Ireland and the British Isles, witnessing to a new and powerful spiritual faith.

The Cross on Which Christ Died

Over the past decade, as I have visited, pondered, and prayed in the presence of Celtic crosses, I have experienced a wonderful consistency: Without fail, they have imparted to me some impression, thought, or insight. What's more, those communications have all been entirely *life-affirming*. The high crosses exude healing, hope, comfort, illumination; they enrich the soul.

This is even more amazing when I consider that the prototype of the Christian cross—a form of execution as cruel and inhumane as the electric chair—was far from any life-affirming qualities. Roman crosses were part of a merciless domination system, intended only to take life and spread terror. Only the most twisted minds would devise such a brutal device. When we think of the cross in this light, the later Celtic stone crosses represent a miraculous reversal, an alchemical transformation from taking life to giving life!

In a sense, Jesus' death was terribly ordinary: He was just one of thousands of people executed on crosses in the ancient world. Egyptians, Assyrians, Greeks, Phoenicians, and Romans all killed their criminals and enemies using this device.[104] In the Roman Empire, crucifixion was the standard form of punishment for violent criminals.[105] When Rome quashed the slave revolt led by Spartacus, for example, they crucified more than six thousand rebels along the 115 miles of the Appian Way.[106]

While Rome inflicted this death on great numbers of people who were enslaved or had committed a crime, Roman citizens shied away from even mentioning the topic. Cicero wrote: "The very word 'cross' should be far removed not only from the person of a Roman citizen but from his thoughts, his eyes, and his ears. . . . There is no fitting word that can possibly describe so horrible a deed."[107] Perhaps much like we often do today when we hear of governmental injustice, the Romans preferred to look away rather than face what their leaders were doing.

Roman executioners were professionals who put considerable thought into their cold-blooded trade; they designed multiple forms of crosses. Some were shaped like a lowercase letter "t" (what most of us imagine when we hear the word *cross* because this is how Western artists portrayed it). Others looked like an upper-case letter "T" (known as the *tau cross* and adopted as a symbol by the Franciscan order); a *furca*—a fork-shaped cross (like an upside-down peace sign or a bird's footprint); or an X-shaped cross (known as a "Saint Andrew's cross"). The earliest depictions of Jesus' crucifixion show a tau cross.[108]

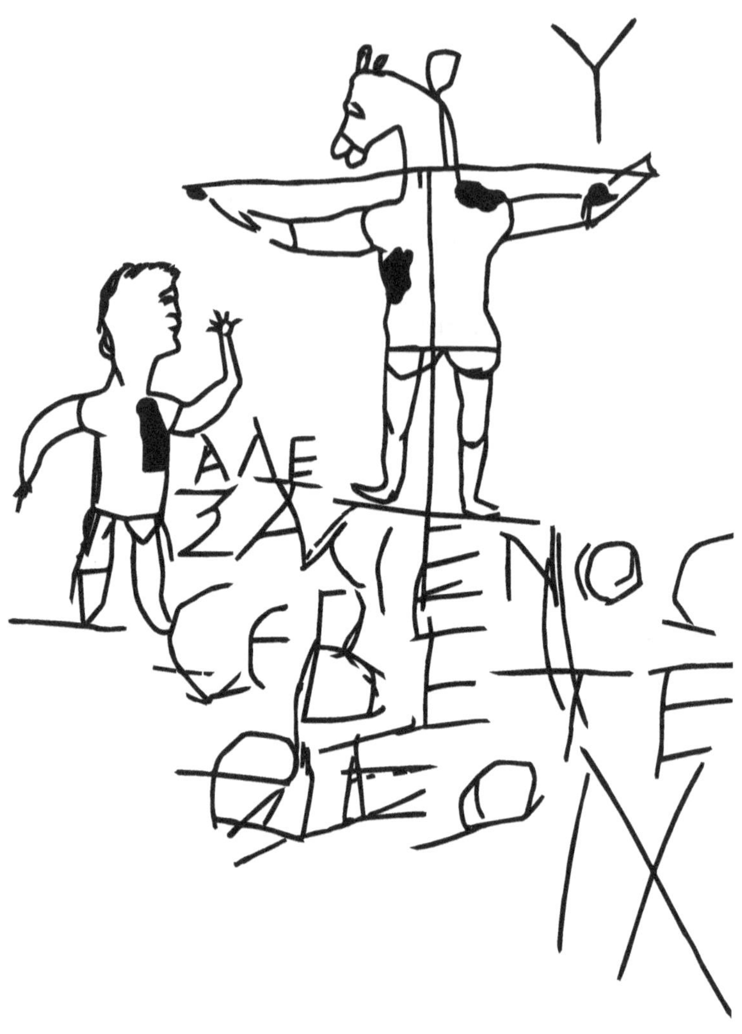

The Alexamenos graffito, at the museum in the Palatine Hill, Rome, is graffiti depicting a man worshiping a crucified donkey. Though apparently meant as an insult, it is the earliest known pictorial representation of Jesus' crucifixion.

From Imperial Weapon to a Symbol of Faith

Roman citizens and their conquered subjects loathed thinking about crucifixion; it was the utmost indignity the empire could inflict. No one wanted to remember the names of people who had been crucified; far better to forget their shame. As a result, a religion built around a crucifixion victim was a hard sell, to say the least. Jesus' earliest followers, however, realized God had performed the most ironic of miracles: God had used the state's weapon of terror to bring about the greatest possible good. (I shall write more about the three-act drama of this great reversal in chapter 10.)

In the early years of the Jesus Movement, the cross was still too associated with violent death to be a symbol of faith—but that changed in the fourth century, when the emperor Constantine granted Christianity his approval. Constantine is responsible for creating the earliest symbol of the crucifixion, the Chi-Rho (*Chi* pronounced "ky" and *Rho* pronounced like "row"), a monogram made by placing the letter "X" (the first letter of *Christos* in Latin) over an uppercase "R" (the second letter in *Christos*). In the year 312, when Constantine won rulership of the Roman Empire in a battle, the victory was attributed to the Chi-Rho symbol he had ordered painted on his legionnaire's shields.[109] As Rome's reach spread across the Earth, the Chi-Rho also traveled through all the reaches of the Empire. As a result, the earliest cross symbols found in the Isles are Chi-Rho emblems, such as one found at Whithorn Abbey (a cradle of Scottish Christianity).

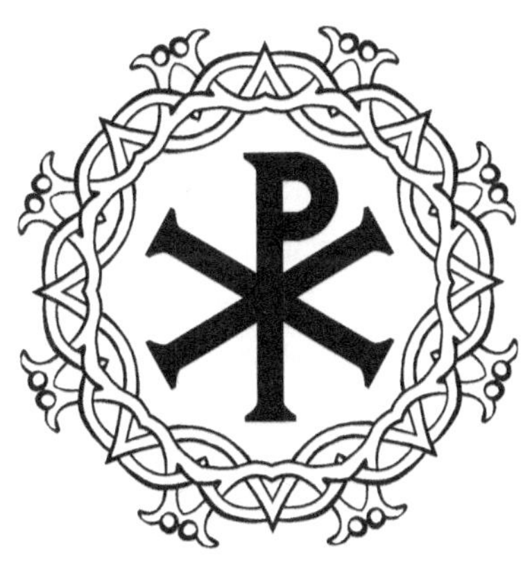

The Chi-Rho symbol combines two letters from the Latin name for Christ.

Author Derek Bryce believes:

> this symbol was the beginning of an art form which, in
> the Celtic lands, led to the production of the beautifully
> sculptured crosses. . . . What happened was that the chi-
> rho monogram came to be enclosed within a circle, and the
> curved part of the P [what I call an "R"] became detached
> at its lower end, and reduced in size until eventually it dis-
> appeared, leaving a circle, or wheel cross.[110]

I disagree; I believe the wheel cross came, instead, from Egypt
(which I'll discuss in the next chapter). Still, Bryce's theory is worthy of
consideration. Something that may support his idea is the enormous
and lavish Chi-Rho monogram in the famous Celtic illuminated
manuscript called the Book of Kells.

The "True" Cross

When I visited the Church of the Holy Sepulcher in 1997, I had a
hard time at first imagining Christ's crucifixion at the site where it
was supposed to have taken place. The place of the cross was crowded
with people and overlaid with glitzy embellishments; all I could think
of was my own claustrophobia.

I came back later in the week, though, at an off time when I was
able to catch a moment alone. Kneeling, I reached down to touch the
hole in the stone where tradition claims the upright post of the cross
was anchored. Emotions swept over me. No one can prove this is in
fact where Christ died—and yet I was deeply moved by the reality
that for more than 1,500 years, Christ's followers have come from
all around the Earth to touch the Divine presence in that same spot.

For many Christians—especially those in the British Isles and
Ireland at the far edges of the Byzantine Empire—the pilgrimage

to Jerusalem was impossible to make. But if they could not come to the place of the cross, portions of the cross came to them. Divided, distributed, replicated, and faked, relics of the "true cross" became the most venerated objects of the Early Middle Ages. The cross as a symbol also rose in esteem.

In the waning years of Rome's power, the message of God's love through Christ spread throughout the European continent and the Isles. A second wave of the gospel came after the Romans withdrew from Britain in the fifth century. Saint Patrick was one of the most influential pioneer missionaries during this period.

The ancient Celts found Christianity to be an easy fit, for several reasons. One of these was the significance of trees. Both early Christians and the Pagan Celtic people perceived trees as having spiritual power and blessings, a factor that likely helped welcome "the tree of Christ"[111]—the cross—into the Gaelic world. For the Pagan people of the Celtic lands, trees were a link between the upper and lower realms; with their roots spreading into the underworld and their branches extending into the sky, trees form bridges between the invisible and visible realms.[112] Meanwhile, early Christians had begun to connect Christ's crucifixion with the "tree of life."[113]

A fifth-century sermon expresses well the merger of Christian and Pagan tree imagery:

This Tree is my eternal salvation. It is my nourishment and my banquet. Amidst its roots I cast my own roots deep: beneath its boughs I grow and expand. . . . This Tree, vast as heaven itself, rises from earth to the skies, a plant immortal, set firm in the midst of heaven and earth, base of all that is, foundation of the universe, support of this world of [human beings], binding-force of all creation, holding within itself all the mysterious essence of [humanity].

Secured with the unseen clamps of the spirit, so that . . . it may never bend or warp, with foot resting firm on earth it towers to the topmost skies, and spans with its all-embracing arms the boundless gulf of space between.[114]

Brown and Herren, professors of theology and art, conclude: "This transformed tree of life became the symbol of Christ . . . and expresses the harmonious co-existence of all nature in the living God."[115]

Cross-ing the Stones

Bede, the first English historian, recalls the instructions that Pope Gregory gave around the year 600 to Augustine, the pope's missionary to England (not the same Augustine who became a saint out of North Africa):

I have, upon mature deliberation of the affair of the English, determined . . . that the temples of the idols in those nations ought not to be destroyed; but let . . . holy water be made and sprinkled in the said temples, let altars be erected, and relics placed . . . that the nation, seeing that their temples are not destroyed . . . may the more familiarly resort to the places to which they are accustomed.[116]

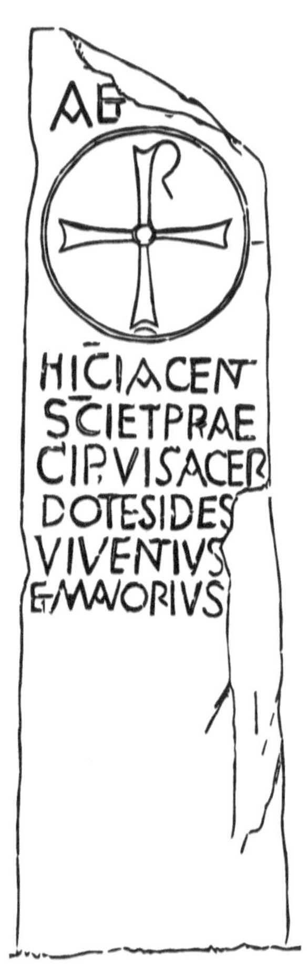

This drawing, based on one of the ancient stones at Kirkmadrine, shows the Chi-Rho influence on the shape of the encircled cross.

Early Christians in the Isles often placed the mark of the cross upon monumental stones their ancestors had erected centuries before. The Kirkmadrine cross-stones, some of the earliest inscribed Christian monuments in Scotland, dating from the fifth or sixth centuries, are an example of such repurposing of sacred sites. Scholars suggest these are prehistoric standing stones that were resanctified for Christian burials. One of these displays a perfect example of what we would now call a Celtic cross: a deeply carved circle enclosing the cross, and—evidence of its antiquity—the vestigial arm of a Roman Chi-Rho.[117]

Another example of a repurposed stone stands at the Reask monastic site in County Kerry, Ireland. Only the outlines of the monastery remain, but the more ancient Reask stone is still a unique and striking monument. (See the drawing at the beginning of this chapter.) Prehistoric workers carved the top of the slab-shaped stone to align with the contours of the hillside behind it (a common practice in monolithic art). The cross and artistic scrolls date from somewhere between the fifth to seventh centuries.[118]

When I see stones like the ones at Kildonan, Kirkmadrine, and Reask, they draw a range of emotions from me. They pull me into the distant past: first, to the Stone Age when the stones were first erected with great effort, and then to a point in time, centuries later, when the hearts of the Isles' people turned to Jesus, the God-Human. Nowadays, of course, if we were to use an ancient artifact for our own purposes, changing or adding to it would be considered an act of defacement, a crime against the past, a destruction of humanity's tale. I doubt, though, the people who carved these crosses had any sense of destroying what came before. Instead, they were claiming the ancient holy places as still relevant to their own lives.

Psychiatrist and spiritual writer M. Scott Peck, in his book *In Search of Stones*, muses about another repurposed megalithic stone at Aberlemno in Scotland, and acknowledges that "throughout history it has been the norm for a conquering religion to build its temples on top of the temple ruins of the conquered one." Peck then recognizes that such behavior could be due to "the opportunity for the new religion to demonstrate its power over the old one"—and yet, standing in the Aberlemno stone's presence, he writes, was "a multicultural, multitemporal monument" that points to a greater potential unity. Despite all our divisions and prejudice, Peck affirms:

> We have a passion for integration. For racial and cultural integration. For religious integration. For the integration of ideas. And perhaps above all, for the integration of the past with the present—and with the future.[119]

The Purpose of Stone Crosses

Clearly, however these ancient crosses came to be—as natural rock formations, as repurposed still-more-ancient monuments, or as sculptures created by early Celtic Christians—creating them took enormous time and effort. Why did the long-ago workers and their sponsors feel that such labor was worthwhile? What motivated them to do the long, hard work of creating these enduring symbols of Christianity? There are several answers to these questions.[120]

Church Worship

If you walk into any Christian church—Protestant, Orthodox, or Catholic—it's a sure bet some sort of cross will be a focal point of worship. This has been true for well over a thousand years, and the ancient people of the Isles readily claimed the cross-symbol as their own.

One of my favorite worship places is a tiny Saxon church in Escomb, near Durham in Northern England. The church today looks pretty much the same as what you would have seen had you walked into the same building just after it was dedicated in the year 675.

Worshipers have attended services at the Escomb church every single Sunday for almost 1,400 years (with the exception of a brief time while the roof was being replaced and worship had to temporarily move elsewhere). I love that sense of continuity!

Northeast England (Angle-land) was Anglo-Saxon territory at the time of the church's construction—but the building is as much Celtic as Saxon. The circular churchyard indicates a Celtic foundation, and architectural details are similar to those found in the most ancient church buildings in Ireland. The cross at the front of the chancel, a bas-relief carved stone slab, has the round center of a Celtic cross.

I've been privileged to worship twice at Escomb, once at a Celtic evening service and then again with my wife and a friend in a private service. Each time, as I prayed in front of that cross, I wondered: Who were the individuals who had stood in the same place over the long centuries, their gaze on that same cross?

Grave Markers

Some ancient stone crosses bear the names of people buried under their reassuring shadow more than a thousand years ago. One example of a gravestone cross is the Tywyn Stone, originally set in the church burial ground in the ninth century. (It now stands in St. Cadfan's Church in Tywyn, Wales.) This stone has drawn scholars' attention because its inscriptions are in Welsh rather than Latin, the language most commonly used at the time for formal and

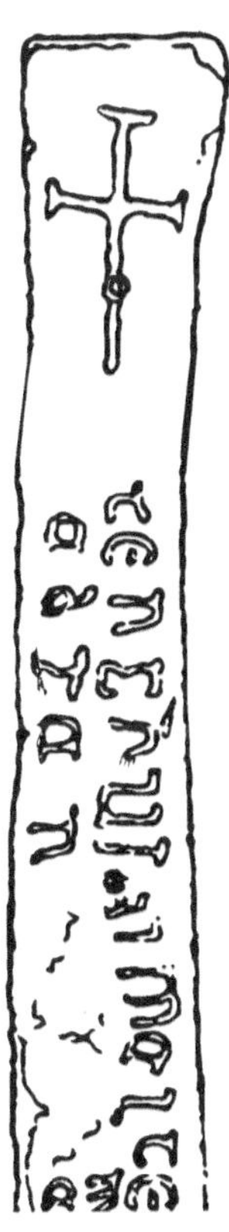

A drawing of the Tywyn Stone, which stands in the church at Tywyn, County Gwynedd, in Wales.

religious purposes. The stone is also unusual because it is dedicated to two women: Tengrumui, wife of Adgan, and Cun, wife of Celen. The words carved on the stone express a timeless expression of grief: "A mortal wound remains"[121]

Modern cemeteries in the Celtic nations also have many fine examples of sculptured stone crosses, and some of them have knotwork and proportions as fine as the crosses made in the ninth and tenth centuries. People who use such monuments to memorialize their departed loved ones are often deliberately connecting to their long-ago Gaelic ancestors. These markers testify to the amazing endurance of heritage and faith.

In 1902, Mary Carbery commissioned another memorial cross, this one to honor her dead husband, Algernon. In the nineteenth century, during the Celtic Revival's renewed interest in ancient arts, Celtic crosses became a fashionable form of gravestone in many English-speaking countries. Lady Mary, a young wife who had just inherited her husband's castle in West Cork, Ireland, wanted to honor her husband's heritage—and she wanted to do so with a memorial cross taller than any other. At 30 feet, that cross is still the tallest memorial cross in Ireland.[122]

Tall or small, these memorial crosses, like the high crosses on Drumalban, all proclaim with the lasting endurance of stone: "This life mattered. This life will not be forgotten by Christ."

Market Crosses

If you happen to be in the center of St. David's, Wales, at the right time on the right day, you'll see vendors selling their wares: produce, market preserves, clothing, handmade jewelry, all set out on tables beneath bright awnings. In the middle of the market, where it has stood since the Middle Ages, is a market cross.

A surprising number of these crosses are still intact and in their original settings in cities throughout Europe. They denoted places of commerce in the British Isles and Ireland since at least as early as the seventh century. These market crosses served more than one function: they proved that the local government had given official permission to do business in that place—and they reminded tradespeople that they conducted their business in the sight of the great and just God. At a deep level, medieval people assumed Divinity was involved in every aspect of life: not only what we would think of today as "churchy" or religious things but also birth and death, planting and harvesting, music and dancing, sex and eating—and buying and selling.

To Sanctify a Holy Well

While walking the Camino, I chanced upon a repurposed place of worship, Nossa Senhora das Neves de Buxante, in Galicia (one of the seven Celtic nations). I was en route to Finisterre, between Hospital and Cee, when I noticed the medieval church. As I explored further, I discovered the church had a holy well, known for its healing powers; a stone *cruciero* (high cross); and an altar with a worn stone statue said to be Mary.

Galician historian Fernando Alonso Romero believes the holy well was the first thing there, long before Christianity came to the Isles.[123] Pagans who worshipped the Mother Goddess may have been the ones who shaped the primitive statue said today to be Mary.[124] Or perhaps the Romans who came later created the statue to portray Furrina, their goddess of springs. Finally, later still, drawn to the place's healing properties and sacred energy (but seeking to hallow it, just in case), Christians built the nearby church and cross. Similar juxtapositions of medieval crosses and ancient Pagan holy wells are common throughout all the Celtic nations.

Preaching Crosses

Do you know someone who says, "I don't go to church on Sunday mornings, but I worship God when I'm outdoors in Nature"? (Maybe that someone is you?) The ancient Celts also worshipped outdoors. The earliest of these crosses were places where priests might read the Gospels and serve the Eucharist, although no shelters were built there. Even after the Celts constructed churches, many of them still had adjacent outdoor preaching crosses. Apparently, the people of the Celtic lands still liked worshipping in the fresh air.

Boundary Markers

If fences make good neighbors (according to Robert Frost), then some really large stones make even better demarcations between what is yours and mine. Some megalithic stones in Europe were boundary markers, some of them erected by the Roman Empire to stake its claim on the land. Although these stones served utilitarian purposes, they were placed with great religious ceremony, in the belief that Divinity watched over the land.[125]

Later, when the Celts replaced ancient standing stones with the crosses, these likewise came to signify the borders of fields, kingdoms, or monastic lands. As with the ancient boundary stones, border crosses served a practical purpose, but they also represented the presence of God watching over the land. Celtic Christians in the Early Middle Ages believed wholeheartedly in the talismanic power of a cross to guard against evil. The great monasteries of Ireland, for instance, had large and ornate stone crosses guarding each gate and each cardinal direction.

Commemorative Monuments

The Latin *Life of Saint Cainnech*, written between 750 and 850, tells this story about Saint Cainnech, an Irish abbot, a friend of Columba, and an evangelizer for Christ in Ireland and Pictish Scotland: As the saint was trudging through the wilderness of Drumalban in the Pictish kingdom on a bitter winter day, he came across a mother and her little daughter. The mother was half-frozen, but the little girl was dead from the cold. Cainnech prayed, the mother was refreshed, and the little girl raised to life. The story concludes: "And in that place there are high crosses to be seen down to this day"[126]

Waymarks

Dartmoor in Devon is an almost surreal landscape, with wild moors, oddly shaped stone formations, dwarf forests, and wild ponies. In the Middle Ages, the moor was downright terrifying, a place where travelers could become lost, mired, or perhaps fall prey to the black hellhounds storytellers described. The presence of strategically placed stone crosses gave hope to anxious travelers. These were situated so that at any point during the daylight hours, people journeying through the moors could always see from one cross to the next. Keeping the crosses in their line of sight, travelers on the moor proceeded safely from cross to cross. Most of these waymark crosses are still in place, and a modern hiker can still navigate between them.

Stone crosses were built throughout the medieval world to mark important points of reference for travelers, especially crossroads, routes to important towns, and hilltops. A walking pilgrimage, where you are dependent on signs to show you the way, is a good way to enter into the experience of long-ago people.

As my wife and I walked the Camino de Santiago, we learned that many of the paths on the pilgrim route are the same ones used since the early ninth century; Roman roads are also visible along the way. Nowadays, the Camino is marked throughout with yellow arrows (*flechas*), signs made by a priest from Celtic Galicia, Father Sampedro, who felt God had called him to prepare for "a great flood" of pilgrims. Over the course of 500 miles, my wife and I learned to keep an eye out for those signs; we were always looking for the next marker. This daily literal dependence on signs even translated into my spiritual life, causing me to be more attuned to the other ways God directs me.

Before Father Sampedro made his *flechas*, other signs marked the trail, though not as thoroughly: *crucieros* (stone high crosses), most dating from the eighteenth or nineteenth century. These typically show the crucified Christ on the front and the Virgin Mary on the opposite side; sometimes Saint James is also portrayed. Seeing these stone crucifixes told pilgrims: "You are on the right path" (both physically and spiritually).

My first walking pilgrimage was the Cuthbert Way, a week-long journey in the summer of 2021, in the company of folk from the United Church of Christ in the United States and the United Reformed Church of Northern England. This pilgrim foot route took us on a 62-mile hike from Melrose in Scotland to the Holy Island of Lindisfarne in England. Signs depicting the reliquary cross of Saint Cuthbert mark the way.[127]

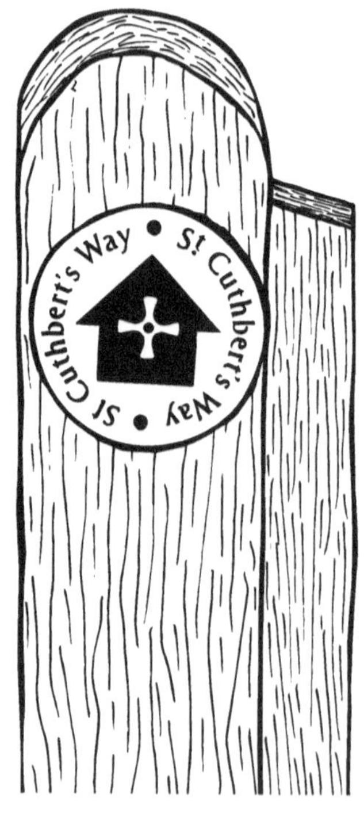

Waymarks keep pilgrims from getting lost as they walk the Cuthbert Way.

Nigel Marns, the author of a book about another pilgrimage route, the Cornish Celtic Way, describes the importance of ancient way-marker wheel crosses on this path:

> More than just stones, they became living stones and companions to me. They energized, propelled me forward, and lead me on with hope and encouragement. I touched each one at the centre of the cross, drawing on the saints of the past.[128]

We might think of all Celtic crosses in a similar way: They connect us not only to God but also to people of faith who lived long ago, allowing us to be encouraged and strengthened by Divine energy. As we journey into exciting new places and new experiences, as well through uncertain, anxious times, the Celtic cross can guide our way.

APPLICATIONS FOR TODAY

Re-Kindling Lost Love

"You have abandoned the love you had at first," writes the author of the last book of the Christian scriptures.[129] He is speaking to a community of Christ-followers, but this diagnosis might just as easily be applied to any long-term human relationship.

As the person who once triggered our passion becomes beloved and familiar, they may, paradoxically, begin to inspire only indifference or boredom. This response to familiarity is a natural human tendency, one most people experience at some time or another. Depending on the relationship, greater depths of intimacy may lie on the other side of the "cold" times—and the same is true in our relationship with God. We may think we know all we will ever know about God (and what we know has grown worn, lacking in passion), but that assumption limits Divinity. When we release God from the boxes we've constructed, Divinity becomes the Mystery that has no end, the Love that has no limit.

Theologian Thomas Andrew Bennett sees a similar dynamic around modern-day Christians' attitudes toward the cross. He says Christians have become "utterly inured" to the cross, so that seeing one no longer causes a shock of emotion. This has happened, he says, because Christians have "stripped [the cross] of any intimation of scandal, . . . sanitized it, . . . rendered it inert and anodyne."[130] The ugly symbol that once shocked well-mannered people has become commonplace, ordinary, lifeless.

But in any long-term relationship that's grown cold, something besides over-familiarity may be going on. Over the years, stuff happens. Misunderstandings happen. Hurt feelings happen. We let each other down. We put up our defenses, and then we hurt each other even more. Meanwhile, the relationship grows colder and colder. It's not so much that we abandoned our first love; it's more that it got stomped out of us.

And just as this can happen within a human relationship, it can happen in our connection to God within Christianity. The church has let us down. It has hurt many of us, and it has demonstrated its hypocrisy in many ways: greed, misogyny, racism, intolerance of others' identities and beliefs, sexual abuse, lying and concealing the truth, self-righteousness, and narrowmindedness. It's hard to untangle our "relationship with Christ" from our experiences with the organizations that claim his name. If we read or hear the words "Jesus loves you," we filter the message through the lens of boredom, rage, disappointment, or pain. The meaning of those three words has become trivialized, sloganized, even weaponized.

Let's Pretend . . .

To clear away the centuries of theological barnacles that have attached themselves to Christ's name and the cross, take a few moments to imagine you are someone different, living in a different time and place, a member of one of the Celtic tribes living in the Isles long, long ago. Your life is filled with crises (births, deaths, violence, hunger) and worry (mostly *about* birth, death, violence, hunger). Just living from day to day, working to care for your family, takes every bit of energy you have. And yet you also have moments of great joy. The love between the members of your community, the way the Moon makes a silver path across the sea, the times you catch a glimpse of the Otherworld, all these make your blood sing. Your life is filled with hard work and much suffering, with shining moments scattered like stars through the shadows. One day follows the next, each one the same as the last, the only changes brought by the turning cycle of the seasons.

And then strangers come to your village. Perhaps one of them is a man named Patrick, or possibly Donan or Ninian; maybe the women are named Lupait, Ita, or Dympna. These people come from afar, and their language and accent are difficult to understand. As your tribe gathers around them, asking questions, there is much searching for words, many hand motions, and a lot of laughter. You and the others in your community learn these travelers have come from across the sea, from Ireland, a trip filled with danger. And yet these travelers have arrived unharmed; they are cheerful and have many tales to share.

You are curious. Who are these people? Why have they come? Why did they take such risks to get here?

At the end of the day, as fires are lit and the day's work is set aside, the community gathers to hear more from the strangers. You settle down on the ground to hear the tales these strangers tell.

They tell about Íosa, a god who came to Earth. He had all the traits you admire in a warrior hero—courage, honesty, inner strength—yet he did not carry a sword, and he refused to use violence against his enemies. Instead, he taught that love can be big enough to embrace even our enemies.

The evening grows late as the strangers repeat the stories Íosa told, the things he did. Some of the stories make you laugh; some of them bring tears to your eyes. Then the strangers describe the death on a cross of this hero, this god, and you sigh in sorrow. At the same time, this makes sense to you; you have grown up on stories about the Warrior King who sacrifices himself for his people. The bards sing these tales, making them come alive, just as these strangers are bringing Íosa to life.

The travelers speak at length about Íosa as Truth and Light, Food and Water, a Way to follow and a Companion who goes with you on the Way. Truth is essential to your culture, light and food are necessary for life and growth, and water is a portal into the Otherworld: Again, this all makes sense to you. The strangers say that Íosa also called himself a Door, and that seems familiar too; after all, druids—the wise teachers of your people—are sometimes called "doors." Íosa, like a druid, is a threshold person, a doorway into the world of the spirit.

Íosa, the travelers say, is the Son of God who came down from Tír na nÓg (the World of Light and Joy) to our Little World to take on all the vulnerability of being human, in order to teach, direct, and inform those who also seek to be Divine. "Íosa," says one of the travelers, "came forth from God's endless love—and Íosa made God's love so we could see it. So we can understand it better. Everything Íosa did was done in love."[131]

As you go to sleep that night, you are still musing on everything the strangers have said, and in the days that follow, you and your community continue to ask questions. The travelers from Ireland seem happy to talk about Íosa for as long as anyone will listen. Something in their stories seems different from the usual tales the bards sing. The more the strangers say about Íosa, the more he seems like someone you might get to know personally.

On a bright morning, one of the travelers stands at the center of the community and speaks these words: "Look at the animals roaming the forest: The same spirit who dwelt in Íosa dwells within them. Look at the birds flying across the sky: The Divine spirit dwells within them."

Just as she says those words, a crow flutters overhead; some people laugh, others gasp softly with awe. You watch as the bird settles on a nearby tree, and you have no problem believing that the Divine spirit lives behind those shiny black eyes, within that black plumage.

"Look at the tiny insects crawling on the grass," the woman continues. "God's spirit dwells within them. Look at the fish in the river and sea: God's spirit dwells within them. There is no creature on Earth in whom God is absent. God's spirit is present within all plants as well. The presence of God's spirit in all life is what makes all things beautiful. In fact, when we see with God's eyes, no aspect of Creation is ugly."[132]

You look up at the sky, then across the green hills, and beauty is everywhere you look. You are not quite sure what the woman's words mean, but the world's beauty has always spoken to you. Now, you feel goosebumps: Everything you see is *God*.

But you're not even sure what that word means to the woman. At first, you thought she was talking about the Dagda, the All-God, the Good-God, or his mother Danu, the Mother of all life—but now you sense that she's referring to something else, something so vast it fills the entire world and yet at the same time, *loves* you, the way your parents love you, the way you love your children. Maybe the Dagda and Danu are part of it; it all seems like a Mystery too big, too lovely for you to grasp. These strange ideas are giving you the same feelings you have before you set out on a journey: nervousness, excitement, eagerness, trepidation, all mixed together.

The Irish woman is still speaking, so you pull your attention back to her. "We see God's love all around us," she is saying. "In the trees, in the flowers, in the sea, in the fields, in the beasts, and in one another. And God wants us to do the same, shedding love into every piece of our lives."

"But how do we do that?" a man near the front of the gathering asks.

The woman smiles. "That's one reason Íosa came—to show us how to love each other and the world around us and even ourselves. He was kind, tenderhearted, quick to forgive. He made it simple for us—'Just treat others the way you would like to be treated,' he told us. And that is what he did. He did not know how to hurt or harm anyone; he only helped everyone he met. He forgave them and loved them, he fed them and healed them—and when we do the same for one another and for God's creatures, we are following Íosa."[133]

The woman pulled from the pocket of her robe a small, painted object. She held it up high so everyone could see. "This is an icon of Íosa's face."

You squint at the little picture of a bearded man; you wonder if later, the woman might allow you to hold it in your hand so you can examine him more closely. From a distance, you can see only that the man's eyes are wide-set and calm, his nose is long and thin, and his mouth gentle.

Then the woman pulls something else from her pocket and holds it up: a small cross carved from wood. It reminds you of images your people make of the Sun and the four corners of the world. The woman says the God-Man, Íosa, this compassionate warrior, died on a structure like this.

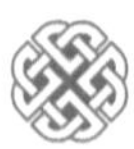 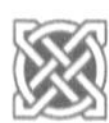 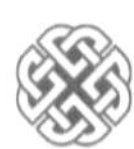

As the days go by, you and your friends and family become more and more curious about Íosa. The travelers help out with farming and fishing, and as they work, they talk still more about their god.

One day, you overhear a man from your village say to one of the travelers, "You say this Íosa is a warrior, but he sounds like a druid too." You stop to listen, because you've had this thought too.

The people from Ireland nod. "Yes, he is a druid," says one of them. "The best of all druids."[134]

You wonder what Biróg, the druid who visits your village most often, will have to say about Íosa. But when she arrives later that summer, she seems as fascinated with Íosa as the rest of you are.

You begin to feel as though something is tugging at you, pulling you ever closer to Íosa. When the call grows too loud to ignore, you talk with a friend and discover he too yearns to know Íosa better. And as it turns out, many people in your village feel the same. One bright morning, all of you gather at the holy well—and one of the travelers immerses each of you in turn into the joy and love of Íosa.

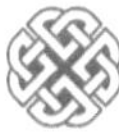 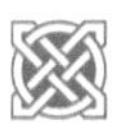 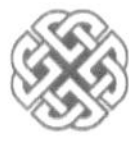

Sometime later, maybe months, maybe even years, after most of your fellow villagers had chosen to follow this new faith, the community joins together around the ancient standing stone that has looked over the land for as long as anyone can remember. You watch as the stone carvers add the shape of the now-beloved cross onto the monument's age-old surface. When they are done, the community joins together in celebration, singing and feasting for the rest of the day. The tall stone, you sense, now holds the joy of Íosa—and the stone will carry it to future generations, long after you have gone to the Otherworld.

SEEING JESUS

It's not easy to "see" Jesus without the layers that have accumulated around the living Person. If this feels like something you yearn for and yet can't seem to achieve on your own, bring your longing to Christ. It might even help you to call him by a different name from the one you're used to, such as Íosa, the Celtic form of Jesus; Isa, the Arabic version of Jesus' name; or Jesu / Yesu, as many African languages call him. Or you can call him by whatever title comes from your heart—*Beloved . . . Light . . . Truth . . . Love . . . Shepherd . . . Teacher.* Then pray something like this:

Jesus, I want to see you with new eyes.
Please, open my heart to see you with a child's vision.
Show me how to make our relationship come alive in my life.

Jesus from a Different Perspective

I hope my story helps you see what it might have been like to hear the Christ-message for the first time. No disappointment or hurt or violence had yet touched the name of Jesus. You would be able to see him standing in his own selfhood, without the centuries of institutional struggle and hypocrisy.

Have you ever run into a close friend, even a relative, somewhere you would never expect to see them? And just for a moment, you don't recognize them. You're seeing them in a new way, without the cloak of familiarity. I invite you to do something similar with Jesus: Look at him from a new perspective.

PRAYING WITH THE CROSS

Consider placing crosses (small statues that stand on a table or hang from the wall—or pictures of crosses that particularly speak to you) where your eyes will fall on them throughout the day: over your bathroom mirror, for example, above the kitchen sink, on your bedroom wall, or by your front door. Each time you see one of these crosses, consciously pause for just a moment and simply, silently say *thank you.*

Prayer does not have to be long or complicated. These two small words, by themselves, can mean whatever you want them to mean:

Thank you for being with me all of my life.
Thank you for helping me not lose my temper.
Thank you for helping me through that medical crisis.
Thank you for my child or grandchild.
Thank you for giving me strength.
Thank you for coming to Earth to teach us how to love.
Thank you for . . . too many things to name!

Crossing Your Life

In the Early Middle Ages, the entirety of life happened in the presence of the cross. Weddings took place before a chapel cross, and so did the christening of babies. Crosses that marked land boundary lines were a familiar part of the landscape. On Sundays and feast days, priests proclaimed the gospel, either inside in front of the chapel cross or, in nice weather, outdoors at the preaching cross. Villagers drew their water from a cross-marked well. They did business, selling farm produce and fabrics, in the shadow of the market cross. When beloved friends and family members departed from this world, the community grieved as they buried them beneath the arms of the cross. Everywhere a person turned, they saw crosses, reminding them: *Everything we do is sacred. Everything we do, we do in the presence of Christ's love. Christ is present in all things.*

Most high glorious God,
enlighten the shadows of my heart.
Give me right faith, sure hope, and perfect charity.
Fill me with understanding and knowledge
that I may fulfill your command.

FRANCIS OF ASSISI
(THE PRAYER HE UTTERED BEFORE THE
CROSS OF SAN DAMIANO, WHICH SPOKE TO HIM)

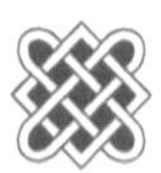

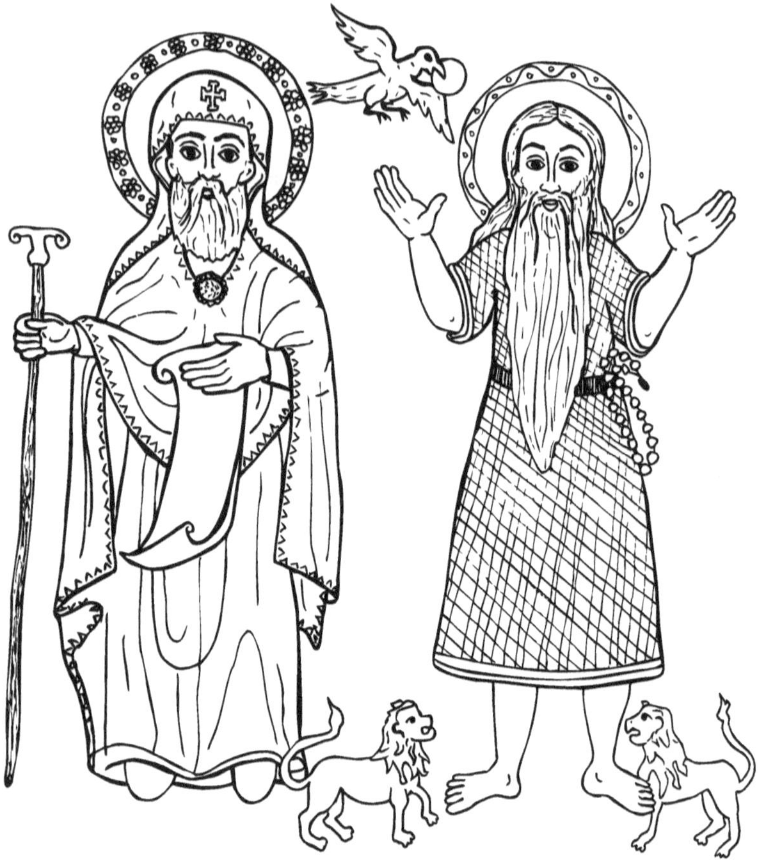

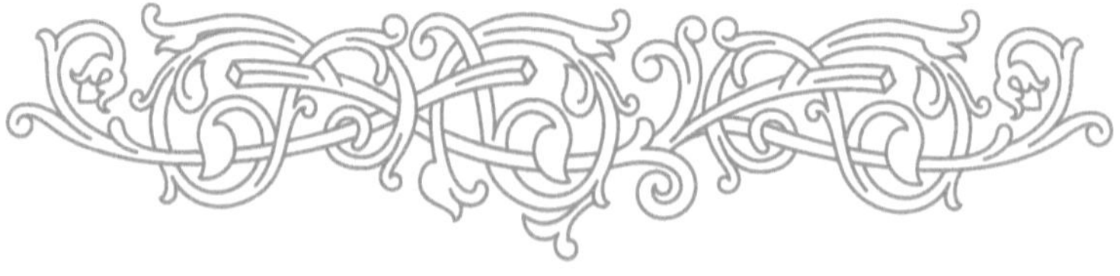

The early medieval Celts loved the story of the two Desert Fathers, Anthony and Paul. Celtic stone crosses often bore artwork that portrayed the friendship between these two old saints, just as Coptic icons from Egypt also did.

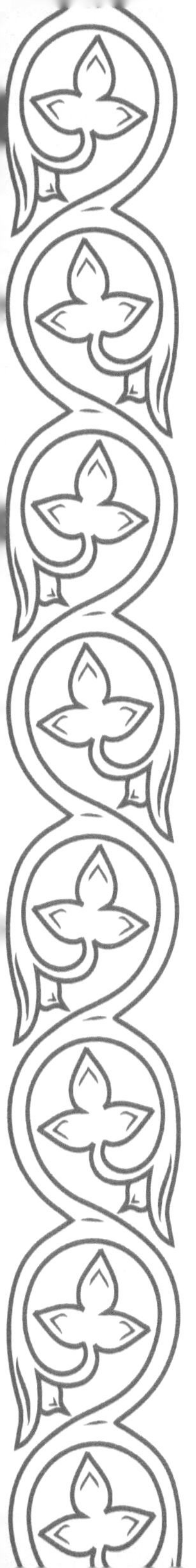

CHAPTER 5

Wisdom from the East

*Now after they had left,
an angel of the Lord appeared
to Joseph in a dream
and said, "Get up, take the child and his mother,
and flee to Egypt,
and remain there until I tell you,
for Herod is about to search for the child,
to destroy him." Then Joseph got up,
took the child and his mother by night,
and went to Egypt and remained there
until the death of Herod.
This was to fulfill what had been spoken
by the Lord through the prophet,
"Out of Egypt I have called my son."*

Matthew 2:13–15

ENCOUNTER

342 CE: The Egyptian Desert (far from any city)

In the morning, before heat made the sands shimmer and a touch of coolness lingered in the air, the man stooped from the mouth of his cave to his sitting-place on a wide, flat stone beneath a broom tree. He closed his eyes and fell into his customary state of waking contemplation, a sense of surrender in the presence of limitless peace, not much different from what he experienced in sleep.

A nearby sound registered in his mind, but he quickly dismissed it. *It is the lion pair, my old friends.*

But the sound came again, and then a voice: "You are Paul, the one I seek."

He turned: There was a stranger, covered head to toe in coarse, patched linen, his beard long and white.

"Are you an angel or a mortal man?" Paul had not spoken in so long that his voice was raspy.

The stranger replied, "I am Anthony, a sinner. I am a hermit also, and I know it is hard to speak when you have not had visitors in a long time. I have lived these past decades in the wilderness, like you, battling demons, treading serpents, lifting high the praises of the Great One."

"Welcome, Anthony." The sound of his own voice still seemed strange, and he cleared his throat and tried again. "Bless you in the name of Christ."

"And the blessings of Christ in return, Paul. I am here because the Mighty One sent an angel to me in my sleep, and told me, 'There is a man who lives in the inner wilderness; the world is not worthy of his footsteps. By his prayers, God brings rain and dew to fall on the soil and brings the flood of the Nile in its due season.' When I heard this, I rose immediately and walked one full day to reach your inner wilderness. God guided me to this cave."

Paul smiled. "Since God called you, then I am glad you have come. Tell me, how were you called to the desert?"

"When my parents died, I inherited their fortune—but then I heard the gospel proclaimed. Christ said, 'Sell what you have and give to the poor, then come, follow me.' So I did. At first, I dwelt among the pyramids, and the demons of the dead came and harassed me. Then I knew God was calling me deeper into the wilderness, to an abandoned outpost. There my soul ascends to God, and I find victory over the forces of evil. Now, others have followed me. Men and women encamp around my dwelling place. They build huts of clay and straw, and the sound of their prayers fills the desert with gladness."

"There are yet more like you and me?" Paul's eyes widened at the thought. He whispered, "I never imagined. I thought I was like Elijah. All alone in the wilderness."

"God told Elijah there were many more people who had not bowed to Ba'al—and just so, many people now defy the world's carnality and worship in the wild places." Anthony hesitated, then asked, "And you, you have been a hermit now for how long?"

Paul took a long time to answer. "As long as I can remember," he said finally. "I have no sense of days, weeks, or months. The heavens turn. The wild beasts are my companions. All days and nights are just drops in the ocean of the Great One."

Anthony nodded. "And what do you know of Christ, from these years of solitary adoration?"

Paul paused again and thought. At last, he said, "He is like cool water when the oases run dry, a secure cave when the sandstorm blows, the embrace of a mother with her child. This is what I have learned. And what say you?"

A long time passed again, and the shadows shifted before Anthony replied, "He is fresh fruit when drought has starved the land, he is the sweetness of honey, he is laughter that feels like it will crack your ribs."

Paul nodded.

The weather-worn, sun-bleached hermits talked slowly, with many pauses, for the remainder of the day; the glories of the threefold God filled every sentence.

As the Sun neared the westward horizon, a raven flew overhead. *Gronk! Gronk!* It landed with a flutter of wings on the sand in front of the two men, carrying in her beak an entire loaf of bread.

Paul laughed. "Now, I am certain you are one of the children of God! All these years, the Lord has been sending me a half loaf of bread, every day, carried by God's servant, the raven. But today, the raven has brought you food also."

Anthony offered Paul a drink from a gourd full of water. Chewing and sipping, the two old men shared silent communion. Then Paul spoke, slowly and carefully: "I am blessed to have met you, blessed to know another soul who loves Christ as I do." He paused, then continued: "Since my hour of eternal sleep has arrived, and because I have always desired to dissolve and be with Christ, a crown of justice is reserved for me. God has sent you to bury my body, to return earth to Earth."

A tear ran down Anthony's cheek, and he begged Paul, "Do not leave me behind. Take me as a companion on that great journey into the Savior's presence."

Paul shook his head. "You ought not seek your own interests but those of another. Although if you cast off the burdens of this life to follow the Lamb in the next, that is a good thing—but it is also profitable for you to stay as a mentor for all who seek Christ in the desert. But I beg of you, hasten, if is not too much to ask, and bring back a cloak to wrap about my wretched body." As he said this, he was thinking: *I do not care at all whether this wrinkled, dried-up body is covered or naked, but I wish to spare Anthony the grief of witnessing my death.*

Anthony bid a tearful farewell and did as Paul had asked.

When he returned, he found the older saint was already dead, his stiff body crouched as if in prayer.

A growl rumbled from nearby. Anthony froze, not in fear but in reverent wonder: Two lions were scratching with their paws at the desert sand. *They are digging his grave!* Anthony realized.

When the great cats had finished their work, Anthony lowered Paul's body into the hole and covered him with sand. Then, before he left, he glanced inside the cave at Paul's meager possessions. Anthony's needs were already met, so he left the spare furnishings for the next seeker of Divine Light. He decided, though, to keep Paul's palm-leaf cloak. He treasured it for the rest of his life, wearing it on feast days.

DEEPENING

Most of us these days are familiar with smartphones and smart TVs. These amazing devices enable us to watch videos that transport us vicariously to far-away places and events. A thousand years ago, people in Ireland, Scotland, and Northern England didn't have any electronic devices, of course, but they did have what we might call "smart crosses."

These immense stone monuments portrayed scenes from the Bible and history, transporting the people who gazed at them to other places and times.

The story I just told about Anthony and Paul is also laid out on Muiredach's High Cross, which stands today at the ruined monastic site of Monasterboice, in County Louth, Ireland. The same story is also told on two other crosses: on a Pictish cross originally standing in a cemetery at Nigg, Ross-shire, Scotland, and on the Ruthwell Cross, near Dumfries, Scotland.

Paul of Thebes and Anthony of Alexandria, two North African saints, were very important to the Christians of the ancient Isles. Paul was the first to carve out the hermit life, while Anthony created the monastic life, two concepts that dominated the Christian faith from the third to the sixteenth centuries. The long-ago Christian faith in Ireland, Wales, Scotland, and England relied upon monasteries for its strength and on the experience of hermits for its visionary wisdom. Gaelic Christ-followers strove to follow in the footsteps of the Egyptian ascetics.

Historians and archeologists of Christianity in the Isles have found abundant evidence of connections to Africa in Celtic art, literature, and spiritual wisdom. Africa's influence in the larger picture of early Christianity is often overlooked, however. Yale-educated author Thomas C. Oden writes: "Africa played a decisive role in the formation of Christian culture. Decisive intellectual achievements of Christianity were explored and understood first in Africa before they were recognized in Europe."[136] The Nile River allowed African cultures to connect via the Mediterranean Sea with the North Atlantic Ocean and from there, to ports as far away as the Isles.

A decade ago, I visited Tintagel Castle in Cornwall, where I saw a display of pottery made in North Africa and shipped to Tintagel in the fifth century. Goods from Africa and the Eastern Mediterranean are often found in the archaeological record, proof of trade and travel between distant lands in ancient times. Egyptian beads found in Wiltshire are more than three thousand years old, indicating that the Isles' contact with Africa dates back to the Bronze Age.[137] An Egyptian map from the second century of the Common Era also includes a detailed and fairly accurate map of Ireland, indicating Egypt was familiar with this northern land.[138]

In our modern world, we often forget Africa's rich history and contributions. We imagine white missionaries bringing the gospel to "primitive people"—but in reality, Christianity was alive and well in Africa a thousand years before the first white missionaries. Ethiopia made Christianity its national religion back in the fourth century, and even before that, early-church writers mention contact with Ethiopians.[139]

While Western Christianity in general owes a great deal to Africa, an especially close relationship existed between Egypt and the churches of Ireland and the Isles. We see this relationship reflected in Celtic art, writing, and theology, as well as historical records; an eighth-century Irish litany, for example, written on Egyptian papyrus by Oengus the Culdee, refers to "seven Egyptian monks" who are buried in Ireland.[140]

Egyptian Origins of the Circled Cross

The most common symbol of Celtic Christianity—the circle around the center of what we now call a Celtic cross—came originally from Egypt, where it derived from a more ancient symbol from the time of the pharaohs.

As with most cultural symbols, tracing the history of the Celtic cross is a complicated and interwoven process. In the preceding chapter, we discussed the Chi-Rho symbol of Roman Imperial Christianity;

the wheel on Celtic crosses may have roots in that shape, but Byzantine crucifixes may have been another influence.

The Byzantine Empire, which coexisted with the beginnings of the Celtic Christian faith in Ireland, Wales, and the British Isles, produced large wooden crosses painted with icons of the crucified Christ. Orthodox icons typically portrayed saints' faces encircled by halos, but when iconographers portrayed Christ, they did something unique to his image: Jesus alone had vertical and horizontal lines marked in the halo around his head, lines that symbolized his cross.[141] The horizontal and vertical lines within Jesus' halo also represent the four corners of the Earth, signifying that the Good News of Jesus is intended for the whole world.[142] This artistic convention from the Byzantine Empire may have helped inspire the shape of Celtic wheel crosses.[143]

Meanwhile, however, Walter Horn, cofounder of the art history department at the University of California, Berkeley, believes the Celtic cross derives from the Coptic wheel-cross design. Early Egyptian Christians adopted the ankh, their pre-Christian symbol of eternal life, as their form of the Christian cross, which they called the *crux ansata*.[144] Byzantine-era variations of the Coptic ankh cross placed an equal-armed cross in the center, creating the basic form of

A drawing from an ancient Coptic burial pall, displaying the image of a cross that clearly resembles the crosses created by the Celts.

what we now call a Celtic cross.[145] On a Coptic Christian fabric burial pall, dating from somewhere in the fifth to seventh centuries, there is an image of a perfect "Celtic" cross.[146] If you didn't know the provenience of this artifact, you'd think it was from ancient Ireland or Scotland.

Other examples of Coptic art from the same time frame, in both fabric and stone, show images of a Latin cross (shaped like a lowercase "t") with an encircled center. Given that the Egyptian circle-cross slightly predates its appearance in Celtic regions, combined with numerous examples of Coptic influence in Ireland, Scotland, Wales, and Northern England, the most significant source for the wheel cross may very well be Egypt. If so, the most ubiquitous symbol of Celtic Christianity owes its origins to Africa (something white supremacists would do well to remember!).

Egyptian Elements on Celtic Crosses

Celtic artwork—with its interlaced knots, spirals, and zoomorphic motifs—is globally recognized and appreciated. Celtic designs have become common on everything from greeting cards to T-shirts, from jewelry to the windows of New Age boutiques. Most people who buy this merchandise have no idea that these designs have an African source.

Some artistic elements on ancient Celtic crosses, such as spirals, are indigenous to Ireland, dating all the way back to the late Stone Age, but other elements have African connections. The dotting and interlace patterns on early medieval Irish artwork, for example, can be traced to Egypt, and Coptic designs likely influenced the basic layout of contemporaneous Celtic artwork found in manuscripts, stone, and metal. Artwork based on plant and animal life is common to both Celtic and Coptic Christian art, as is the depiction of the soul as a bird.[147] Motifs from Pharaonic Egypt even inspired the images of Christ on Celtic stone crosses, where he holds holy objects with crossed arms, a posture identical to the way Egyptians portrayed Osiris.[148]

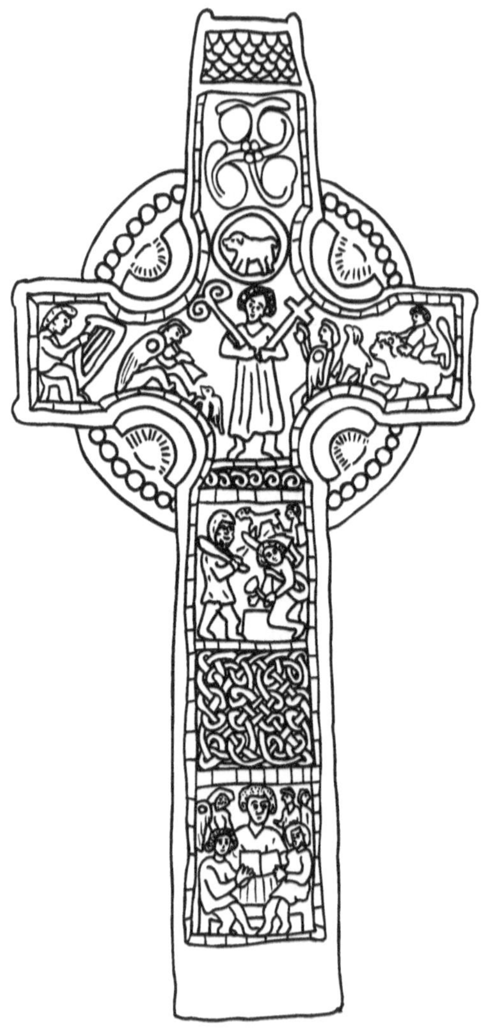

The image of Christ on the east side of the Durrow high cross shows
Christ in a pose similar to that of Osiris in Egyptian statues.

APPLICATIONS FOR TODAY

Many people, including me, are drawn to Celtic Christianity because it is part of our family or ethnic heritage. We love the culture, history, music, and art, and it may become a vital part of our self-identity. This is all good and healthy. We all need to find our tribe.

But tribal pride holds a significant danger: We may cross the line from "I like who we are" to "we are better than other people." I wish this were merely idle musing, but the problem is more serious than that. I have seen overt and subtle expressions of racism and Celtic superiority, online and in person.[149] All God's best gifts can be misused; art, theology, and heritage can be twisted into tools of explicit and implicit oppression against people we think of as different or "other."

The ancient Celts delighted in learning about far-away lands and people; they believed their own art, stories, and inner lives became richer when they incorporated influences from Africa and other regions. I believe Celtic art and spirituality appeal to people today because the Celtic tradition incorporated delightful elements from so many cultures. The appeal of Celtic art is not that it is unlike anything else; it is beautiful because it is so globally connected!

If we seek to practice the theology that created the beauty of ancient Celtic crosses, we will continually work to learn from cultural expressions that differ from our own. We will listen to stories that span national, racial, and spiritual boundaries. We will especially attend to the expressions of marginalized people.

CROSSING BOUNDARIES

Some practical ways to venture outside familiar boundaries:

- Watch movies, read books, listen to music, eat food, and attend cultural events that represent cultures you know little about.

- Make friends and engage socially with people of diverse backgrounds. Ask questions about their lives and beliefs. (And never express judgment!)

- Worship with a church or other spiritual gathering where people's racial identity, language, and ideas differ from your own.

- Volunteer at local food banks, charitable institutions, or other community settings where you'll encounter folks from all walks of life and differing cultural and ethnic backgrounds.

The most vital element of a truly Celtic Christian faith is to whole-heartedly embrace Christ, the One whose identity is made up of all humanity—and at the same time, Christ comes as God available to everyone. In Christ, each human's suffering is recognized, honored, and given meaning. He told his followers: "Whatever you do to those who are overlooked and forgotten, you do to me."[150] Ultimately, if we treat others with intolerance or disdain, that is how we are treating Christ—and if we commit ourselves to unconditional kindness, openness, and a willingness to learn, that is also how we interact with Christ.

A NEW HABIT

As you go through an ordinary day, consider developing a new habit: Whenever you encounter someone—on the street, at work, in a social gathering, at the gym, in a store, on a remote web meeting, on a phone call, or even a text or email, take just a moment to truly recognize and honor the other person's presence. Then say to yourself:

Hello, Jesus.

Dearest One,
Jesus of my heart,
Christ of the world,
let me see your face in every person I meet,
hear your voice in every word anyone utters,
and touch your hands in anyone I serve
and anyone who serves me.
I am open to you,
Living One,
in the glorious expression
of each fellow human being.

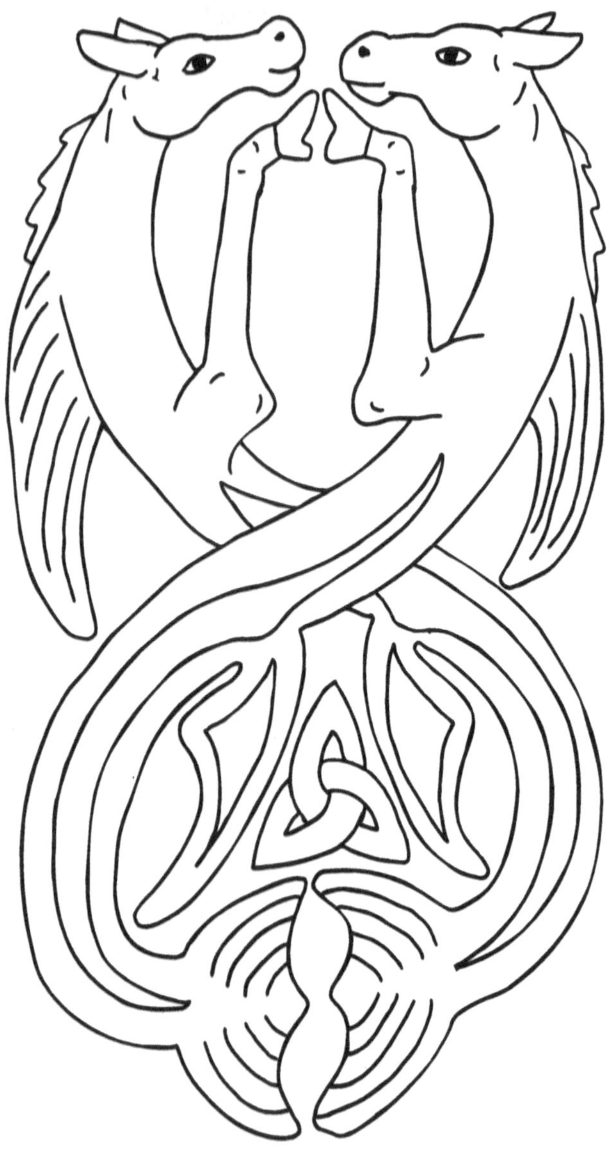

*The lower panel of one of the Aberlemno Stones shows
two hippocamps—seahorses—twined together.*

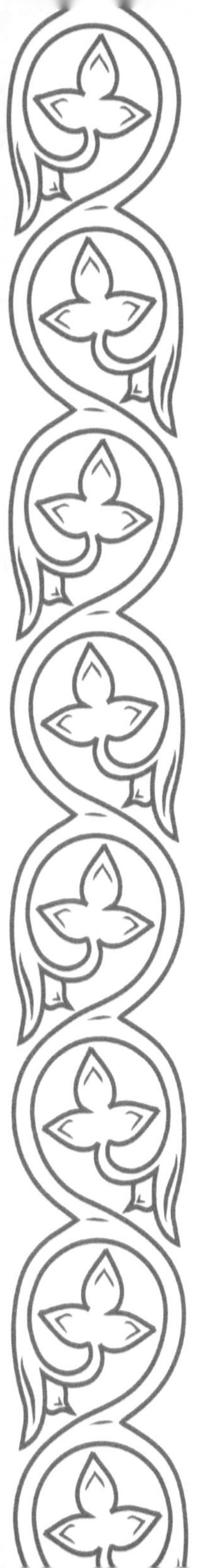

Monsters and Mysteries

Can you draw out Leviathan with a fishhook
or press down its tongue with a cord?
Can you put a rope in its nose
or pierce its jaw with a hook? . . .
Will it speak soft words to you?
Will it make a covenant with you
to be taken as your servant forever? . . .
Can you fill its skin with harpoons
or its head with fishing spears?
Lay hands on it; think of the battle;
you will not do it again!
Any hope of capturing it will be disappointed. . . .
No one is so fierce as to dare to stir it up.
Who can stand before it?
Who can confront it and be safe?
—under the whole heaven, who?

JOB 41:1–11

ENCOUNTER

564 CE: The Shores of Loch Ness, Kingdom of the Picts

Columba looked at the corpse and twisted the scraggly hairs at the bottom of his beard, an unconscious habit of his when deep in thought. He had never seen anything quite like it.

He was used to death; he had sat with scores of people as they passed from this life to the next. He had survived a plague, when death felt like an enormous dark shadow all around him. And he had known the horrors of warfare, ministering to warriors savaged by their fellow man. Yet he had never before seen such brutal maul marks.

The Picts were washing and wrapping the body for burial, while the abbot's companions—Luigne, Cained, and Cathel, all from Iona in the Kingdom of Dalriada—stared at the bloody body. Cathel knew the Picts' tongue, so Columba nodded at him, indicating he requested translation for what he was about to say.

"Give these people our condolences, ask forgiveness for our intrusion—and then ask what befell this poor fellow? We will be following this ness afoot to King Brule's dun—better we know what dangers may be here."

Cathel pulled back the hood of his monk's garment, revealing the long red hair behind his tonsure, and walked toward the group on the bank slowly, his hands held wide so they could see his good intentions.

He noticed an older man with a grief-stricken face and a gold torc around his neck; Cathel guessed he was the father of the dead man. The two women who were gently cleaning the corpse seemed unperturbed by the amount of blood; perhaps they were healers and accustomed to such ministrations? Cathel noted that all three Picts wore finely woven clothes and well-crafted jewelry.

They turned toward him as he approached, their eyes wide as they took in these strangers with their robes and shaved heads.

While Cathel spoke with the Picts, Columba waited serenely. After a few minutes, Cathel turned back to Columba and said, "The departed soul was Braden. He was swimming in the river when an enormous beast burst from the depths—black and shiny like a seal but of enormous size, with a long mouth full of teeth like daggers. After the beast departed, some men from their settlement put out in a currach to rescue Braden, but he was dead when they got to him. The whole community is terribly afraid, for they rely on fish caught from this water."

Columba fingered his beard again as he thought. "Tell them they need not fear," he said at last. "Our God is High King over all beasts. I shall pray and exorcise this monster."

As Cathel translated, Columba could tell by the Picts' expressions that they were not convinced.

"They say it is nice of you to care," Cathal told Columba, "but their river god and the spirits of their ancestors rule over this waterway. They don't believe the prayers of an unheard-of deity will have any effect."

"Tell them that we must cross today for we have business with the king a few days hence, and we must not delay. One of us will now swim across the river while I pray, proving we serve the Creator of all beings."

Luigne stepped forward, pulling his cassock over his head to reveal a well-muscled torso. "I'll go, Father. You know I am the best swimmer."

The abbot nodded, and Luigne waded into the current. When he was waist-deep, he dove under the water. The river flowed swiftly, and he had to stroke hard to keep a straight course.

As the others on land watched, an enormous form emerged from the water. The onlookers gasped. A great head reared out of the waters, its jaws opened wide enough to envelope a man, and blasted the air with an unearthly howl.

Columba made the sign of the cross with large, sweeping gestures in the air. Then his voice rose above the tumult: "In the name of Christ, go no further! Do not touch the man! Go back at once!"

At the sound of the abbot's voice, the beast turned, stared at Columba for a moment, and then wheeled around and swam quickly in the opposite direction. After a few moments, it disappeared beneath the water's surface.

One of the Picts turned to Columba and uttered a few quiet words.

Cathel translated: "What is that gesture you made? And what is the name of the God you serve?"

DEEPENING

Mysterious Monsters

We all love a good mystery. That may explain why the Loch Ness monster has excited our imagination ever since the eighth century when Adomnan described Columba's encounter with the creature. A famous photograph taken in 1934 seemed to indicate that yes, *something* was in Loch Ness, but that photo turned out to be a hoax.[152] In 2023, a new search—with scores of volunteers and expensive technology—combed the loch for a trace of the monster; they reported they heard "four mysterious and previously unheard loud noises from the depths of the loch" and saw a "giant shadow" moving just beneath the surface.[153] They failed to capture any direct proof of Nessie's reality, however. Still, a lack of evidence has not deterred enormous numbers of people from believing in Nessie. Like Fox Mulder in *The X Files*, we want to believe.

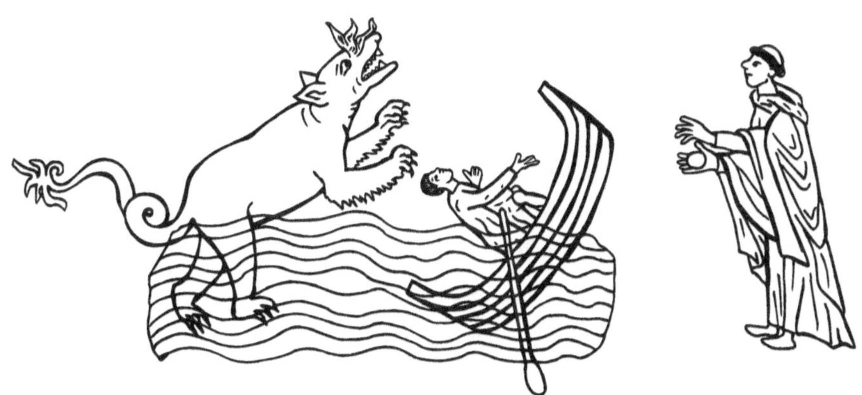

A 12th-century manuscript portrayal of Columba with the Loch Ness monster indicates a creature quite different from the one we picture today!

And what does Nessie have to do with a book on ancient Celtic stones? Well, because artwork on Pictish stone slabs may depict Scottish legendary beasts that gave rise to the Loch Ness mystery. Scholars refer to some of these stone carvings as hippocamps—legendary water creatures with horse's heads and fishtails. A pair of hippocamps appear in detail, for example, carved on the west face of the churchyard cross in Aberlemno, Scotland.

Strabo and other ancient Greek writers described these seahorses in detail, believing them to be real.[154] Their appearance on a stone from the early Middle Ages in Pictland may simply show that the Picts were familiar with the traditions of the Mediterranean world, possibly from seeing Roman carvings. Other scholars suggest the Picts were, initially at least, depicting the small sea creature we call the seahorse today.[155]

Hippocamps are similar to the *eich uisge* (water-horse) and kelpies of Irish and Scottish folklore. A folklorist relates: "The kelpie would strike the water three times with his tail so heavily that the sound was like thunder, while his disappearance into a pool was like a lightning flash."[156] An expert in Pictish archaeology says, "The kelpie is a Caledonian spirit described as the personification of water. It can be as gentle as a rock-pool, as unpredictable as a squall, and as dangerous as a torrent." She goes on to say, "Just as Nessie is the biggest tourist attraction in the Highlands today . . . so the Picts may have regarded the water-horse as real."[157]

Hippocamps appear multiple times on Pictish stone art, but there are also dozens of somewhat different images, which scholars refer to as the "Pictish beast." This is the most common design found in the Picts' stone art,[158] so whatever it is, it must have been significant to their culture. This creature has a curled tail like a cat's, a long body like a seal, two sets of long flippers like a plesiosaurus, a long mane or horn extending backward from its head, and what might be a trunk like an elephant's or a long beak like a crane's. Scholars' opinions vary greatly when asked, "What is the Pictish beast?" Suggestions include a stylized dolphin, an elephant, and a beaked whale.[159]

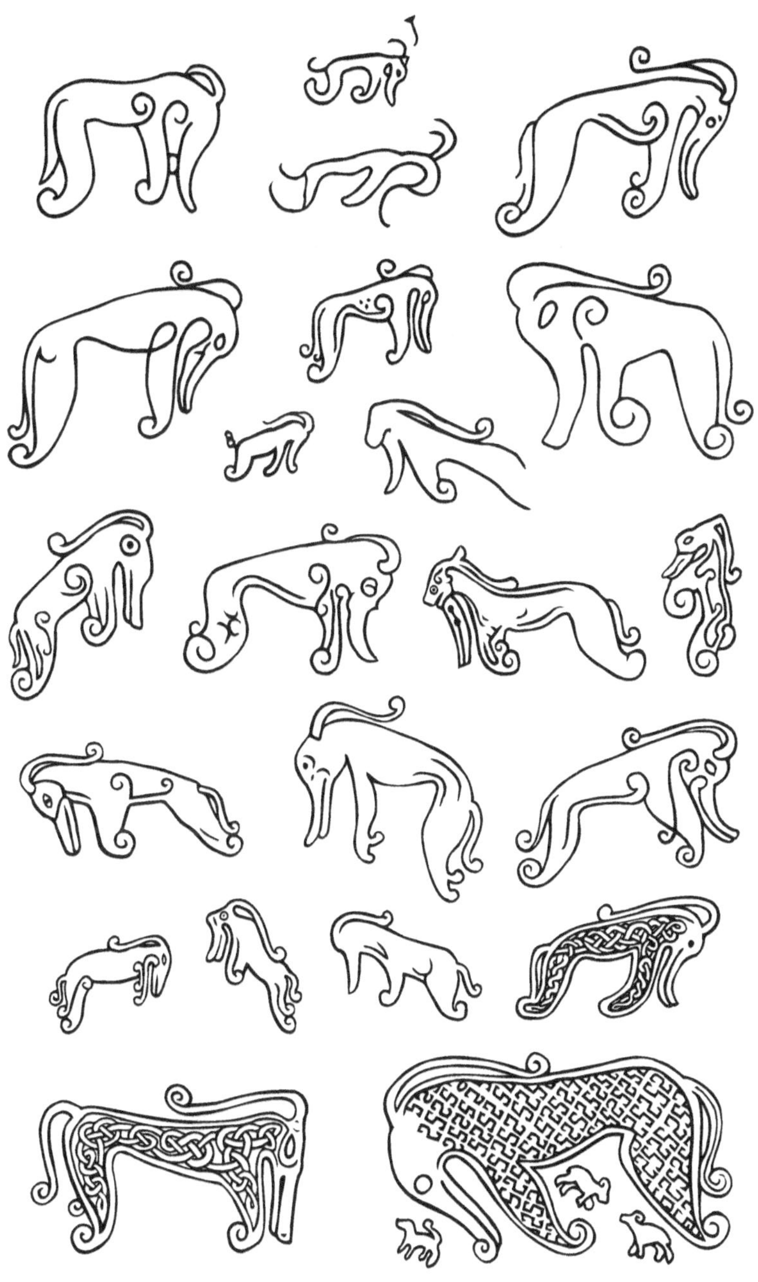

These drawings, traced from Pictish stones, portray both the variations and the common characteristics of the Pictish beast.

Were the ancient Picts trying to portray something like the Loch Ness monster with their stone art? Or are these images fanciful interpretations of creatures that are familiar to modern marine biology? Or were they something else altogether? A recent theory, based on the Pictish beasts' similarities to other ancient drawings found in Asia and Africa, is that it corresponds with an ancient zodiac, and thus, it indicates an astrological point of time (perhaps, some archeologists have hypothesized, the birth of Christ).[160]

We don't understand what may exist in Loch Ness, and neither do we understand what the ancient Picts were trying to communicate with their monumental stone sculptures (despite historians' and archaeologists' ongoing research). The Pictish beastie is a mystery depicting a mystery. The one thing we do know is that these mysterious aquatic creatures were part of the worldview that led at the same time to beautiful depictions of the cross. Whether portraying an animal that's still known today or a legendary creature, the images had a deeper spiritual meaning.

The Picts

When Rome first ventured into the land now called Scotland, they called the people they encountered "Picts," meaning "Painted People." This has led to an unfortunate stereotype: Novels and movies often portray the Picts as naked savages, cavepeople covered in blue woad who lacked a material culture. For the Romans, anyone outside their own culture was a "barbarian" (in other words, a person whose non-Latin tongue sounded to the Romans like "ba, ba"), an expression of extreme prejudice. Even Roman writers admitted, however, that some people outside Rome had sophisticated civilizations, and archaeology shows that these original inhabitants of what is now Scotland possessed a rich culture with highly sophisticated stone- and metal-work, as well as a well-organized society.

Pictish culture was present in the Scottish Highlands from the Iron Age through the Early Middle Ages. The Scoti—people from Ireland—gradually moved into the area, and by the tenth century, Scots culture largely replaced Pictish culture, and the Pictish language was lost. As a result, we lack the sort of written records that exist from Wales, Ireland, and Scotland during the same time periods, a fact that may contribute to our sense that the Picts are mysterious.

The Picts began to convert to Christianity when they encountered Saint Ninian in their southwest kingdom around the year 400; they then had subsequent encounters with Saint Columba who traveled throughout the Highlands a century later. Stone crosses indicate a significant number of Picts accepted this new faith, but scholars debate the extent to which the Picts were Pagan or Christian (or a hybrid of both) between the years 400 and 800.

The Picts left behind more than three hundred stone monuments, carved in the Late Middle Ages and concentrated along Scotland's eastern coast north of Edinburgh. Pictish stones often display abstract symbols, repeated from stone to stone: crescents, rods, discs, as well as various kinds of life-forms. These carvings obviously communicated ideas; although we do not know what the symbols stand for, the Scottish Archeological Research Framework believes they likely formed a symbolic language[161] that may have begun as early as the fourth century.[162] Were they proper names? Clan totems? Spiritual admonitions? Speculation is abundant, but the language of Pictish stones is like having Egyptian hieroglyphs without a Rosetta Stone: So far, no one can prove they've cracked the code.

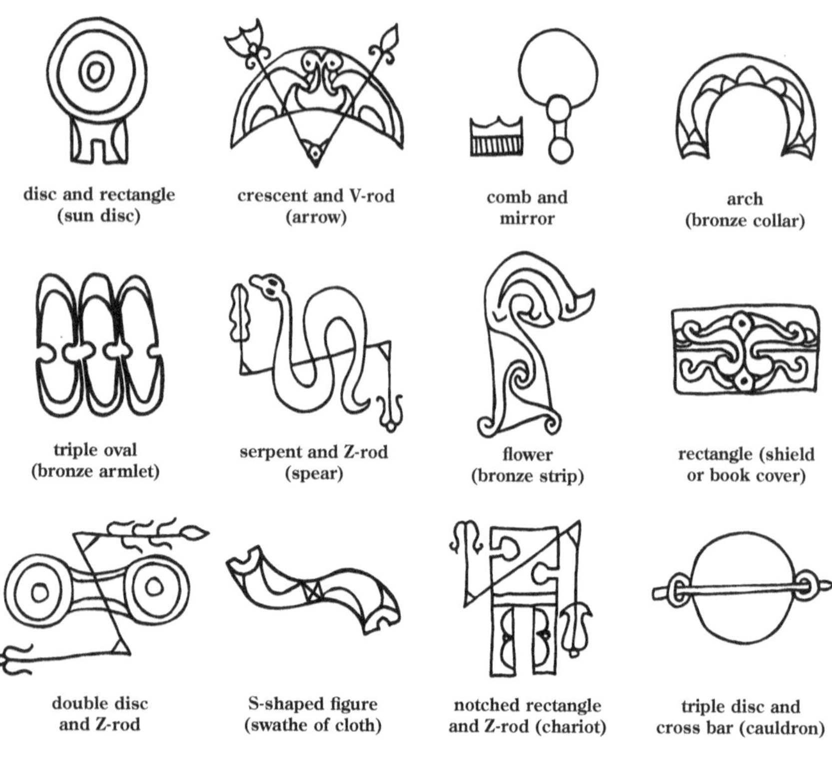

Pictish abstract symbols.

Alongside these abstract symbols, the Picts also portrayed objects that were apparently significant to their culture: mirror-and-comb (denoting women's beauty), horseshoe, broken sword (possibly denoting a warrior's death), hammer-and-anvil (blacksmithing), and bow-with-helmet. The Picts also carved detailed realistic creatures: serpent, salmon, eagle, bull, boar, wolf, goose, stag, and horse. (I will discuss these in more detail in chapter 8.)

And, besides the Pictish beast, the Picts portrayed other fantastical creatures: centaurs, gryphons, dragons, a sphynx, and bird-headed humans. The mythical menageries of Pictish stone masons seem like a mash-up of Greek legends and the medieval surreal paintings of

Hieronymus Bosch. We might think of them as monsters—and yet the Picts carved them side by side with clearly Christian crosses. In their eyes, these sinister-looking beings inhabited the same world as Christ. These slab crosses are among the earliest Celtic monumental crosses, and their detail and artistic vision are breathtaking.

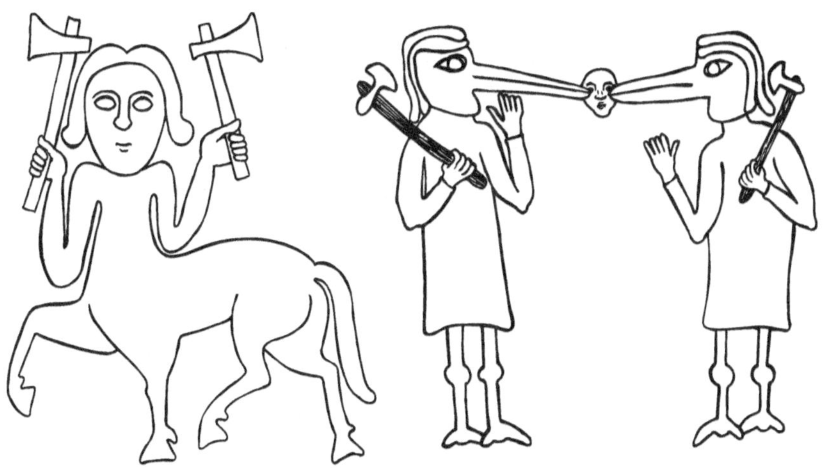

Pictish images like these blur the lines between human and animal.
These two—the centaur from the village of Glamis in Scotland, and the
bird-headed creatures from the village of Papil—seem particularly threatening.

Ancient Celtic Art

The four elements that comprise what today we know as Celtic artwork—plait work, knots, key patterns, and spirals—also occur on Pictish crosses in dizzying, interlocking arrangements. At a seminar I attended on Celtic artwork, one participant commented: "There is something about the patterns in Celtic artwork that people, whatever their background, recognize as spiritual and comforting." I believe she's correct. These designs point to a Divine harmony.

They also have incredible continuity. A pattern of swirls carved on the entrance stone at Newgrange (3,000 BCE) is very much like that on the shaft panel of the Cadboll Pictish stone (around 700 CE)—and today a famous Scottish single malt whisky uses the design for its logo. These patterns have passed from hand to hand, artwork to artwork, across the Celtic nations for five thousand years.

While these design elements appear throughout the Celtic lands—including the far-flung regions of Galicia and the Isle of Man—Pictish and Welsh regions have them in greater profusion, dazzling extravaganzas of interconnected patterns. The Carew Cross in Pembrokeshire, Wales, is a fine example of combined symbolic patterns. By contrast, the high crosses of Ireland and Northern England feature more pictorial or wildlife elements.

The meanings of Celtic design patterns cannot be definitively proven. Unlike Pictish symbols, however, there is an artistic continuity of these designs and folkloric explanations that have survived along with them. Using the patterns in Celtic artwork, we may be able to solve some mysteries, though we can't prove that neolithic stone carvers thousands of years ago understood symbols the same way that craftspeople in later historic times understood them.

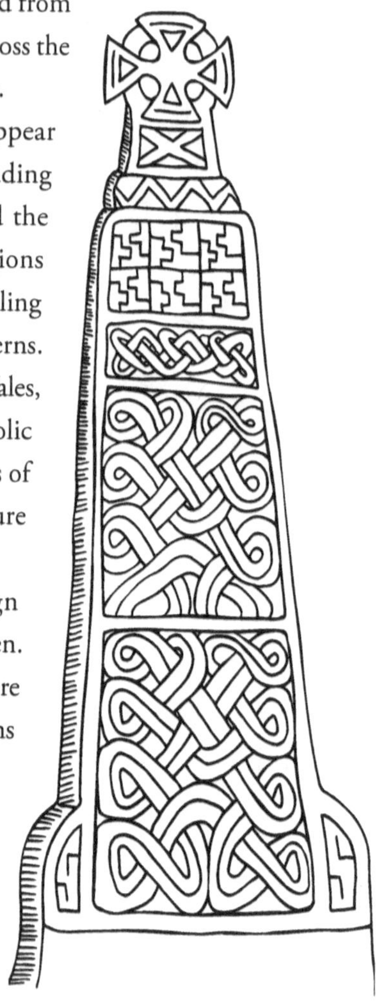

The Carew Cross in Pembrokeshire, Wales, displays several different Celtic design patterns. The cross stands 4 meters tall and dates back to the 11th century.

Knotwork

Interwoven knots are the most famous elements of Celtic artwork. The Celts used the same designs in weaving, but although stonework knots may have originally derived from textile patterns, they may hold deeper significance. The patterns are apparently endless: You can't tell where a knotwork strand begins or ends. If the knot was made of string, taking out any bit would cause the whole pattern to unravel.

The interwoven, unending patterns point to the Celtic understanding that all life is interconnected. According to Scottish researcher Derek Bryce, these motifs can signify "the great cosmic loom of the universe. . . . [T]here are no loose ends, and the symbol is one of the continuity of the spirit throughout existence."[163] More specifically, knotwork patterns may symbolize the binding of the soul to the world, with the tiny breaks where the lines cross indicating the soul's release from the world at the end of life.[164] Personally, I think the patterns look like branches interwoven to make medieval wattle fences and also like the patterns of chainmail armor. Either of these would be a symbol of protection, a representation of Divine care.

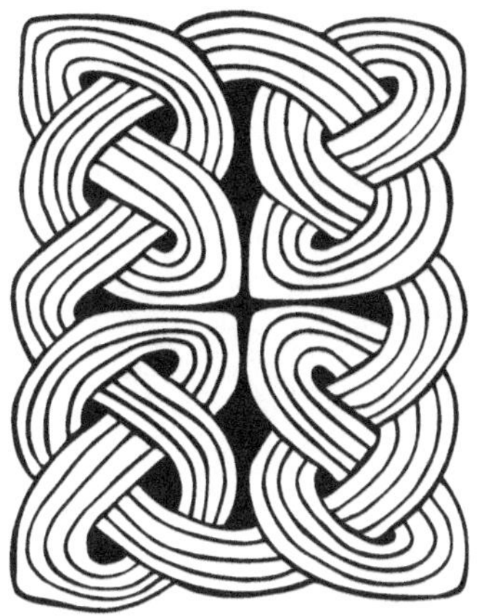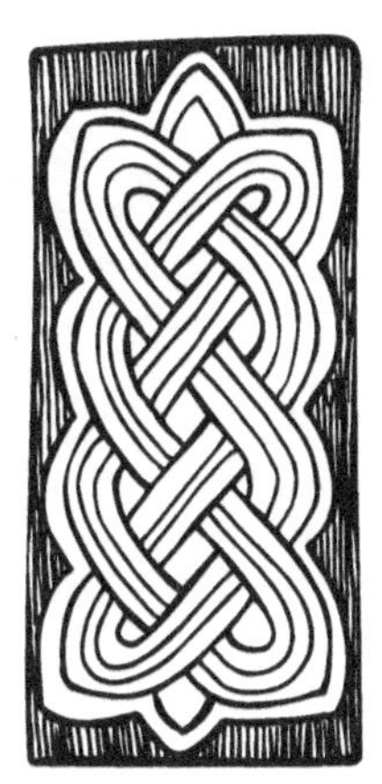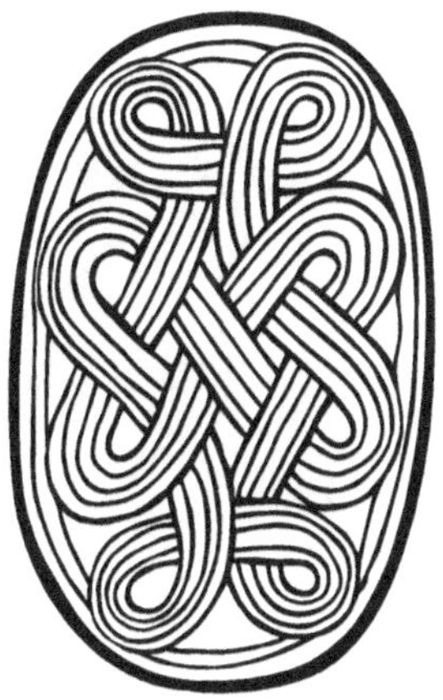

Examples of Celtic knotwork.

Key Patterns

This pattern is common in both Pictish and Celtic artwork; it may have been adapted from the ancient Greeks or Egyptians.[165] However, this is not "mere copying, but the sign of a society open to such change as it chose to accept and adapt on its own terms."[166] Although they may have borrowed stylistic features, they gave those motifs their own cultural and spiritual meanings.

Despite how common this pattern is in Pictish stone art (as well as Celtic manuscripts and carvings), we cannot be certain what those meanings were. One art historian suggests they were designed to confuse the eye, and perhaps act as charms to ward off evil.[167] A mathematician suggests that these repetitive patterns reflect an understanding of reality similar to today's quantum physicists', where the "fabric of space and time is best understood as a densely woven skein."[168] If nothing else, these designs indicate the Picts had a sophisticated sense of mathematics, which was necessary to create such consistent and complicated patterns.[169]

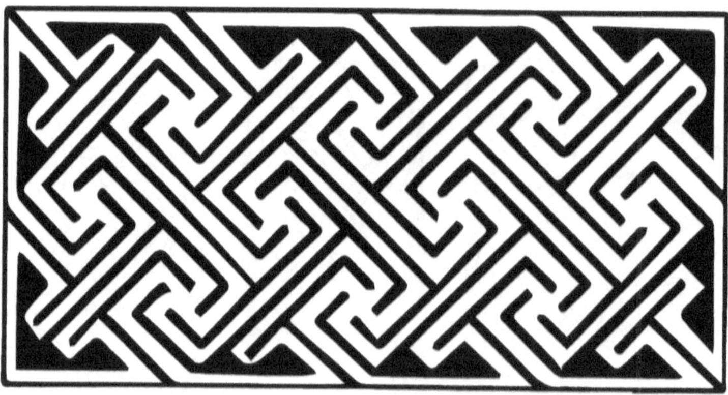

An example of a key pattern. This pattern is also sometimes called a "meander." Archeologists speculate that for the Greeks, this interlocking pattern represented both unity and infinity.

Spirals

The spiral is a cross-cultural symbol that goes back to the Stone Age, but the Picts and the Celts made this pattern central to their artwork. To my mind, spirals evoke the curl of a wave rolling over its top; the Hilton-Cadboll Pictish stone in Easter Ross, Scotland, overlooks the ocean, and I can't help but wonder if the sea inspired its playful profusion of spirals.

In the perennial spiritual traditions, spirals represent journeying. Labyrinths are ancient designs derived from spirals, used throughout history for a walking meditation that symbolizes each soul's spiritual journey. A labyrinth is basically a spiral pattern with meanders (reversals) added into the design, so the walker moves back and forth rather than in a single direction. Labyrinths are often confused with mazes but differ in that mazes have false trails and dead ends, designed to confuse the walker; labyrinths have a single path that always leads to the center. These wandering path patterns appear as miniatures a person can "walk" with their fingertips, and they also exist as full-scale pathways for walking. The labyrinth has accrued many sacred meanings over the centuries, and labyrinth walkers report improved mental health, spiritual connection, and guidance for their lives by sauntering through the winding pattern.

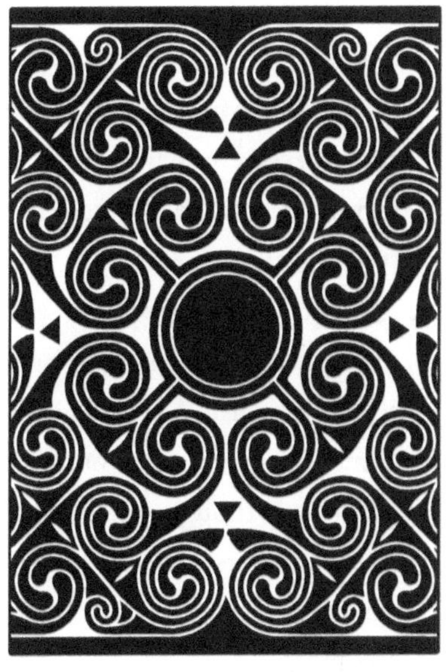

These typical Celtic spirals are based on a stone found in Hilton of Cadboll in Scotland. The stone dates back to about 800.

In June 2024, as I walked the Portuguese Way of the Camino pilgrimage through Galicia, the ancient Celtic region of Spain, I noticed a broken sign pointing up a steep, forested hillside: "PETROGLIFOS." It was raining and we had already walked many miles, but we decided to venture uphill. After a few minutes of climbing, we found the world's oldest labyrinth design. Four thousand years old, the design is sharply visible in the stone, several feet wide, a classic labyrinth with seven layers of twists and turns leading to its center and back. This design, originating in the late Stone Age, was reused time and again over thousands of years.

At the Rock of Cashel, County Tipperary, a castle-church that was the ancient seat of ecclesiastical authority in Southern Ireland, the central cross—known as Saint Patrick's Cross—has an ornate labyrinth design that covers an entire side of the base of the cross. The center of this labyrinth shows a strange creature that has been interpreted as the Minotaur, the monster that inhabited the labyrinth of Crete in ancient Greek legend. A labyrinth's primeval pattern—combined with a Greek legend on a twelfth-century Celtic cross—reminds us that these ancient stones record human thought from around the world and across centuries. Perhaps the minotaur in the labyrinth was a reminder that each soul must meet her fears in the course of life's journey.

Barney McLaughlin, who has done an immense amount of research into the ancient Celtic crosses, describes the meaning of spiral patterns: "A spiral has movement. We might think of a spiral as moving in toward or out from the center. Spiritually the center has often been thought of as the Holy, God, the Ground of our Being. As we spiral in, we move deeper into relationship with the Holy. As we spiral out, we move from our Divine source into service to others. The inward and outward dimensions of spirituality are in constant dynamic tension. Both are necessary to the spiritual journey."[170] This description of the spiral's symbolism also describes the most common form of meditation for walking a labyrinth.

Messages in Stone

The Picts of the Early Middle Ages have left us messages carved on stone. Those messages tell of an enchanted world overflowing with mystery and wonder. They transformed the stillness of stone into lively scenes teeming with God's creation. Consider, for example, the Rossie Church cross slab in Perth. The cross has two faces on each side of the slab, both containing complex patterns of interlace and key designs, while the panels on each side of the crosses overflow with creatures in movement. On the front of the slab, we see:

- a beast with a human head and curling tail

- a beaked figure attacking a bird with an ax

- a beast with its tail curled over its back

- a beast attacking a naked man

- a fish-tailed monster

- a pair of beasts that are each swallowing a bird

- a beast swallowing a serpent

- a big-eyed animal that looks like it might be a cow

- a pair of monsters with human heads, the fins of a fish, and beast-headed tails, bodies intertwined as they face in opposite directions

And that's just the front of the slab. On the back, we find:

- five horsemen

- a pair of hunting dogs

- an angel

- a figure holding a pair of birds by the necks

- a crescent

- a Pictish beast

- a kneeling animal that has a second head at the end of its tail

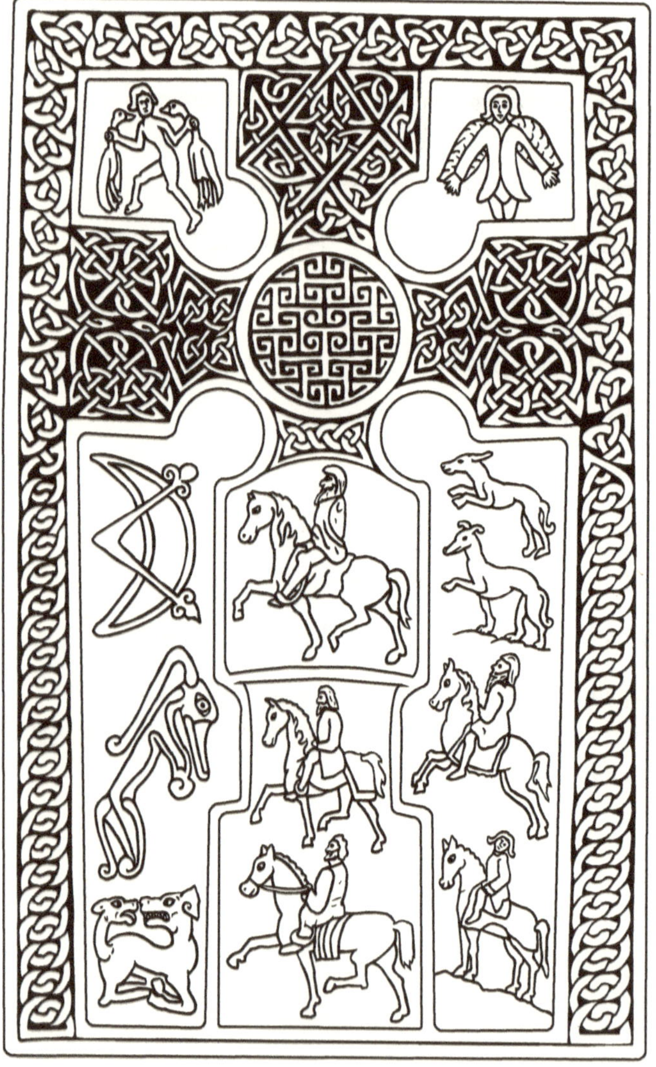

The back side of the Rossie Church cross slab.

What this tapestry of fantastic images meant we can only guess; doubtless, each visual vignette evoked some myth familiar for the artist and their original audience. It's hard to imagine how any artist could create such complex patterns without the use of modern technology. I think it is sad that we know the names of famous European Renaissance sculptors like Michelangelo and Bernini, and we have no idea who the genius was that created this Pictish tour de force.

And yet the Picts' messages to us remains, enduring through the centuries. We may never know the precise meanings of these wild, even bizarre images—but they were all contained with the cross. Nothing was outside its scope.

"Set in Stone" May Not Mean Forever

All ancient stone art has an allure: Aboriginal Australian markings, Native American petroglyphs, Egyptian hieroglyphs, and Celtic monuments, all share a feeling of mystery due to their extreme age and enigmatic designs. But while stone is durable, it is not eternal; even stones suffer the ravages of time.

In 2019, as I followed the Easter Ross Pictish Trail, I observed several approaches to the preservation of Scotland's Pictish legacy. A great many ancient stones are safe in museums, but the downside to this is that the crosses are no longer in their original settings; the placement of ancient monuments is often integral to their meaning and artistic form.

We found the Shandwick Stone, on the other hand, in a field near the roadside, exactly where it has stood for 1,200 years. It is enormous—encased completely in a huge plexiglass box. This does preserve the stone in its original place, but the glare of the glass makes the modern vessel much more obvious than the ancient monument itself.

The original cross that stood at Hilton of Cadboll is safely preserved in the National Museum in Edinburgh, but we discovered that a stone duplicate had been put in its place. That seems to me a near-perfect way to honor Scotland's Pictish legacy, preserving the original object indoors while replacing it with a clone in its original location. Unfortunately, it is an expensive and time-consuming endeavor: The replica Hilton of Cadboll stone was made possible by a donation from Glenmorangie Distillery, which uses a design from the stone for its signet on whisky bottles.

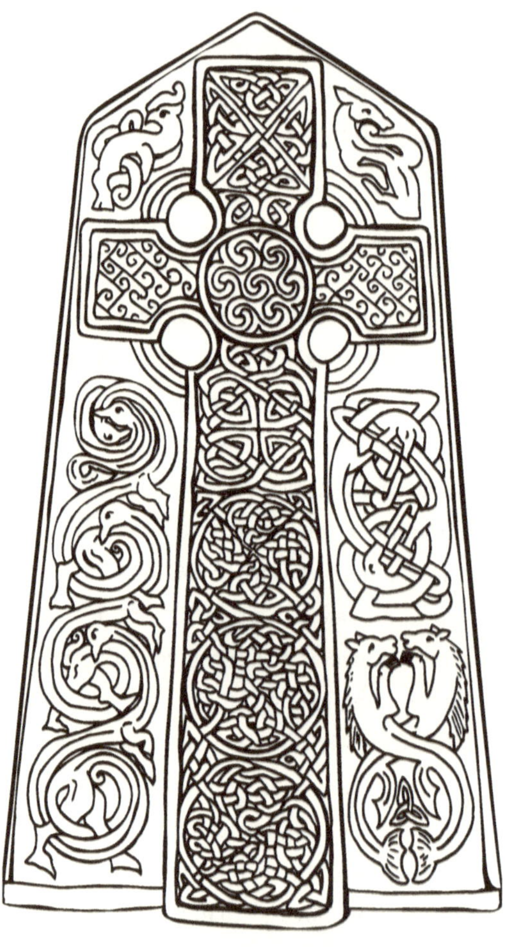

This cross, found in the churchyard at Aberlemno, stands 2.3 meters tall and dates back to the mid-9th century. It combines several features of Celtic and Pictish carvings: knotwork, spirals, and zoomorphic images.

Seeing the stones where they have always stood, weathered but still bearing witness in the same way they have done for more than a millennium, their power overwhelmed me. And yet I also felt queasy seeing lichen growing into the Serpent Stone at Aberlemno in Scotland, realizing that stone is vulnerable to Nature and time—and violence. A crazy vandal could destroy over a thousand years of heritage with just a few moments of terrible destruction (other sites in the UK have received such mistreatment).

As archaeologists dig into the earth, and historians delve into archives, we are slowly learning more about the Picts, these enigmatic indigenous people of Scotland. It would be utterly tragic if anything marred their records in stone while so many mysteries remain.

APPLICATIONS FOR TODAY

Chaos Monsters

George and Isabel Henderson, who have devoted their lives to studying Pictish art, suggest that the Pictish beast may be the Leviathan from the Bible's Book of Job.[171] If so, that could explain the presence of the Pictish beast alongside the cross and other Christian symbols. (See the Bible's description of Leviathan at the beginning of this chapter.)

In the Book of Job, the hero has done all in his power to serve God, yet he suffers greatly. God never actually explains to Job why he has suffered so, but he does receive a tour of God's cosmic power in the book's last section, an overwhelming journey that ends with one of the biggest and scariest things God made: Leviathan. No human dares even approach Leviathan, God tells Job, but the Holy One has made a covenant with the horrific creature; it—like Job—is God's servant. At the end of his tale, Job still doesn't understand the specific reasons why he has experienced so much hurt. He realizes, however, his place in God's universe, and as he catches a glimpse of God's magnificence, he is willing to again trust Divine rule over his life.

At this point, you may be asking: What exactly *is* a leviathan? To identify a leviathan on a Pictish stone only solves one mystery with another. Various Bible scholars have suggested that Leviathan was a whale or a crocodile. Some cryptozoologists point to a late-surviving dinosaur, like they believe Nessie to be. According to the Jewish Zohar, Leviathan is an ouroboros, a creature that eats its own tail. (The Zohar also states that God plays with Leviathan for three hours every day!)

Bible scholars steeped in the cosmology of the ancient Near East point to a more universal identity. In the Fertile Crescent, even before Hebrew scribes committed their people's oral legends to written form, priests and storytellers portrayed the universe as a struggle between the elemental forces of order and chaos. As Yale Divinity School professor Gregory Mobley explains, Leviathan is an archetypal monster, an ancient Semitic avatar of "every chaos monster in the human imagination." According to Mobley, God is saying to Job: "I have a covenant with chaos. Chaos is part of the plan." Mobley goes beyond any literal statement in the Bible and suggests: "The Creator designed a world with terrifying freedom on the off chance that love might emerge from the chaos."[172]

To be human is to be curious, and over the long ascent of our evolutionary heritage, our species has gained a vast amount of knowledge about everything imaginable. And yet there are still hidden corners, closets of reality our vision cannot penetrate. What we do not know or understand fascinates us (as shown by the ongoing popularity of Nessie, UFOs, and conspiracy theories). At the same time, though, what we don't know or understand frightens us. Often, we are like children lying in bed, imagining monsters lurk beneath us where we cannot see.

The future is one of the great unknowns. Fear about what lies ahead—whether it's our own and our loved ones' health, our finances, our relationships, or the overall state of the world—wraps us in anxiety. As I write this, a hurricane is pummeling Florida, but you don't need a category-five hurricane to experience the dread that chaos brings. We are all capable of conjuring up in our minds all manner of life-threatening (or ego-threatening) monsters.

YOUR PERSONAL MONSTER

We each have our own version of a chaos monster. What is yours? Can you describe it? What does it look like? What danger does it threaten?

There's a children's book titled *I'm Coming to Get You* that tells the story (with illustrations) of a hairy, howling outer-space monster that's heading for Earth to get little Tommy Brown. The suspense builds throughout the book—until we discover that the monster is less than an inch tall.

Sometimes, when we describe our fears, bringing them out into the light where we can take a closer look at them, we may discover they're not as enormous as we imagined!

The Ruler of Mysteries

The unknown may be the realm of chaos, but it is also the realm where God lives; that, ultimately, is the message Job receives from God. What is unseen need not frighten us, for God is there. "The light shines in the darkness, and the darkness did not overtake it."[173]

The *Saltair na Rann*, an early medieval Irish poem, says:

> *All the many creatures of God—*
> *Beloved and clever, a mighty multitude—*
> *After the fair shaping of each of them*
> *I have no true understanding of any.*

The poet is expressing his finitude: How can he possibly comprehend even a small portion of God's universe?

We have learned much since the Middle Ages, and yet today we are no better off than this ancient Celtic poet. When we gaze at the night sky, we see only the tiniest fraction of the septillion (1 followed by 24 zeros) or more stars in the universe; we can only imagine the mysteries that space's untold reaches hold. If we turn our attention instead to the tiniest things in creation, the infinitesimal components of everything we see and touch, we must humbly admit we cannot comprehend these subatomic realities. Like the long-ago poet, we too must conclude: "All the many creatures of God—I have no true understanding of any."

But the ancient Irish poet doesn't end on a negative note. He goes on to affirm:

> *My King of Mysteries, of fair fame,*
> *Wherever in his creation he dwells above the world,*
> *Mighty and glorious—in my life*
> *I can do nothing but worship him.*

Here is a ray of warmth that reaches into every cold cranny of the unknown: God is the Ruler of Mysteries. Reality may seem too much to handle, and our fear of what *could be* reality may be even worse—but when are co-creating alongside the All Giver, we have nothing to fear. Our much greater Companion in life has us covered.

As the apostle Paul said: "For I am convinced that neither death, nor life, nor angels, nor rulers, nor things present, nor things to come, nor powers, nor height, nor depth, nor anything else in all creation will be able to separate us from the love of God in Christ Jesus our Lord."[174]

Why should chaos monsters appear on Pictish stones, alongside, even sheltered by the cross of Christ? Perhaps to affirm that Christ contains realities we can only guess at, that nothing is outside the scope of Divine love. Divinity is the biggest Mystery of all.

Since the Enlightenment, the Western mindset has focused on intellectual reason. If we cannot "make sense of something," if we can't verbalize it or put it into words, and if we can't analyze it and break it down into manageable pieces, it must not be real or true. This may cause us to doubt or discard the concept of God. But life holds many things we do not understand; that does not stop them from being real. Love, death, time: These are all realities beyond our comprehension.

Most Christians take for granted the tenets of their faith. But take a moment to consider: Can anyone really understand that a human woman became the mother of the God-Human? What do we mean when we say Christ is fully human yet fully Divine? How is it that Jesus' crucifixion enacted the redemption of all Creation? And how can a human being who is thoroughly dead rise again to sit at the right hand of universal Power? Theologians can debate endlessly; they can analyze and quote scripture and refer to the great theologians of the past. But when all is said and done, we cannot reduce Mystery, we cannot contain it in a small box where we can see it clearly. In *Summa Theologica* (Summary of Theology), Thomas Aquinas employed elaborate semantic analysis to his faith—and in the end, he confessed: "It is all straw."

Ultimately, our human brains are not equipped to grasp some mysteries. Can you imagine what a five-dimensional—or a ten-dimensional—object looks like? Yet the mathematics involved in quantum physics indicates such a reality. Can you measure a memory? Quantify consciousness? Explain why animals can find their way without a map? As physicist Niels Bohr said: "Everything we call real is made of things that cannot be regarded as real."[175]

When it comes to spiritual mystery, theologian Steven Boyer indicates it "involves a penetration into or a participation in a depth that is a source of nourishment and life." We can "feed upon the mystery," he says, in much the same way as when we sit down to eat a meal: Our goal is not to determine an accurate analysis of nutrition's chemical steps but rather " to eat and to savour and to grow strong."[176]

Ultimately, the Bible indicates, what we don't know points us toward God. According to the Amplified Bible, God "planted eternity" within us as "a mysterious longing which nothing under the sun can satisfy, except God."[177]

A PRAYER PRACTICE

Whenever your personal chaos monster starts to writhe and breathe fire within the haunted spaces of your mind, here's a prayer practice I recommend:

First, take time to recognize what it is that frightens you. Very often, our bodies know our fears before our consciousness does, so you may want to look for clues in physical sensations such as your heartbeat, your breath, the way your skin and stomach feel. We cannot slay the dragon we do not see, so dare to ask your body what it knows. As you look into the shadows, sit somewhere safe, surrounded by comforting objects (or possibly your dog or cat), and stalk your chaos monster. Why does it frighten you? Can you give it a name?

Now, take up the cross you have been using in the various exercises suggested in this book. Simply gaze at it for a moment. Imagine Christ's hands reaching out from the crossbeams to contain—even welcome!—your monster. Your monster is Christ's servant, for Christ is the Ruler of Mystery.

Now imagine the cross lighting up with the Divine Light that existed before the Big Bang. Watch as the Light spreads, and your fears are caught up like vapors that vanish within it.

Conclude this practice with the end-of-chapter prayer.

Creator,

Beloved,

Guide,

Majesty of Mystery,

I cast at the foot of your cross

my anxieties, my imaginings,

my bogies and nightmares and horrors,

every phantasm born from my fear of the unknown.

You are my light in shadow, my safe place.

Majesty of Mystery,

Savior,

Friend,

Dear One of my heart,

I cast my fears upon you

for you care for me.

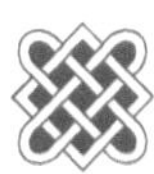

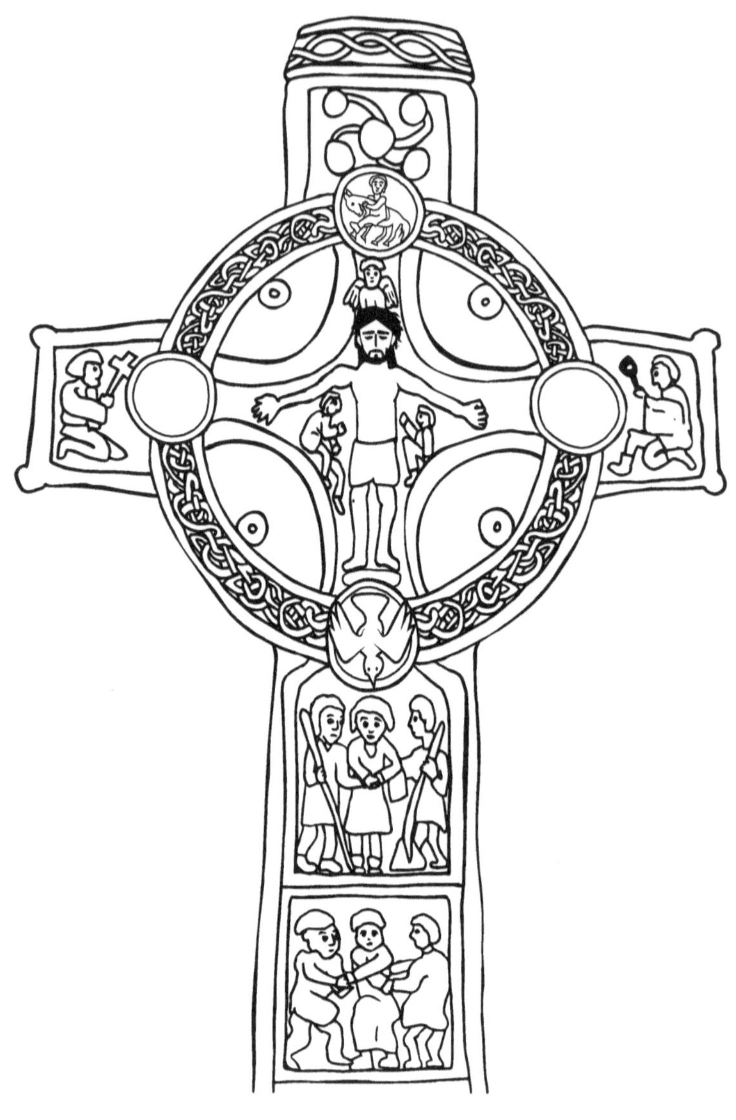

*The cross at Clonmacnoise is one of
the masterpieces created by the Muiredach Master.*

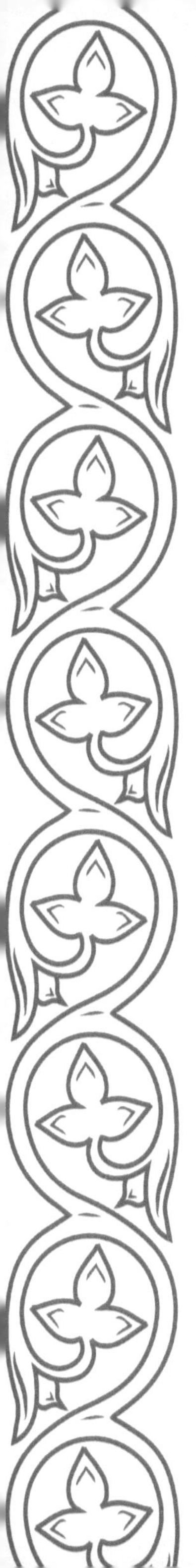

CHAPTER 7

Scriptures in Stone and the Still-Speaking God

Then beginning with Moses and all the prophets,
he interpreted to them the things about himself
in all the Scriptures.

ACTS 24:27

These crosses will stand out as
wonders in the story of art,
not just in Ireland but in the world.

OLIVER CRILLY[178]

ENCOUNTER

August 1973: Portage, Michigan

I was fourteen years old, just entering into the well-known rebellious-teenager phase of life. All the cool kids were talking about a recently released movie, *Jesus Christ Superstar*. There was a lot of buzz about this movie, both pros and cons. Religious critics were aghast that the movie gives no explicit resurrection account (though the fact that the singer who plays Jesus is missing at the end of the film may imply his continuity). The comparison of Mary Magdalene's relationship with Jesus to her other relations with men also upset traditional thinking.

At the same time, the film generated fresh conversations about Jesus and the Gospels. The fact that it was a *rock* opera and had the word *Superstar* in place of "Messiah," pointed to the potential value of the show; this was Jesus *made modern*. It forced people to think: How would we view Jesus if he did his great deeds *today*?

My father, known for his mild manner, was not so tranquil about the rock opera. I had the vinyl album before the movie came out; I recall playing the record on my stereo one day, and my father slammed his fist down so hard that the whole house heard it. He was furious that rock music had desecrated a classic work of literature like the Bible.

If it upset my parents and excited my schoolmates, then I had to view the movie, right? I announced to my parents that I was going to the theater to see it. My father's cousin Hazel, who happened to be visiting at the time, asked if she could go with me. She was in her late seventies, though she seemed ageless, and even to a cynical teenager, Hazel was fascinating. She knew something about any topic and was willing to talk about things other grown-ups would not. She was a mystic (though I lacked that word at the time) and one of the few "religious people" whom I respected.

After we returned from the theater, my parents quizzed Cousin Hazel: What did she think of the movie? She said, "I am glad I saw it. It shows that Jesus is modern and relevant—he is still with us." I did not come to believe in Christ until four years later, but I think this utterance by my father's cousin was one of the small events that paved the way for my coming to faith.

May 2011: Clonmacnoise Monastery

Three decades later, I was in a very different place, both spiritually and geographically. After years of longing, I was in the heart of Ireland, visiting Clonmacnoise Monastery, standing in the room that encloses the Cross of the Scriptures, a masterpiece of early medieval art. The cross stands tall, and its sculptors covered all four sides with panels portraying biblical and other pictorial scenes. It was breathtaking.

One detail jumped out at me: On a west-face panel of the cross were two soldiers guarding Christ's tomb. An interpretive plaque pointed out that this scene—portraying an event from the first century—depicts the guards not as Roman legionnaires

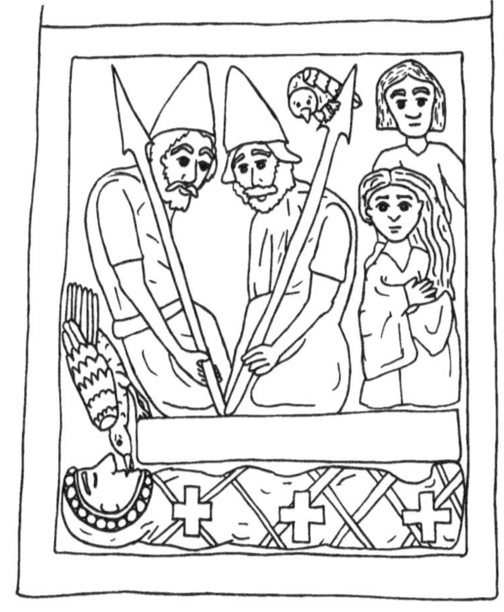

Portrayed here is the west-face panel of the Cross of the Scriptures, depicting Christ's tomb.

or as Irish soldiers of the artist's time. Instead, the plaque stated, they wear "the distinctive peaked helmets of . . . Christianity's persecutor, the pagan marauding Vikings." (In chapter 9, we'll consider a different picture of the Scandinavian impact on Celtic nations.) This was my first encounter with the way in which early medieval craftsmen contemporized the biblical messages.

The Irish scripture crosses of the ninth and tenth centuries were, in their time, similar to *Jesus Christ Superstar* or *Godspell* in the 1970s. These monumental works of art, with intricate portrayals of Bible scenes carved on all their surfaces, did more than remind people of scripture stories: They portrayed holy history in ways that were relevant for the people of their time, connecting well-known ancient narratives with contemporary political, social, and spiritual realities.

Today, the crosses, constructed from grey or reddish stone, are monochrome, but the original artists painted the pictorial scenes with bright, lifelike colors. Those vivid hues gave an even stronger impression that the stones were alive.

DEEPENING

The Bible and the Celts

The church I serve has a motto: "God is still speaking." As a past church president explains, "We believe the Gospel is still revealing God's truth in new and important ways for our living today. The ancient texts speak to us in new ways and provide for us new insights, as we live in a very different world from the ancient world."[179] This same still-speaking God has been bringing forth new meanings from ancient texts for a long time—as the Irish scripture crosses attest.

The scripture crosses are the most complex and impressive of the Celtic high crosses, the apex of the art form. To understand them better we must first examine the Bible's role in Ireland and the British Isles in the Early Middle Ages.

"One of the noblest gifts of the Holy Spirit is Holy Scripture, by which all ignorance is enlightened, and all worldly sorrow comforted, by which all spiritual light is kindled." That is how *An Leabhar Brac,* a medieval Irish manuscript, describes the value of written sacred words.[180]

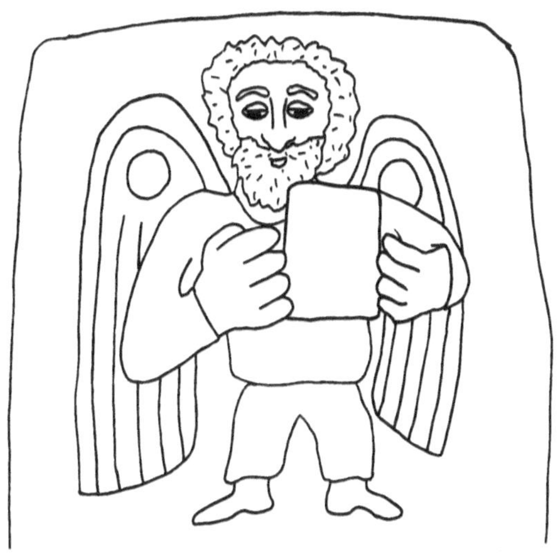

This drawing from the cross in Gulval, Cornwall,
depicts Matthew the Evangelist with his Gospel.

The gift of written scripture took a while to reach the Celtic lands. Ireland and the land of the Picts were outside the Roman Empire, so the first century's missionary efforts barely touched them. Not until the early fifth century, when Patrick and Ninian spread the news of Christ into Ireland and Scotland, did the Christian scriptures reach the Isles.

Imagine reading the Bible for the first time! Far from finding it dry or irrelevant, the Celts fell head over heels in love. They did not lay claim to scripture as a bludgeon to prove their point nor as literature from a faraway place and time; instead, the Celts saw themselves and their world in scripture; for them, the Bible was an endless source of wonder, beauty, and delight. Patrick, a former slave in Ireland, claimed to be poorly schooled, and yet he was steeped in the scriptures. In the two short writings he left us, he quotes or alluded to scripture 340 times, citing forty-nine different books of the Bible.[181] One of the legends of Saint Brigid tells how she miraculously produced an entire text of the Gospels, pulling it out from her chest. (Such fabulous tales often have an allegorical meaning; in this case, the story shows that the Gospels were so close to the saint's heart that they flowed out from her.[182])

Complete Bibles were rare, costly, and bulky, however, so most of the Celtic saints only had access to the four Gospels, a selection of scriptures, or the Book of Psalms. Since monks used the psalms for their prayers, bound collections became common. All these Bible texts were written in Latin, the common language of the Roman Empire; translators had only recently rendered them from Greek and Hebrew into Latin.

While book learning came late to the Celtic people, they readily embraced it. They already knew words held intoxicating power; language, for the Gaels, was a potent form of magic. Bards were the most honored members of society, since their words could influence the people to raise up or pull down chieftains and kings. With the introduction of literacy, as it rode the wind of God's written words—the Celtic love of wordplay transferred from oral to written form.

The Celts loved story and poem. The Christian faith brought new narratives, with exotic lands, mighty heroes, and the breathtaking figure of the God-Human, and these inspired the Celtic wordsmiths. Song and poetry were already in their blood, and now suddenly, they had been enriched with a hundred and fifty new poems, the Psalms. This contact with a new spirituality invigorated their creativity.

Before their introduction to Latin writing, the Gaels had used the Ogham alphabet, comprised of cross-hatched straight lines cut into wood or stone. Now, the new form of expression, made of curving brush strokes flowing smoothly onto animal hide, opened up new worlds of artistic expression. The Celts saw words' shape and meaning as intertwined, inseparable. Art historian and manuscript expert Benjamin Tilgham writes: "Insular calligraphers were consciously playing with the fact that a letter can be twisted and abstracted into a seemingly infinite variety of forms."[183]

Two to three hundred years after they first encountered the texts of the Bible, Irish scholars in their native island, as well as in Wales and Northern England, produced some of the greatest works of calligraphy ever made by hand. Illuminated manuscripts such as the Book of Kells and the Lindisfarne Gospels still draw crowds to gaze at their marvelously embellished pages. Small teams of artists and scribes, working together in monastery scriptoriums, spent decades producing one such masterpiece.[184] The effort, artistic genius, and precious materials that went into making a scribal tour-de-force like the Book of Kells made Gerald of Wales in the twelfth century call it "the work not of men, but of angels."[185] These expressions of Celtic manuscript art were produced at the same time that Pictish stone masons were pushing their artistic talents to create striking slab crosses with designs inspired by the manuscripts.

Clearly, the early medieval Celts were passionately in love with scripture—but it might be hard for you to generate the same enthusiasm. For people in the twenty-first century, the Bible may be a stumbling block more than a source of inspiration. Bible verses (taken out of context and with disregard for scholarship) have been weaponized to shame and disempower people. Thoughtful readers struggle with immorality and cruelty instigated not only by Bible characters but also by the biblical God. And ultra-literal readings of texts related to the Earth's history fall flat (like a flat Earth!) when compared to the consensus of paleontology, genetics, and geology.

For my entire adult life, the Bible has been my daily companion, but I also went through a phase of having to deconstruct what authority figures taught me about it. My relationship with the Bible has been like a turbulent romance, with a passionate beginning, disenchantment, then a rekindling of ardor. What rescued me from my cynicism was studying the methods of Bible interpretation common to scholars of the Early Middle Ages.

John Scotus Eriugena, whose name means "John the Irishman from Ireland," was a poet, mystic, philosopher, and theologian, famed in ninth-century Continental Europe. "For there are many ways, indeed an infinite number, of interpreting the Scriptures," he wrote, "just as in one and the same feather of a peacock and even in the same small portion of the feather, we see a marvelously beautiful variety of innumerable colors."[186]

Eriugena expresses the assumption of most Bible readers in the late Classical Period and the Early Middle Ages: that the scriptures should be viewed from one angle and then from another to reveal surprising and life-giving truths. Surely, they reasoned, a miracle-working God could produce Divinely inspired words hosting a multitude of meanings.

Irish Bible interpreters in the Early Middle Ages distinguished three layers of meaning assumed to be present in any biblical text: *stoir* (as in storehouse, referring to the literal level: that of physically observed reality), *sens* (allegorical meaning), and *run* (the "hidden" or mystical meaning).[187] In the third century, Origen defined three layers of Bible reading—literal, moral, and spiritual—which may have inspired the medieval divisions; they also correspond to the three elements of each human being (body, mind, and spirit).[188] I think of this as reading the Bible in "three dimensions": literal, symbolic, and imaginative. Using this method of interpretation, many passages of scripture shine with a brighter light.[189]

At the same time when Eriugena compared biblical texts to the multihued splendor of a peacock's tail feathers, stonemasons in Ireland were creating high crosses that were taller, more elegant, more complex, and more marvelous than anything attempted previously. An anonymous Michelangelo was leaving his mark on art history with enduring masterpieces in a small cluster of monasteries in the center of Ireland.

Some scholars surmise that ancient sculptors created these crosses as a memory device. Picture a crowd of unlettered Celtic villagers huddled around a cross while a monk points at the panels: "Now, this is Adam and Eve, the first people. This is Abraham. This is King David . . ." This scenario imagines the scripture crosses as simple mnemonics in stone for the biblically illiterate. The reality is far more complex.

People well-versed in the multivalent meanings of scripture produced the monumental crosses of the ninth and tenth centuries, knowing a Bible-literate audience would meditate on their work. These crosses depicted the levels of Bible meaning understood in their time: a literal sense *and* a higher level of metaphorical meaning *and* a yet higher level of imaginative application to the sculptor's own time. The ideas may have been set in stone, but they conveyed the messages of a Divinity who was still producing new meanings from the ancient texts.

The Irish Scripture Crosses

The amazing Celtic crosses of the late ninth and early tenth centuries would not exist were it not for a spiritual movement. The entire history of faith is a story of ebb-and-flow; the Spirit moves in striking ways in a certain place and time, energizing human beings to achieve works of great love—and then, as time goes by, the principles of this spiritual movement become institutionalized and stale, while spiritual leadership devolves into the pursuit of money or power. Then the Spirit must descend again, and the cycle renews.

The inspired geniuses who brought the gospel to the Celtic nations—Saint Patrick, Saint Brigid, Saint Ninian, Saint Ita, Saint David, Saint Aidan, and their like—made their world-enriching marks on the Gaelic world between the years 400 and 650. Their spirituality tended to be inclusive, mingling easily with the indigenous beliefs already present. Their successors, from 650 to 800, however, fell into predictable patterns of privilege and greed. While the scriptoriums produced some masterpieces during these years, the spiritual life of the monasteries declined.

Scholar and priest Oliver Crilly describes what happened next: "The unconquerable human spirit was at work, and . . . there was a new surge of spiritual energy among the monks and the faithful people of the Irish church. In the year 774 St Maelruáin founded the monastery of Tallaght in Co. Dublin," which was "full of the spirit of unity and of renewal." From this fountainhead, "A movement of spiritual renewal spread around the country," a movement that "came to be known as the Céilí Dé, which means the spouses or close friends of God."[190] The Céilí Dé (also spelled *Culdee*) movement spread across Ireland and the British Isles, sparking spiritual ardor and artistic splendors. Artists created most of the scripture crosses during this time of renewal.

The term *scripture cross* can refer to any early medieval cross that contains at least one biblical image. Out of 235 Irish high crosses catalogued, eighty-five contain biblical scenes, so slightly more than one in three crosses have this feature. Twenty-one of these crosses contain seven or more biblical images.[191] The ten most common images from the Hebrew scriptures are, in order of their frequency:

1. the sacrifice of Isaac

2. the fiery furnace (where King Nebuchadnezzar put Shadrach, Meshach, and Abednego)

3. Adam and Eve know nakedness

4. Eve gives Adam the apple

5. David slays the lion

6. Cain kills Abel

7. Noah's ark

8. David as a musician

9. Daniel in the lions' den

10. David and Goliath [192]

The top-ten most-portrayed images from the Christian scriptures are, again in order of frequency:

1. the Crucifixion

2. the baptism of Jesus

3. the Last Judgment

4. multiplication of loaves and fish

5. marriage feast at Cana

6. the second mocking of Jesus on his way to the cross

7. adoration of the Magi

8. the twelve apostles

9. first mocking of Jesus on his way to the cross

10. the Great Commission (Jesus' instructions to carry the gospel into the world)[193]

Out of the many Irish scripture crosses, art scholars recognize seven with craftmanship above the rest. These date from the end of the ninth or beginning of the tenth century, and all of them are in the center of Ireland, at the monasteries of Clonmacnoise, Durrow, and Kells (the preeminent monasteries after the Céilí Dé renewal).

People who carefully study art can recognize an artist's style, even without a signature; in fact, anyone familiar with some of the most famous artists—Van Gogh or Da Vinci, say—can usually recognize their work, even without an inscription or caption. In the same way, medievalists have determined that this set of outstanding crosses is the work of a single artist, an anonymous Irish Michelangelo (who likely had a small team of artisans working alongside him). He is referred to as the "Muiredach Master," though Muiredach was not his name. Abbot Muiredach (890–924) commissioned the cross at Monasterboice and made sure an inscription included his name. Alas, while the abbot ensured his own place in history, he was not so generous as to name the artist who created this masterpiece.

Reading Scripture Crosses at the Literal Level

On what I call the *literal level* of biblical interpretation, the grand Irish crosses were a stone tapestry of scripture references, with commonly understood artistic motifs to aid in identifying the subject. On the west face of the Clonmacnoise Cross of the Scriptures, for example, we see Jesus' crucifixion as it's detailed in John's Gospel; we know this is from the Gospel of John because the spearing of Jesus' side is portrayed in an obvious manner, which is only described the fourth Gospel. The panels beneath this imagery depict events connected with the Crucifixion: soldiers divide Christ's garment (one is holding a knife, a reference to the debate over dividing the article of clothing); soldiers torture Christ, one holding a nasty staff or flagellum; Christ rises from an open tomb while two soldiers sleep (they are, as noted earlier, portrayed as Danish warriors).

On the flip side of the cross, are a large, robed figure and lines of figures on each side. This is Christ at the Last Judgment: To his right, the saved souls face Christ, following an angel playing a horn, a sign of praise; while to his left, another angel pushes away figures with downcast heads, the damned en route to suffering. Beneath that, is a depiction of Christ giving Saint Peter the key to Paradise, while he hands a book (probably the Gospels) to Saint Paul. Other panels include a figure playing a lyre and a figure leading sheep, both references to King David who was both psalmist and shepherd.

Reading Scripture Crosses at the Symbolic Level

The details of the Cross of the Scriptures also carry messages that transcend literal identification with Bible passages. These are difficult to interpret with complete accuracy, since the symbols of our cultural milieu have changed a great deal over the centuries. However, we can make some educated guesses.

If we turn back to the cross's west face and look more closely, for example, we notice that the soldier is spearing Jesus' right side; normally, however, portrayals of this event position the soldier on Jesus' left because that's the side of the body where the heart is. So why did the artist portray the soldier on the "wrong" side?

The Muiredach Master may be giving us a subtle but profound hint about the meaning of the Crucifixion. The body of Christ is associated with the new temple of God, the place where humanity goes to be reconciled with God. The mystical vision described in Ezekiel 47:1 had the water of salvation flowing from the *right* side of the Jerusalem temple. This may be why John's Gospel emphasizes blood and water flowing from Christ's side—it is the water of salvation flowing from the new place of God's salvation. By placing the soldier on Christ's right side, the sculptor could have been implying these rich layers of symbolic meaning.[194]

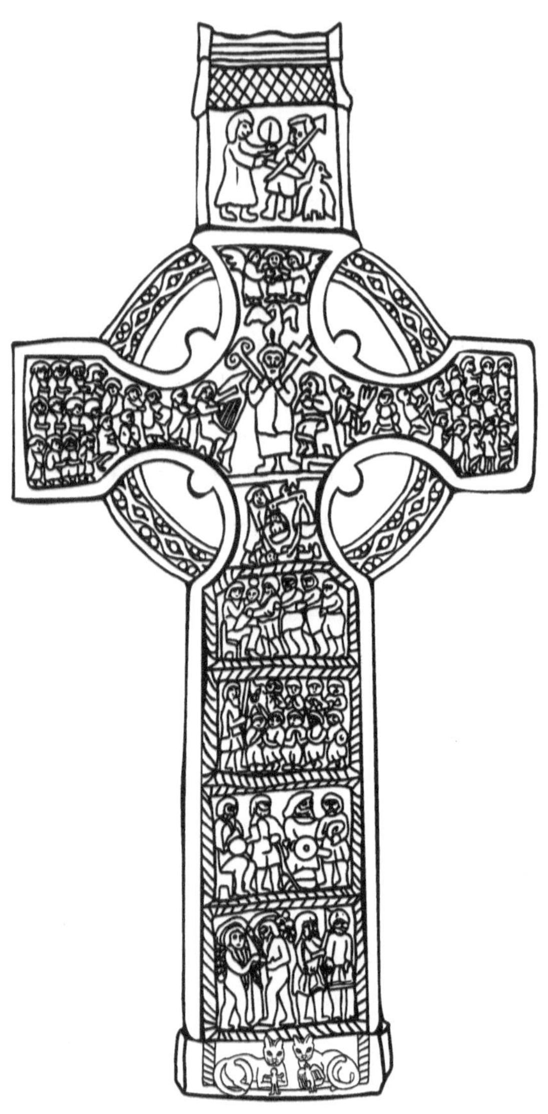

Muiredach's High Cross at Monasterboice, by the same artist who created the Cross of the Scriptures, also portrays an image of the Last Judgment. Note, however, the little figures beneath Christ at the center. They are meant to portray the weighing of the soul, a concept with roots in ancient Egypt. While the devil lies beneath the scales, trying to pull the soul down to him, his power cannot overcome the counterforce from the Archangel Michael who is standing beside the scales. Divine mercy, the stone proclaims, is powerful, reaching out to save and redeem all souls.

Artistic details derived from Egypt may also convey symbolic meanings in the biblical scenes. In one image, Christ holds two ritual objects, crossed; this artistic motif hearkens back to Egyptian portrayals of Osiris judging the dead, which reinforces the biblical scene of the Last Judgment.[195] In the scene of Christ rising from the tomb, a bird places its beak into the mouth of Christ, possibly indicating a connection to the Egyptian portrayal of the human soul (*Ba*) as a bird: God is returning the soul to Christ's body for his imminent resurrection.

Even the cross's interaction with light and shadow has symbolic meaning. The north side of the cross, which was in shadow for most of the day when the cross was in its original outdoor location, portrays human figures struggling with temptations, while the south side, which is illuminated for much of the day, depicts people basking in Divine grace and protection.

Another image with symbolic meaning on the Cross of the Scriptures is an image known as the Hand of God. This carving is a bit harder to see, since it is under the cross's southern arm. The hand's placement above scenes that may portray the king and abbot could indicate that God's hand is above all earthly authority figures. Heather Pulliam, a Scottish scholar who specializes in medieval art, says the meaning goes even deeper, however:

Suspended over the head of its audience, the hand of Clonmacnoise hangs in the air like a query or command awaiting a human response and presence—whether imagined, remembered, or corporal. It is an open, ambiguous, and flexible sign. Anyone standing beneath it and sheltered with the arms of the cross may envisage themselves under God's protection or blessing. Like the use of the first person in the Psalms, the hand's position on the cross creates a direct and intimate relationship between the praying supplicant and God, the visual equivalent of "I" and "you."[196]

Pulliam also points out that the hand can be viewed as either the Divine left hand with the palm facing the Earth—or as a right hand raised up toward Heaven. "Such polyvalence and ambiguity," she writes, "collapse time and convey the omniscience and omnipresence of God." The Divine right hand blesses the resurrected in Heaven, and the left "offers benediction to the dead buried in the grounds surrounding the cross, awaiting the Resurrection."[197]

Expanded meaning comes not only from the way the scripture crosses portray biblical subjects but also from the *selection* of scenes they portrayed. With so many Bible stories to choose from, why did so many of these crosses portray the same biblical events? These scenes may have alluded to a common liturgical hymn of the ninth century, made popular by the Céilí Dé. Known as the "Help-of-God" chant,[198] it includes these lines:

> *Adam's seed, by Jesus has been freed.*
> *Free me, Jesus, as thou saved Noah from the flood.*
> *Free me, O Jesus, as thou saved Isaac from his father's hand.*
> *Free me, O Jesus, as thou saved David from Goliath's sword.*
> *Free Me, O Jesus, as thou saved Daniel from the den of lions.*
> *Free me, O Jesus,*
> *as thou freed the Hebrew children from the fiery furnace.*[199]

Notice the overlap between the scenes on the crosses, and the salvation events listed in this popular hymn. The scripture crosses offered visual parallels to the words of a familiar chant.

These crosses can also refer to theological concepts with symbols from outside scripture. For example, Irish and Pictish crosses marked with five bosses (half globes) represent the five wounds of Jesus on the cross.[200]

Vine motifs, common on Northumbrian, Pictish, and Irish crosses, reminded viewers that Christ is the "the vine of life."[201] The many grapevine designs on Celtic stone crosses also point to the Eucharist. In the Celtic regions, hymns, liturgies, sermons, stories in saints' lives, art in illuminated manuscripts, ornate liturgical objects, and designs on the stone crosses all expressed the central role of the sacred meal in the Early Middle Ages.

On many crosses, the vine designs also include birds and beasts feeding on grapes. This feeding motif reminds viewers that, as Saint Ambrose said in the fourth century: "Christ is the new drink brought down from heaven to earth . . . who just like the grape on the vine, hung in the flesh from the wood of the cross."[202] The birds and furred creatures included in these eucharistic images denoted the ancient inclusion of all Nature, both flora and fauna, alongside humanity in the redemption of all Creation. Christ's death, descent to Hades, and resurrection restore everything God had ever made. (For more on this, see chapters 10 and 11.)

Reading Scripture Crosses at the Imaginative Level

The third way of deriving meaning from scripture, the "hidden" level, requires simply reading the Bible the way you would any good narrative. A well-told story connects you to the lives of its characters; through the powers of imagination, you enter the story, seeing beyond the words to the sensual details of the surrounding scene, the emotions of the characters, and the motion of their actions. At this level, you don't perceive the story as someone else's creation, a suspended, unmoving moment outside time and space; instead, the characters take on a life of their own. You wonder, "What will happen to them next?"

The ancient Celts loved stories, and they integrated this passion with their faith. Theological historian Ian Bradley says, "The Celtic saints were associated with an approach to expressing and explaining the mysteries of the Christian faith through story, symbol, and verse, rather than through intellectual proposition."[203]

Many good stories begin with the author asking, "What if?" Like the creators of *Jesus Christ Superstar*, Celtic artists of the Early Middle Ages played with sacred scriptures in light of that question. *What if this story from the Bible were happening today, to people I know? What if I had been present at the Crucifixion (or the Nativity or Resurrection)? What if the story of Jesus was transposed into the familiar details of my own ordinary life? What if Bible stories took place in today's political environment?* One way the creators of the scripture crosses answered these questions was by using their own contemporary styles of clothing and hair for their biblical figures. As I mentioned earlier, the Cross of the Scriptures at Clonmacnoise portrays Roman guards wearing Viking garb.

APPLICATIONS FOR TODAY

Study the Master

For every art form, there are women and men whose achievements shine through the years: Frida Kahlo, John Coltrane, Jane Austen, Michelangelo, and others. What an unfortunate fluke of history that the greatest sculpture of the Early Middle Ages remains anonymous! But that doesn't stop you from appreciating their work.

PONDERING THE MUIREDACH MASTER

You should be able to find online images that cover the many panels and sides of the great crosses by the Muiredach Master. They are:

1. the Cross of the Scriptures at Clonmacnoise
2. the North Cross at Duleek
3. the Durrow High Cross
4. Muiredach's Cross at Monasterboice
5. the Tall (or West) Cross at Monasterboice
6. the Tower Cross at Kells
7. the Market Cross at Kells

Set aside some time to compare these works. What features do you notice in common? What features are unique to certain crosses? How would you describe the sculptor's style of human portrayal? Sketch some of the designs.

Scholars have spent years poring over the details of these Irish masterpieces; surely, they are worth a leisurely hour or two of contemplation!

Read the Bible the Ancient Way

Has Bible study become wearisome for you? Does scripture seem irrelevant to your life?

Earlier in this chapter, I mentioned the Celtic "three-dimensional" way of Bible interpretation. I believe churches and their leaders could have prevented many of the painful abuses of scriptural authority in our time by using this multifaceted way of Bible reading. Try applying the three ways to your own experiences with scripture. Look beyond the literal meanings of the words to see what deeper meanings Bible passages may have for you. What symbolism do you see? If you allow your imagination to play with the scripture, what emerges?

SPENDING TIME WITH SCRIPTURE

This application, like the previous one, requires a commitment of your time. Take one Bible vignette, perhaps a familiar one like the Crucifixion or the birth of Christ. Decide to live with it for a length of time—a week, a month, or go big and commit to it for a year. Determine to *find every possible artistic interpretation* of the tale that you can. Cover the history of painting and sculpture for that story, and cross geographic, racial, gender, and other boundaries to get a panoramic view. Look for novels and short stories. Stream videos. Listen to music, from ancient to Classical to Baroque to Pop and Jazz. You may want to keep a journal, complete with sketches and images printed from the internet or cut from magazines. See how many fresh insights you can produce from just one story. Summarize these at the end of the time span to which you committed for this exercise.

What have you learned?

How might your life be changed if you applied these insights to your heart and actions?

The scripture crosses remind us how many bright revelations await us if we can see with renewed eyes. As we listen to the messages of these ancient crosses and read the Bible the Celtic way, we embark on fresh journeys of adventure and wonder.

May I read the Sacred Words with the Trinity:
with the High First-Sower,
with the King of Mysteries,
with the Divine Breath filling me.
May the Holy Pages restore all that is broken in me,
and may I be transformed into Christ,
the Brightness that outshines the Sun,
the Holy Child that gives everything,
desiring nothing in return
but the joy of my affection.

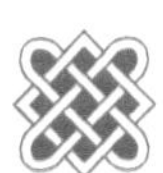

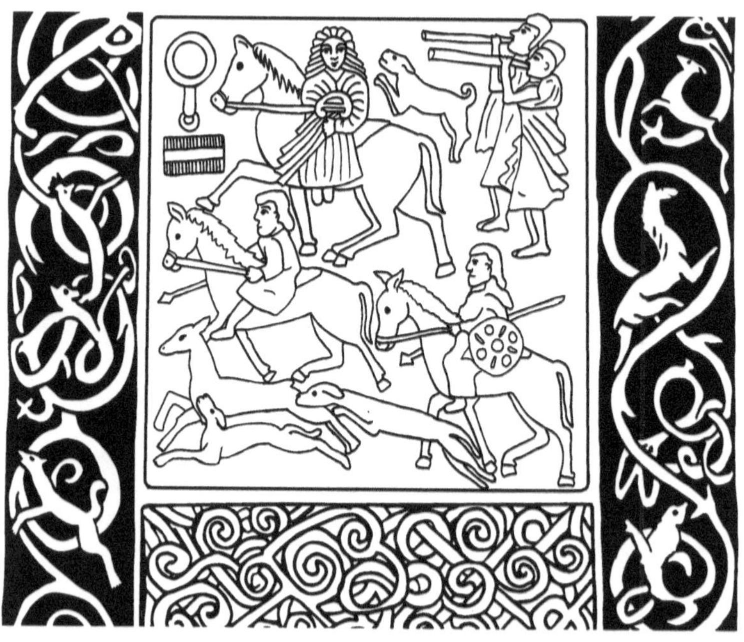

The Shandwick Stone in Easter Ross, Scotland, shows a hunting scene.

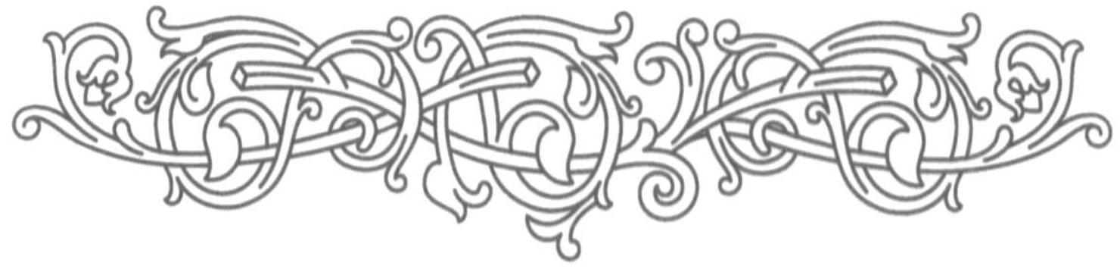

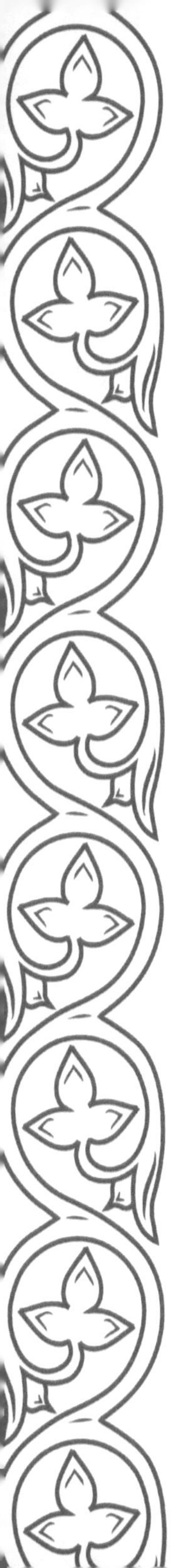

CHAPTER 8

All Creatures of Our God and King

But ask the animals, and they will teach you,
the birds of the air, and they will tell you;
ask the plants of the earth, and they will teach you,
and the fish of the sea will declare to you.
Who among you does not know
that the hand of the Lord has done this?

JOB 12:7–9

Perceive the eternal Word of God
reflected in every plant and insect,
every bird and animal, every man and woman.

SAINT NINIAN'S CATECHISM[204]

ENCOUNTER

500 CE: Kildare, Ireland

The knock on the door came sharp and insistent.

"Your Grace, Your Grace!"

Brigid's mind came back from the Ocean of Light where it was dwelling in contemplation. *It's Brother Niall, what now?*

"Honored Lady, there is urgent news—it cannot wait!"

Her legs stiff from sitting in the pose for holy meditation, she pulled herself upright and opened the door.

Brother Niall was but a lad, his face flushed and his voice high-pitched as he explained the situation. "As you know, Abbess, the King of Leinster has been building on his fortress this summer season, and he hired workmen who came from all over Éire with their families. And as you are also aware, Your Grace, the king has a trained pet fox, which does amazing feats of agility at his command. It is his greatest joy. Yesterday a workman, Colm by name, saw the king's fox headed toward the barnyard. He knew not that it was the royal pet and—thinking to assist his employer—he grabbed a bow and killed it with his arrow. When the king heard, he was beyond enraged. He swore in the presence of all his underlings that Colm, his wife, and his children shall be hanged today at sunset. Your friend at the court, Mavern, begs you to come and intercede for the man's life, and for the lives of his family members. He is entirely innocent! The king will listen to no one else, but perhaps because of your great reputation for sanctity, you might prevail?"

Brigid clapped her hands. "Brother Niall, ask the stable workers to make ready my chariot and the four fastest horses—the three black stallions who have not been gelded, plus the one that is dappled. As soon as they are ready, I leave for Leinster. And then ask Sister Winfrey to lead the prayers at terce, in my absence."

She hastened to the refectory, grabbed a piece of bread and some cheese for nourishment, then dashed to the barn where the stable hands had already prepared her chariot and horses. After only a few moments, she was racing through the woods. She stood on the chariot's wooden bottom with a firm stance, her knees bent to yield to the vehicle's jerk and sway. Lesser mortals would have been afraid in this forest, for it was frequented by brigands, but Brigid had been through these roads alone many times before; she knew no one would dare assail her.

Majesty, she prayed, *protect me from that numpty oaf's hatred. Give me a level head to confront him. Help me remember he is more stupid than evil, like a spoiled child. May I be your agent to free Colm and his family, and . . . O Beloved, I have no idea how to do this—so let it be as it is written in Saint Mark: "Do not worry beforehand about what you are to say, but say whatever is given you at that time, for it is not you who speak but the Holy Spirit."*

As she finished her prayer, a reddish blur dashed past, narrowly avoiding her right wheel. Then, to her amazement, it turned and leapt into the chariot. *A fox!*

"Well, hello little fellow!" Brigid said softly. "Who might you be?" She reached down her hand and stroked the furry creature. When he did not flinch from her touch, she lifted him into her ample satchel.

O Beloved, Maker of all creatures, you have sent your servant the fox to aid me! O Dearest One, you always provide!

Brigid's horses were the stuff of legend; none could match their speed and endurance, and so the Sun was just past its zenith when her chariot clattered past the open gates of the king's stronghold. Few people were permitted to walk unquestioned from the courtyard into the great hall; she was one of those few.

The king sat atop a dais, under a mountainous pile of leather and fur garments that made him appear—to Brigid's eye—ridiculous. The queen sat beside him with the same glazed expression Brigid had seen before. *Is she terminally bored or merely drunk all the time?*

"Your Majesty." Brigid bowed.

"You're here to plead for the life of that bastard who killed my fox. I know you, Brigid of Kildare, all mercy and sweetness, you think you'll just sweep in here and change my mind. Not a chance! Turn around, go home. Stop wasting my time."

"Your Majesty," Brigid continued, "You are sorely aggrieved, and most sadly grieving. I know the pain of losing a beloved companion such as your fox. But why pile loss upon loss? Why add the grief of a family to your grief from the loss of a beloved pet?"

"Fine words and a waste of breath," the king snarled. "You plead for kindness, but what kindness was shown to me? Hmm? I only know my fox is gone. Unless you can bring him back, get back to your convent and let me see no more of you."

"Your Majesty." Brigid spoke slowly, making sure she had the king's full attention. "I cannot raise your beloved fox from the dead, but what if I could supply a replacement for your companion? Many people find solace in the love of another furry creature, after their animal friends go to the next world."

"Hah! Stop bothering me with foolish words. My fox possessed great nimbleness of body. He knew how to do tricks like a dog. You'll find none other like him."

"Well," Brigid smiled, "let us see." She lifted the fox from her satchel and set him down in front of the king's dais. "Okay, my little friend," she whispered, "uh . . . roll over." She made a circular motion with her hands and held her breath.

The fox rolled over thrice. Brigid clapped her hands with joy.

"Hmph!" the king snorted, "Coincidence! The creature is merely stretching itself after being in your bag."

"Wait, Your Majesty. See what else this clever beast can do." She bent down to the fox and said, "Now, my friend, please go up the steps and beg before his Majesty." She motioned toward the king.

The fox bounded up the steps, stood erect on its hind legs, and gestured with its paws, his tongue lolling, his bright eyes pleading as he looked into the king's face.

"Not bad," the king admitted. "Still, not the equal of the clever one I have lost. My fox could dance. No one has ever seen a creature that could perform so nimbly."

"Sire, if this lovely creature who stands before you can do as well, do you then promise to release the workman Colm and his family? Will you remit any claim you have on their lives?"

The king hesitated. At last, he nodded his head.

The fox looked up at Brigid, his head cocked as though he waited to see what she would ask next. The abbess smiled and made her hands dance in the air. Immediately, the fox sprang upright on his rear legs, skipping up and down on one and then another foot, his back straight and head high.

The king could not hold back a smile. He lifted the fox onto his lap.

"The workman and his family will be released." Brigid was issuing a command rather than asking a question.

"Let it be so." The king nodded to his guard.

"Thank you, sire." Brigid bowed her head to hide her laughter. "I knew you would judge wisely."

As she took her leave of the king's residence, Brigid saw in the courtyard a haggard man, his face covered with tears of relief, accompanied by an equally joyous wife and a son and daughter. They climbed into their wagon and headed out the gate. She watched until they were out of sight, lost in the woods' shadows.

Dearest One, I praise you for this dear creature who has granted this man and his family a new lease on life.

Brigid climbed into her chariot. Her horses seemed eager to be off, away from the king's lair, but she held them back. *All's well save for that fox. The king is such a callous oaf. I fear, my Love, to leave the wee fellow at his mercy.*

Brigid put her fingers in her mouth and gave a piercing whistle. Moments later, she saw a streak of red fur dash out of the great hall, past her chariot, and straight out the gate into the deep forest. Brigid grinned. "Go in peace, little friend," she called.

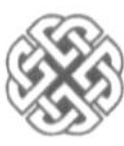 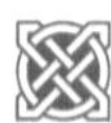 

Several days later, after Brigid was once more at home, she got word that the king's servants scoured the woods, beating the brush for any sign of the fox. But they never found him. Brigid saw him in her mind's eye, nestling snugly in his well-concealed den. She smiled to herself.

Many mouths told this tale, and the people throughout Celtic lands gave praise to Christ for the deeds done through God's servant Brigid of Kildare.

DEEPENING

The Celtic Connection with Animals

Cogitosus, a monk of Kildare, recorded this incident in his *Life of Saint Brigid*, the first biography of an Irish female saint, written around 650, about a century after Brigid's death. A century after the time of Cogitosus, an anonymous Pictish artist depicted a fox on a fine stone cross slab on the eastern coast of Scotland. Was he alluding to the story of Brigid and the fox?

In the Early Middle Ages, people of all classes recognized the tremendous value of their fellow creatures—wild, domestic, and mythical.[205] Animals were fellow citizens of the enchanted world, possessing great powers in the old legends, and they served in Christian understanding to communicate God's kindliness and faithfulness. No wonder then that Pictish and Irish pictorial crosses portray many different representatives of the animal realm.

Celtic Christians' love for animals had its roots in the pre-Christian Celtic world, hearkening back to the shamanistic practices of druidism. Pagan sages sought to gain power and insight by associating with the skills, instincts, and special gifts of the animal world. Tales of shapeshifting might reflect such skillful practices as perceiving like a hawk, running through the forest with the agility of a deer, or swimming like a salmon. Using meditation or entheogens (psychoactive natural substances), shamans could experience the powers of the animal world.

Shapeshifting

"The Song of Amergin" tells the story of one of the seven sons of Mil, the Milesians who traveled from Galicia to populate Ireland. They were able to take the island in part due to Amergin's magical song, which reflects the ancient shamanistic view of the natural world:

> *I am a stag: of seven tines,*
> *I am a flood: across a plain,*
> *I am a wind: on a deep lake,*
> *I am a tear: the Sun lets fall,*
> *I am a hawk: above the cliff,*
> *I am a thorn: beneath the nail,*

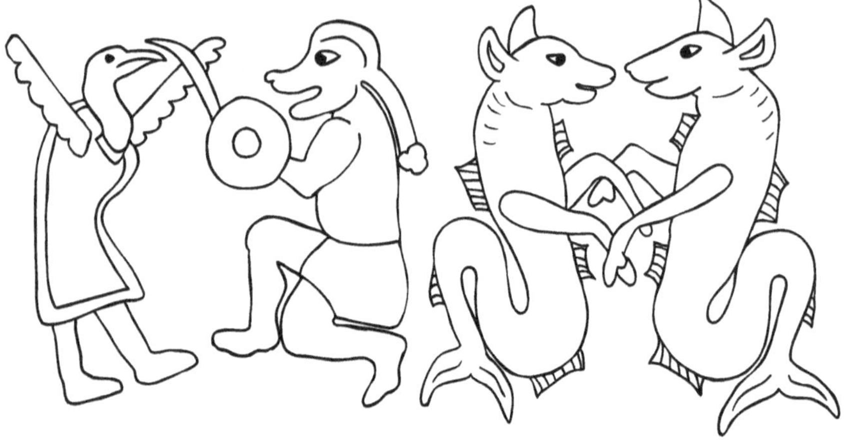

A farmer discovered a small stone bearing these images while plowing his field. Archeologists speculate that the site may originally have been a chapel, and the stone is a piece of a larger cross. These drawings—a man with a bird's head, a man with a dog's head, and two fish with what look like the heads of mice (which are what the experts call hippocamps or seahorses)—indicate the fluid boundary between human and animal in the Celts' imagination.

Pagan Celts believed humans could shift into the forms of animals, or perhaps more correctly, into the *reality* of animals. Stories about Celtic gods and heroes often mentioned their shapeshifting abilities: Tuan MacCarell lived as a stag, an eagle, and a salmon. The Goddess Morgan was said to be someone who "has learned the use of plants . . . ; she knows, too, the art of changing her shape."[207]

Shapeshifting could also work the other way around: Animals might sometimes turn themselves into humans. The selkie, the

Scottish seal-woman, is one example; the God Cernunnos, both stag and human, is another.

The ancient Celts perceived a sense of spirit, even consciousness, in river and mountain, loch and marsh, tree and stone; no wonder, then, they sensed this same sense of awareness and personality in furred, feathered, and finned life. What's more, the barrier between humans and animals was far more permeable than we perceive it to be today. Consciousness could even pass back and forth between them.

Since all things are connected, like the endless interwoven pattern of Celtic knots, there is no hierarchy, no first or last, no beginning or end.

Kentigern

Saint Kentigern (560–612), patron saint of Glasgow, also known by the nickname Mungo, is an example of the Christian Celts' ongoing love of animals. When Kentigern was a child studying at a monastery school, his fellow students were playing with a robin and killed it. The young saint took the bird in his hands, "signed it with the sign of the cross, and lifted his hands in prayer. Straightaway the bird revived and flew with joy."[208]

Years later, when he was a bishop, Kentigern and some monks sought a location for a new monastery:

> And while they went together over abrupt mountains, hollow valleys, caves of the earth, thickset briers, dark woods, and open glades in the forest, lo and behold, a wild boar from the wood, entirely white, met them, and sometimes advancing a little, and then returning and looking backwards, motioned to the saint and his companions . . . to follow him.

The monks praised God and followed the boar to the perfect location for their new place of worship. The boar then came before Kentigern "and by his frequent grunts seemed to ask something of the bishop." So Kentigern uttered a blessing for the boar, wishing that: "God Almighty, in Whose power are all the beasts of the forest, the oxen, the birds of the air, and fishes of the sea, grant thee for thy conduct such reward as . . . is best for thee."[209]

My favorite story of Saint Kentigern, however, concerns an unfaithful queen and a special salmon. Kentigern's hagiographer relates that "Queen Languoreth, living in plenty and delights, was not faithful to the royal chamber or the marital bed." She had an affair with a guard, and in the course of their adultery, the queen's wedding ring was accidentally lost in the River Clud. The king, suspecting his wife's betrayal, demanded to know the whereabouts of her ring. She claimed to have mislaid it, and the king gave her an ultimatum: If she could not produce the ring in three days, the queen would die "a most disgraceful death."

Queen Languoreth sent a messenger to Saint Kentigern, pleading for his help. The saint in turn directed the queen's messenger to take a pole and fish from the banks of the Clud; he did so, quickly reeling in a salmon—with the queen's ring in its mouth! The messenger gave it to the queen and, "when she saw it and received it, her heart was filled with joy, her mouth with praise and thanksgiving. Therefore the queen returned to the king the ring he required, in the sight of all," and the royal couple "were recalled to the grace of peace and mutual love."[210]

Salmon and boars are both magical creatures in Pagan Celtic mythology, and these tales show their continued importance in the age of the Gaelic saints. The story of the ring also shows Mungo's Christ-like character, favoring restoration over retribution.

The Spiritual Significance of Animals

Christians in the Early Middle Ages universally agreed that the universe was a vast web of analogies; hidden likenesses connected the tangible world with unseen truths. Scripture declares, "From the greatness and the beauty of created things their original author, by analogy, is seen."[211] When Job sought to teach others God's ways, his advice was: "Ask the animals, and they will teach you, the birds of the air, and they will tell you."[212] In the early years of the medieval period, most people believed God had arranged the "Book of Nature" as a source of instruction for humanity; it was a second scripture. If all Creation proclaims God's qualities,[213] then animals, who share so much in common with humankind, were considered especially valuable forms of Divine revelation. Each species of creature was thought to convey truths about the Creator and how to live in God's world.

Pagan Hellenists had also written about animals' significance for centuries before the Christian era, and the early and medieval church absorbed these ideas. *Physiologus*, written by a Greek anonymous author in Alexandria in the fourth century of the Common Era, briefly describes each animal and then provides a Christian allegorical interpretation. *Physiologus* was a bestseller in the ancient world, translated into the languages of Europe and western Asia and eventually one of the most widely distributed books in Europe (after the Bible). Around 600, Hispano-Roman archbishop and theologian Isidore of Seville wrote *Etymologiae*, a massive encyclopedia that in the following centuries became the standard scholarly reference work throughout Europe; Isidore devoted Book XII of his encyclopedia to birds and animals. Later, other writers combined ideas from the *Physiologus* with Isidore's animal section, resulting in many more books, known since then as *bestiaries*.[214]

The well-established ship routes between Northern Iberia and Ireland created opportunities for Isidore's scholarship to influence the Irish scholar-saints.[215] As Celtic Christians came in contact with these ideas, they readily combined them with their own ancient shamanic understanding of beasts and birds. Meanwhile, at least one theologian in the sixth century stated the belief that images of animals could serve the same purpose as scripture, because uneducated people "see through them what they must accept; they read in them what they cannot read in books."[216]

Animal Friends

They say there are two kinds of people: cat lovers and dog lovers. In fact, there are three kinds of people, for there is a third category who love *both* cats and dogs. (Actually, there is a fourth category as well: people who like *neither* cats nor dogs.) When I wrote *Water from an Ancient Well* more than a decade ago, I counted myself in the category of dog people. During the years of our children's adolescence, we had both dogs and cats, but the dogs were my favorites. I have been fortunate to have loved two sheepdogs and to have been loved by them in return. Both Duke, a border collie, and Bryn, an Aussie heeler, came to us as rescue dogs; both were intelligent and—once they learned their new owners were dedicated to their welfare—dotingly affectionate. Duke and Bryn, in succession, lived to old age with us and passed away in our home. We grieved, then went for several years without any furred companions.

And then we received a surprise gift from our grown daughter: a rehomed Scottish fold cat we named Bunty. She has the softest, most extraordinary silver-and-brown coat and a unique owl-like, short-nosed face; I have dubbed her a "proximity cat" because she remains steadfastly alongside us (but never sits in our laps). Her quiet companionship has transformed me now into someone who loves *both* dogs and cats.

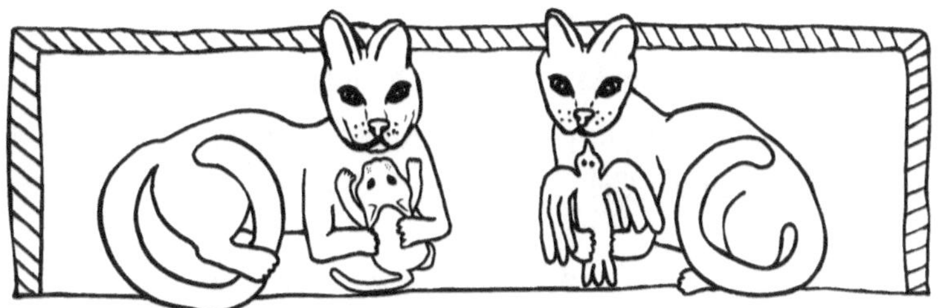

*These two cats are carved on the base of Muiredach's Cross at Monasterboice.
Are they about to eat their helpless prey? Or do they symbolize the scriptural
concept of a Peaceable Kin-dom, where lion lies down with lamb?*

Felines

A Stone-Age artist carved the earliest known depiction of a cat in
the Celtic lands, within a passage tomb at Fourknocks in Ireland's
County Meath.[217] Centuries later, the anonymous Irish Michelangelo
portrayed cats on two of his masterpieces—the Cross of the Scriptures
at Clonmacnoise and Muiredach's Cross at Monasterboice. According
to medieval scholar Roger Stalley:

> The artistic interest in cats was not an arbitrary matter, for
> they were highly valued in Irish society, principally for their
> ability to catch mice. In monasteries they guarded the pantry
> and granary, and even protected the bread of the eucharist.[218]

Medieval bestiaries indicate people in the Middle Ages appreciated
cats for some of the same reasons we still do today: They reduce mice
populations, have extraordinary night vision by night, and politely cover
their droppings. They were also kept as pets, however, and sometimes
pampered, as a thirteenth-century household account reveals when it lists
cheese being bought solely for the manor cat. An unknown scribe wrote
in the margin of a manuscript about "a golden, milk-drinking, furry,
purring beast," while another medieval account gives this description
of cats: "They delight in being stroked by the hand of a person and they
express their joy with their own form of singing."[219]

I believe Celtic monks in the Early Middle Ages loved their cats as much as I love Bunty. The poem "Pangur Bán" expresses the affection of one ninth-century Celtic Christian for his cat:

> *I and Pangur Bán my cat,*
> *'Tis a like task we are at:*
> *Hunting mice is his delight,*
> *Hunting words I sit all night.*
>
> *Better far than praise of men*
> *'Tis to sit with book and pen;*
> *Pangur bears me no ill-will,*
> *He too plies his simple skill.*
>
> *'Tis a merry task to see*
> *At our tasks how glad are we,*
> *When at home we sit and find*
> *Entertainment to our mind.*
>
> *Oftentimes a mouse will stray*
> *In the hero Pangur's way;*
> *Oftentimes my keen thought set*
> *Takes a meaning in its net.*
>
> *'Gainst the wall he sets his eye*
> *Full and fierce and sharp and sly;*
> *'Gainst the wall of knowledge I*
> *All my little wisdom try.*
>
> *When a mouse darts from its den,*
> *O how glad is Pangur then!*
> *O what gladness do I prove*
> *When I solve the doubts I love!*

So in peace our task we ply,
Pangur Bán, my cat, and I;
In our arts we find our bliss,
I have mine and he has his.

Practice every day has made
Pangur perfect in his trade;
I get wisdom day and night
Turning darkness into light.[220]

We know the author lived in Germany at the same time Pictish stoneworkers were doing some of their grandest work, and we know Pangur's owner was Irish because he wrote the poem in Old Irish. His location in Germany is evidence of the widespread influence of Celtic monastics across Europe at the time; the poem attests to the Celtic love for both animals and written knowledge.

Humanity's "Best Friend"

Hunting deer or boar on horseback, armed with spears, was Celtic aristocrats' primary recreation from the beginning of the Iron Age through the Middle Ages. Good hounds were an indispensable part of that activity, and kings and chieftains probably gave more love to their hounds than they gave to their less fortunate human servants. Ninth-century Pictish cross slabs include hunting scenes, complete with hounds. The cross embraced these dogs, just as they did all life.

An article from the American Kennel Club states, "Sir Walter Scott referred to the Deerhound as 'the most perfect creature of Heaven'. . . . Those who know the breed appreciate its sterling attributes, in no small respect because of how those traits have withstood the test of time." The article goes on to explain, "The earliest clues to breed origins can be found in stones sculpted by the Picts, the tribal folk who peopled much of Scotland through the Dark Ages until the arrival of the Scots from Ireland in the mid-ninth century. Many of these 'Pictish stones' . . . depict a Greyhound-like dog in pursuit of deer. Some historians believe this dog may have been the Deerhound's ancestor."[221]

You may not be familiar with the Scottish deerhound, but maybe you've gaped at an Irish wolfhound? With an average height of three feet at the shoulder, weighing as much as a typical adult human male, they are impressive creatures. They proved the skill for which they were bred, doing their job so well, in fact, that no wild wolves are left in Ireland. At the end of the fourth century, Roman statesman Quintus Aurelius Symmachus wrote a thank-you letter to his brother for the gift of seven Irish hounds, noting that "all Rome viewed them in wonder."[222] Their popularity continued into the Christian era in Ireland, when monasteries kept wolfhounds to guard their sheep against wolves. As the twentieth-century Celtic scholar Eleanor Hull notes, the whole of ancient Irish literature "is filled with accounts of the esteem in which the large hounds were held."[223]

Medieval dog owners valued their pets primarily for their practical service (few could afford to feed an animal merely for companionship), but early medieval Christ-followers certainly loved their dogs. Brigid's biographer, Cogitosus, tells the story of how the saint gave meat to a hungry dog, despite a scarcity of

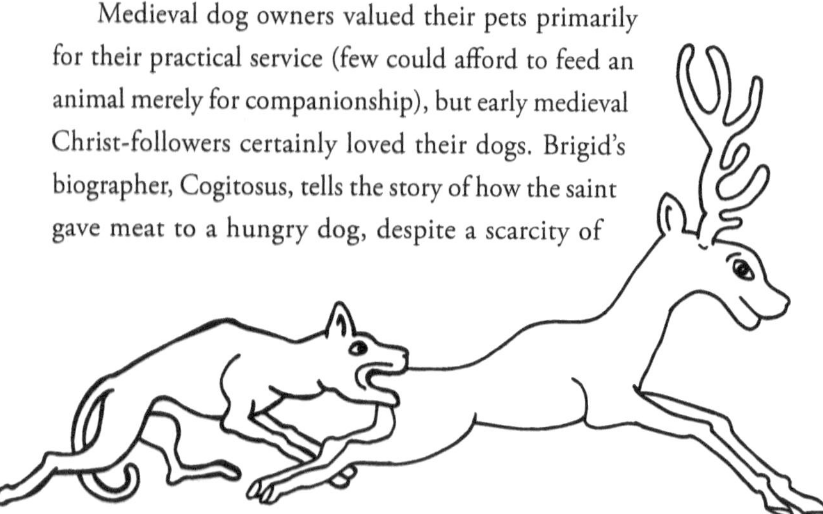

The cross slab at Kirriemuir bears the image of a hound taking down a stag.

meat for her human companions; God mercifully multiplied the remaining meat (like Christ's miracle of loaves and fishes) so that neither humans nor canines went unfed. Another time, when Brigid fell into a trance, her loyal dog guarded her for weeks until the saint came to herself.[224]

Medieval bestiaries name three kinds of dogs: guard dogs, hunting dogs, and sheepdogs,[225] canine breeds that are still valued even in our technologically enhanced world. And, the bestiaries explain, dogs have a spiritual meaning to share: "The dog's ability to heal wounds by licking them represents how the wounds of sin can be cured by confession."[226] Symbolically, dogs represented fidelity;[227] canine loyalty caused one medieval English scholar to place dogs as the best and first of all domesticated animals.[228]

Horses

Pictish monuments often depict horses bearing warriors or huntsmen. Historian Elizabeth Sunderland says, "To the Iron Age Celt, the horse was the embodiment of majesty and nobility. Epona, whose name means 'great mare,' was one of the few goddesses to be worshipped by both the continental and Insular Celts." Sunderland says the horse carved on the Cadboll Cross may very well be meant to portray Epona, the horse goddess.[229]

Not only warriors and chieftains but also Celtic monastics prized their horses. Adomnan's *Life of Columba* records that one day, as the elderly saint was walking back from the barn on Iona, he sat down for a few minutes' rest (for he was wearing with age). And then, "behold, a white horse came to him, the loyal work horse. . . . It approached the saint and—strange to tell—put its head against his bosom, inspired I believe by God for whom every living thing shows such understanding as the Creator bids; it knew that its master would soon be going away so that it would see him no more, and it began to mourn like a person, pouring out its tears in the saint's bosom and weeping aloud with foaming lips."[230]

Columba's companions thought this a miracle, and I do not argue; I have heard first-person accounts of interactions with four-footed companions that are no less astonishing. Two reliable and intelligent people have told me how a pet literally saved each of their lives; one was a cat, one was a dog, and they each showed extraordinary empathy and intelligence that led to their respective owners' rescue. There are also documented modern instances of horses rescuing their owners. In England, when a farmer was trapped beneath a cow in a pasture, her horse, which shared the pasture, ran over and kicked vigorously until the owner could escape. An Arizona cowboy passed out in a winter storm far from his home, and his mare continued walking for miles under its own direction until it brought the man back to his home.[231] I suspect the artisans who chiseled equine subjects onto the stone crosses knew of similar occurrences. Horses, like all animals, carry the Divine Spirit—and the Spirit always works on behalf of love.

Deer and Snakes

Oddly, at least at first glance, the Celts connected the same spiritual meanings with both snakes and deer. Both were considered to represent transformation and renewal: the snake because it sheds an old skin to reveal a new one, and the deer because stags shed their antlers and then grow them again.

Especially in pre-Christian Celtic artwork, snakes and deer are often depicted together. The ancient Celtic god Cernunnos was usually portrayed as an antlered man holding a snake. Elizabeth Sunderland tells us that Cernunnos "represented the spirit of the forest, the Horned One . . . who bore antlers on his brow. His power was essentially peaceful, and his symbolism represented fertility and prosperity. He also stood for chieftainship."[232]

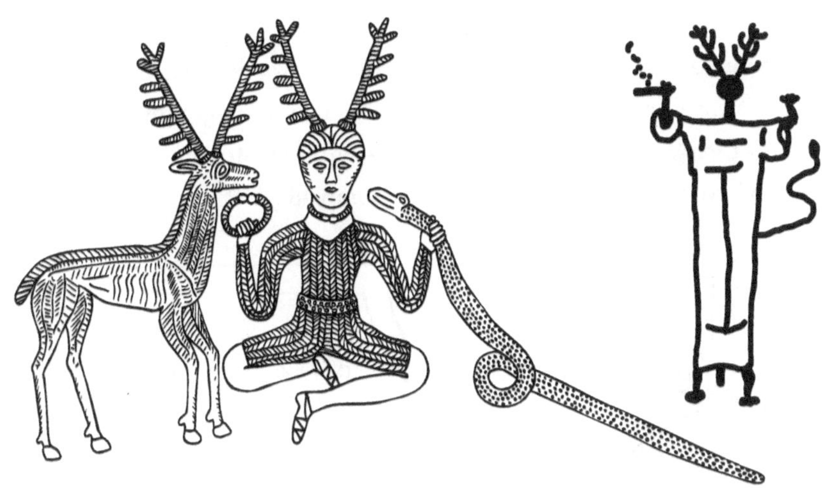

*The image on the left, taken from the 1st- or 2nd-century
Gundestrup Cauldron, shows Cernunnos—a man bearing deer antlers—
grasping a snake while a deer stands beside him. (The cauldron also
shows many other animals, but the deer seems to be his closest companion.)
The Bronze Age image on the right predates the Gundestrup Cauldron by
at least 1,000 years, but it also shows an antlered man with a snake.*

Archeologist Phyllis Fray Bober suggests that for Pagan Celts,
the snake and the deer represented both fertility and death (or the
underworld).[233] The symbolism points to the Celtic understanding of
life's eternal renewal. Indo-European scholar David Flickett-Wilbar
believes Cernunnos, a deer-man grasping a snake, represented a "medi-
ator between opposites"; he reconciled life with death, humans with
animals, and the wild forest with domesticated farmland.[234] Although
Christianity later identified Cernunnos with the devil, his image
appears on the North Cross at Clonmacnois.[235]

The Celts considered white deer to be particularly magical, a sign
the Otherworld is nearby.[236] In Celtic mythology, sometimes the
white deer is a warning not to go further in a particular direction, but
in other cases, a white deer draws the hero into a quest for a greater
good. While the white stag was sometimes connected to kinship and
masculine sovereignty, the white doe represented the Divine Feminine.

Saint Gobnait, a sixth-century Irish woman, was led to her "place of resurrection"[237] by a series of white does (always in groups divisible by three), and Saint Ita, another sixth-century Irish woman, was said to have a blue-eyed white doe as her companion.[238]

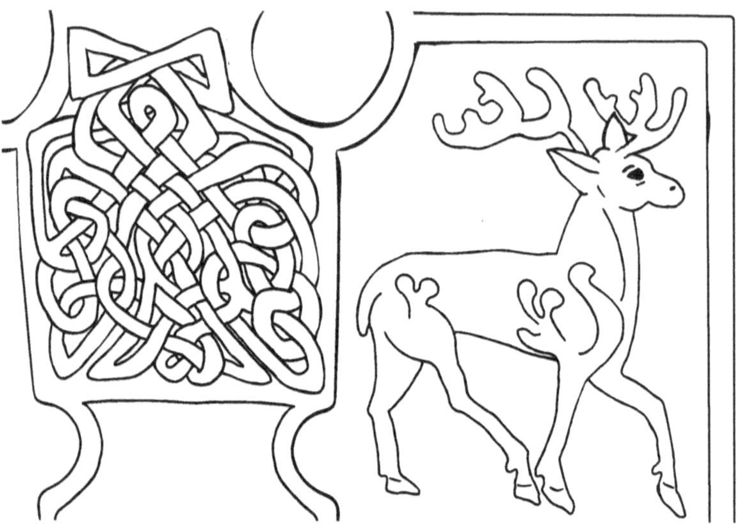

The Eassie Stone, one of the earliest examples of a Pictish cross slab, dating to the late 600s, bears a perfect image of an antlered deer. The cross slab is now housed in a shelter with see-through walls within the roofless shell of the old Eassie parish church.

Although we often think of the serpent as a symbol of evil, the Celts and other ancient people perceived snakes quite differently; snakes brought wisdom and healing. Even the Bible does not consistently portray snakes as representing evil: In the Hebrew scripture, Moses creates a statue of a serpent and lifts it up on a pole; people bitten by poisonous snakes had only to look at the bronze serpent to be healed.[239] Later, in the Gospel of John, Jesus compares himself to Moses' bronze serpent: Jesus too will be "lifted up" in order to bring healing. Jesus also mentions his own ability to cross between the worlds (the heavenly and earthly dimensions),[240] an attribute of snakes, according to the ancients.

In the fourth century, Saint Ambrose employed both the snake and the deer as symbols of Christ. For Ambrose, the snake represented the power of transformation and renewal, and he called Christ's followers to be like Christ, who was the "Good Serpent." Ambrose also described a deer who manages to subdue and tame a snake. According to theology student David Voprada, both the snake and deer symbols allowed Ambrose's "audience to understand God's activity as a present-day reality which the faithful can enter into."[241]

According to early medieval bestiaries, when a stag becomes old and weak, he draws serpents from their holes with his breath and then eats them. The snakes bring new strength to the deer, renewing his youth. Here, once again, we see snakes and deer as intertwined symbols representing transformation and healing.[242]

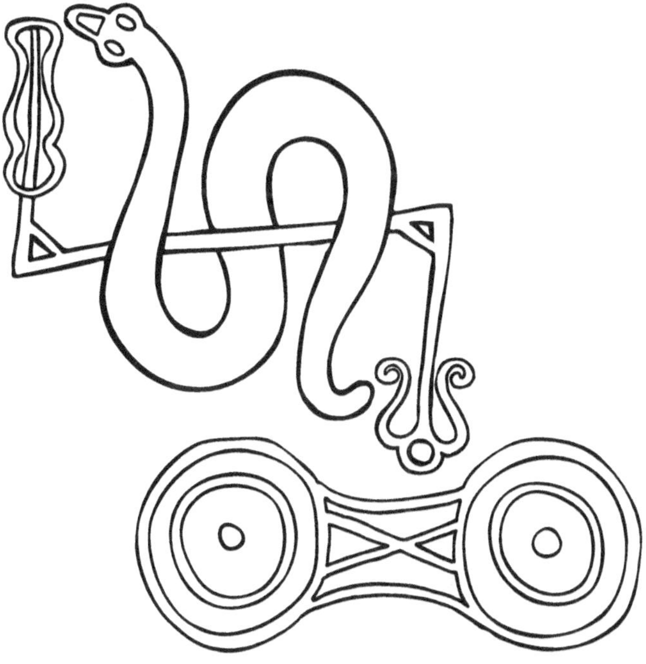

A Pictish serpent appears on a stone found at Balmacaan, near Loch Ness.

Snakes and deer are common images on Pictish cross slabs and Irish high crosses. Sometimes, hunters atop horses, accompanied by hounds, are shown pursuing deer. However, deer also appear apart from hunt scenes, such as on the elaborate sculptured cross stone at Eassie Kirk, in Angus, Scotland. Snakes, meanwhile, can be seen on the stone crosses on Iona, on Muiredeach's Cross, and many others; in fact, snakes are the most common creature carved on ancient Celtic crosses. Sculptors in Scotland, Ireland, Wales, Northern England, and the Isle of Man chiseled them over a span of at least three centuries.

Many times, Picts carved snakes in a standard S-shape (often with a "Z-rod" intersecting it), but on other Celtic crosses, snakes merged into interlaced knotwork. A cross at Dromiskin, Ireland, shows a possible hunting scene with a man, a dog, and a deer on one arm, while the center has a circle of intertwined serpents. Although these serpentine patterns are often interpreted as "the snares

The well-known association of snakes with the devil does appear on some of the Celtic crosses, like the Gallen Priory Cross of County Offaly, Ireland, portrayed here. From the center of the cross, four serpents spiral outward, perhaps a vivid reminder of the devil's deadly power. However, there is room for another interpretation here. The snakes' spiral forms a solar image, and the snakes may instead represent the healing power of the cross to consume all sin.

of base or animal desires,"[243] I suspect their original meanings were sometimes quite different.

The first-century Roman naturalist Pliny writes about a "serpent stone" formed by the spittle from a tangle of hissing snakes; druids throughout the Highlands and Islands used this magical amulet, Pliny claimed, as a healing charm.[244] The druids were not the first to associate snakes with healing; the story of Moses' bronze snake hints at the Rod of Asclepius, the ancient symbol of a snake winding around a staph that's still used to represent the healing arts.

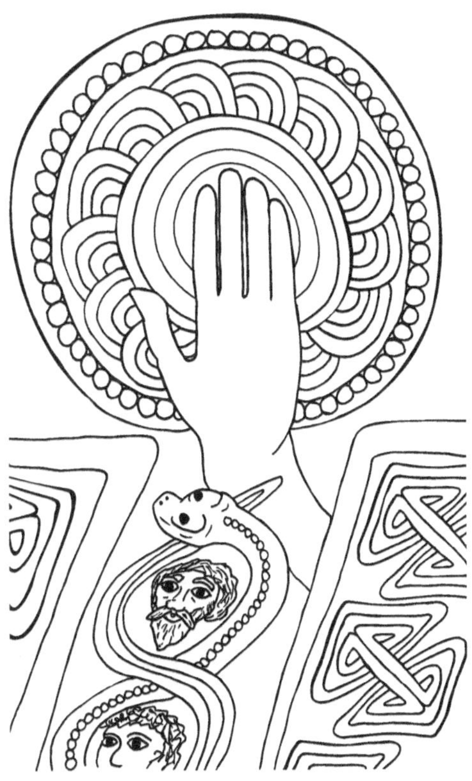

Carvings on Muiredach's Cross at Monasterboice, Ireland, indicate serpents' healing power. On the underside of the north-facing ring is a portrayal of God's saving hand, and entwined about the people beneath it is the serpent-pole of Christ.

In both Ireland and Pictland, the snake was a symbol of wisdom. According to Elizabeth Sunderland:

> The snake is a creature of the earth both wise and dangerous, a symbol not only of healing and fertility but also of death and rebirth. Its spiraling body represents the journey to the Otherworld where it sleeps until it emerges in early spring from its hole in the ground and sheds its old skin to appear new-born.[245]

In Celtic folklore, Brigid, the Goddess of marriage, childbirth, and the hearth (before she was a Christian saint), is also associated with the serpent. In the *Carmina Gaedelica*, Alexander Carmichael records a charm recited on February 1, Brigid's Day (or in Scotland, Bride's Day):

> *Today is the day of Bride.*
> *The serpent shall not come from the hole.*
> *I will not molest the serpent,*
> *Nor will the serpent molest me.*[246]

While we look to the groundhog and his shadow to predict the end of winter, the Scots hoped Bride's snake would remain in its lair, forecasting a soon-to-be spring thaw.

Like their companion the snake, deer also play prominent roles in stories of the Celtic saints. In Muirchu's *Life of Patrick*, the High King of Tara intends to kill the saint and his companions—but "Patrick, knowing the thoughts of this most evil king, blessed his company. . . . The king was counting when they approached, when in an instant he could no longer see them. All [they] could see was eight deer and a fawn going, as it were, into the wilds."[247] The mention of the fawn may be a reference back to Oisín, the legendary Irish poet whose name means "young deer."

While later legends attribute the extermination of all Irish snakes to Patrick,[248] this story connects Patrick to an ancient druid tradition that humans with supernatural knowledge could transform themselves into deer.[249] Muirchu's account implies the liminality of Patrick and his followers; like Cernunnos, the Pagan god, they are able to shape-shift from human to untamed animal. Patrick then escapes into the wild forest, indicating that Christianity at this time was still connected as much to Nature as to the human world.[250]

Because of these layers of interwoven meaning, the hunt scenes on Pictish and Irish crosses may be more than just hunt scenes. Sometimes, a snake is just a snake, and a deer is just a deer—but in the case of the ancient stone crosses, they possess deeper symbolism. Hunting deer could represent our pursuit of union with Christ. The juxtaposition of deer and snake also points to transformation, renewal, and the reconciliation of opposites.

Ravens and Crows

If you reside in the Americas, Ireland, the United Kingdom, or Continental Europe, you have likely encountered feathered beings whose intelligence approaches that of a young human child. Scientists have discovered that corvids—a bird family that includes ravens and their smaller cousins the crows—possess self-awareness "and can ponder the content of their own minds, a manifestation of higher intelligence and analytical thought long believed the sole province of humans and a few other higher mammals." These birds' brains possess physical features that resemble a human's prefrontal cortex, the portion of our brains that makes spiritual and intellectual thought possible.[251]

Our ancestors recognized the keen nature of the corvids who flew in and out of their daily lives. Cultures from around the world, including Greco-Roman, Hebrew, Islamic, Hindu, Siberian, African, Norse, Indigenous American, and Celtic, attributed spiritual and supernatural qualities to these birds.

In Luke's Gospel, Jesus points to the corvids as models of going with God's flow: "Consider the ravens: They do not sow or reap, they have no storeroom or barn; yet God feeds them."[252] Living in a rural area where crows—and more rarely, ravens—are a common sight, I've noticed they never seem hurried or troubled; they lounge around on trees or poles, with their sharp eyes open for the next meal, which humans or natural events consistently provide. Truly, God feeds the ravens.

Remember how I highlighted three different levels of Bible interpretation in the

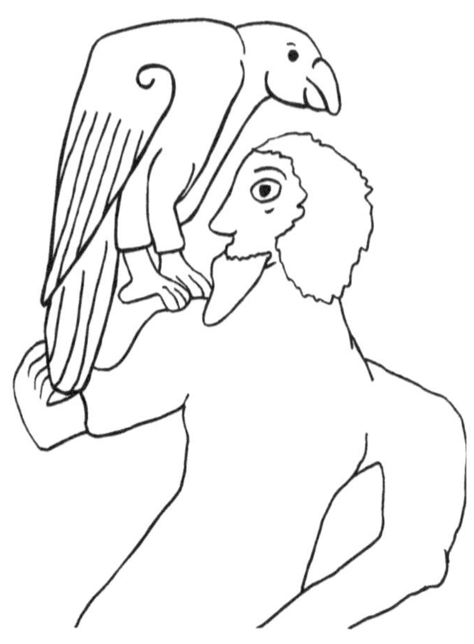

This stone reveals the transition in the Viking world of Pagan beliefs to Christianity. For a short time, both creeds coexisted, as Thorwald's Cross reveals: One side shows the Norse god Odin with a raven perched on his shoulder, while the other side has Christian symbolism.

last chapter? If we use a higher, imaginative level to think about Jesus' raven sermon, we can see new layers of meaning. Ravens would remind Jesus' listeners of the time recorded in the Hebrew Bible when a raven fed Elijah in the wilderness. While Elijah had been bent on retribution, the ravens were God's messengers conveying mercy; according to ancient rabbis' interpretation, if these birds fed Elijah, how much more should Elijah have "fed" the people of Israel with gentleness? As we apply this to ourselves, we see not only that God will provide for our physical needs but that we need not covet and grasp. The story contains a gentle reminder that we should freely share God's bounty with others; if we have no worries for our own well-being, can we not—as Elijah should have—offer mercy to all? The story of the raven feeding Egyptian saints Anthony and Paul teaches us the same lesson. (See chapter 5 for details on this event.)

The Pagan Irish associated ravens with the Goddess Morrigan and also linked them to the God Lugh, the "Shining One." The name *Bran*, referring to the gigantic Welsh deity thought to be the protector of the British Isles, means "raven." Druids used ravens for prophecy, interpreting the birds' utterances and flight patterns as omens, especially for fortune-telling related to war and the outcomes of battles.[253] Norse folk who settled in Ireland and the British Isles after the ninth century told of Odin's two ravens, Huginn and Muninn, who sat on the God's shoulders, informing him of happenings on Middle Earth.

Both Pictish and Irish cross sculptors most often portrayed ravens feeding saints Paul and Anthony. Ravens also appear on Irish and Pictish stones in battle scenes, perhaps influenced by ideas from Norse mythology.

The bestiaries understood the ravens' feeding patterns as a spiritual metaphor. "Ravens refuse to feed their young until their feathers grow and become black, and the parents can recognize them as their own. . . . As the raven will not feed the chicks until it recognizes them as its own, so the teacher should not tell his students of the inner mysteries until he recognizes that they are ready to receive them."[254]

Next time you see these brilliant birds, consider your own pursuit of deeper spiritual insight!

The King of Beasts

How could a list of animals be complete without the noble "king of beasts"? The sculptors of the Irish high crosses apparently concurred. They depicted on scripture crosses the stories of David's defeat of a lion and Daniel in the lion's den.

Although insular Christians lived far away from any literal lions, they learned from scripture that "like a roaring lion your adversary the devil prowls around, looking for someone to devour"—and they were comforted by the promise that "Christ, will himself restore, support, strengthen and establish you."[255] While lions in this reference represent the evil Adversary, at the same time, in the New Testament, Jesus is called the "Lion of the Tribe of Judah."[256] The king of all beasts was an apt metaphor for the God-Human's majesty over the cosmos.

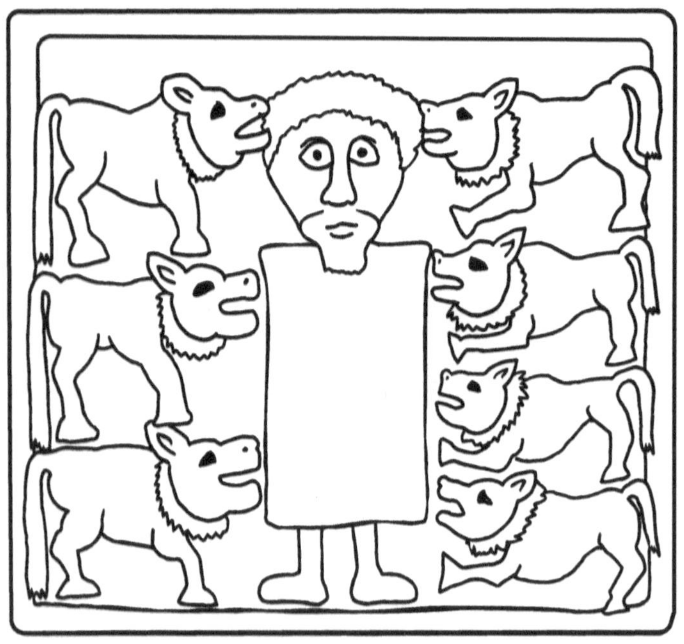

The Moone High Cross in County Kildare, Ireland, shows Daniel in the lions' den.

This may explain the lion's primacy—and positive portrayal—in medieval bestiaries, which list lions before all the other animals and devote more writing to the lion than to other creatures. According to these writings, the lion has three major attributes: When a lion sees hunters in pursuit, it erases its tracks with its tail; it sleeps with its eyes open; and lion cubs are born dead, but their parents bring them to life on the third day by breathing in their faces or roaring over them. Each of these has meaning in Christian symbolism. "The lion erasing its tracks with its tail represents the way Jesus concealed his divinity, only revealing himself to his followers. The lion sleeping with its eyes open represents Jesus, physically dead after crucifixion, but still spiritually alive in his divine nature. The lion roaring over his dead cubs to bring them to life represents how God the Father woke Jesus after three days in his tomb."[257]

The lions on stone crosses are another good example of how Celtic Christians in the Early Middle Ages looked at the world: not as "either/or" but as "both/and." The lion is both a threat and a source of danger (as was the case with David and Daniel)—and it is also the One who protects us, the God-Human. The ancient Irish artists were pioneers of nondual thinking, a concept that has only recently gained currency in spiritual thinking.

The Gryphon

If you're like me, the first thing you think of when you hear "gryphon" (or griffin) is Buckbeak in the Harry Potter tales (though Buckbeak is actually a hippogriff, part horse rather than part lion). According to the bestiaries, "The griffin is a winged, four-footed animal. It has the body of a lion, but the wings and head of an eagle."[258]

The gryphons on Pictish slabs are proof the Picts were not the wild, isolated barbarians falsely portrayed in Hollywood movies and novels. These early residents of Scotland interacted with Europe,

Egypt, and the Mediterranean. Their use of gryphon images indicates their awareness of Christian symbolism cataloged by bestiary writers in Egypt and Spain.

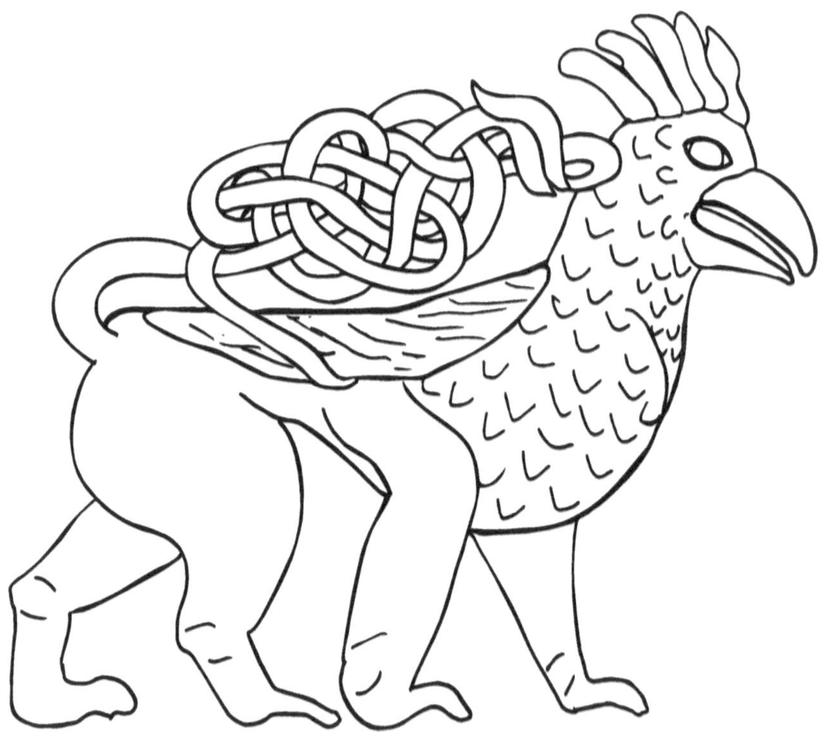

A Pictish image of a gryphon found on a stone in Meigle, Scotland.

Gryphons served in Greek mythology as guardians of Apollo's treasures. Later, in Christian art, they were ambiguous symbols of either good or evil. Legends that noted their great power and rapaciousness used them as warning symbols of Satan. At the same time, their combination of bird and mammal forms symbolized the union of Christ's Divine and human natures.[259]

APPLICATIONS FOR TODAY

Joining a Community of Furred and Feathered Neighbors

I conclude a chapter in my book *Water from an Ancient Well* with this paragraph:

> Wild creatures live according to their own designs, allowing us a glimpse of their routines only when they please. . . . So pay attention when your fellow creatures share their lives with you. Watch closely. Listen carefully. Open your heart. Let God speak to you through these furred and feathered neighbors.[260]

I believe the same concept is fitting for this chapter of *Sacred Stones*.

KEEPING COMPANY WITH WILD CREATURES

Here is a practice that requires considerable time and consistency but is freely available to anyone.

Find a place where wild things live and return there frequently to observe them, every day if possible (even better, in both morning and evening). Even if you live in a city, you should still be able to find a spot frequented by sparrows, pigeons, or squirrels; foxes, coyotes, and raccoons have also taken up residence in many of our cities.

If you make time to visit these creatures over the course of a few weeks, you will begin to recognize individual animals. As you watch them, quietly and patiently, you will do what my wife Marsha has done during her morning walks along a nearby marshlands: She has progressed from "There's a heron," to "There's 'Harold,'" a large heron always standing by the same inlet. Because Marsha has given a name to Harold as well as assorted muskrats, birds, and other fauna, these wild animals have begun to seem like friends and neighbors.

Frequent retirement to a wild community can pay off in glimpses into the animals' personalities and habits. I will never forget one fall day when, as I walked Duke, my border collie companion, a large raven dropped straight down onto the trail about sixty feet in front of us. She then hopped up and down, *gronking* in a most irritating manner. *What is this bird doing?* I thought. *Does she not realize a dog will charge at her?*

And indeed, Duke bolted straight at the raven. She stayed where she was, waiting . . . waiting (I was growing worried) . . . and then, a split second before Duke reached her, the corvid flapped upward as quickly as she had come down. Duke leapt and snapped, but he missed her by about six inches. Then, to my amazement, the same shiny black trickster lit in the same manner, some sixty feet further down the trail. Again, Duke flew at her; again, she waited until the last moment to narrowly escape the collie's bite. When she lit a third time, her cry was different; I swear she was laughing at us! After a third failed attempt, Duke gave up. The raven tried again, but when she realized we were no longer playing, she flew away. Now, when I "consider the ravens," as Jesus recommended, I am reminded that good neighbors trust each other enough to play jokes—and even wild creatures like to have fun.

Animal Meditation

Have you ever sat down to pray and meditate, only to have your pets assume—since you're sitting down, apparently doing nothing—now would be a perfect time for you to pay attention to them? In this practice, consider your pet or pets' presence as the practice itself rather than a distraction. Put your hands on your furry friend; if they are small enough, allow them to sit in your lap if they want. If you have a "proximity pet," like our Bunty, just be aware of their nearby presence.

Focus on the *feelings* (not thoughts but emotions) your pet's presence gives you. Do you feel warmth? A sense of deep mutual love?

Now imagine (or gaze at) the cross you selected in an earlier exercise. Feel the same sense of warmth and unconditional love emanating from it that you feel from your pet. Extend the same love you feel for your animal friend toward Christ, whose presence indwells the image of the cross. Relax; dismiss any thoughts that arise; soak in and radiate warmth and love.

Experiencing Mutual Love

A woman at my church, a federally licensed wildlife rehabilitator, cares for any local indigenous feathered or furred creature that's injured or needs other assistance. Equipped with an array of feeding devices, handmade nests, incubators, and aviaries of various sizes, she has returned many healed birds to their natural habitats. When she takes in baby chicks, she must feed them every twenty minutes; that's dedication!

Even after the birds are fully healed and grown, many of her adopted birds keep coming back to visit her whenever she is outside. She recognizes each of her former wards and delights in seeing them; often, they sit beside her or perch on her shoulders or her hat. Her familiarity with these feathered friends resembles the artistic depictions of Francis of Assisi with the birds, as well as the legends of the Celtic saints and their animal companions. Her farm is a model of the peaceable kin-dom of God.

Our furred and feathered friends sometimes embody God's love better than humans do. My wife and I have been blessed to experience the unqualified affection displayed by our pets. They ask very little, and even if we are late to fill their bowl or empty their litter box, they persist in their affection. They demonstrate more love and loyalty to us, in their uncomplicated way, than we, with our convoluted minds and wide-flung loyalties, can convey in return.

I saw Christ today,

hungry,

outside my windows in the winter cold,

and I filled my birdfeeders

that He might be filled.

I saw Christ today

in the glad face of my dog

as I greeted her at the end of the workday.

I saw Christ today

in the moth that beat against the window

until I let it out into the night.

Each time I saw Christ,

He blessed me,

in the Holy Name of the Trinity,

and the bird outside my window sang

again and again,

"Often and often, goes Christ

on wing and hoof and paw."

Ellyn Sanna [261]

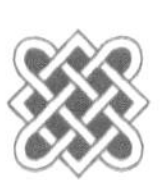

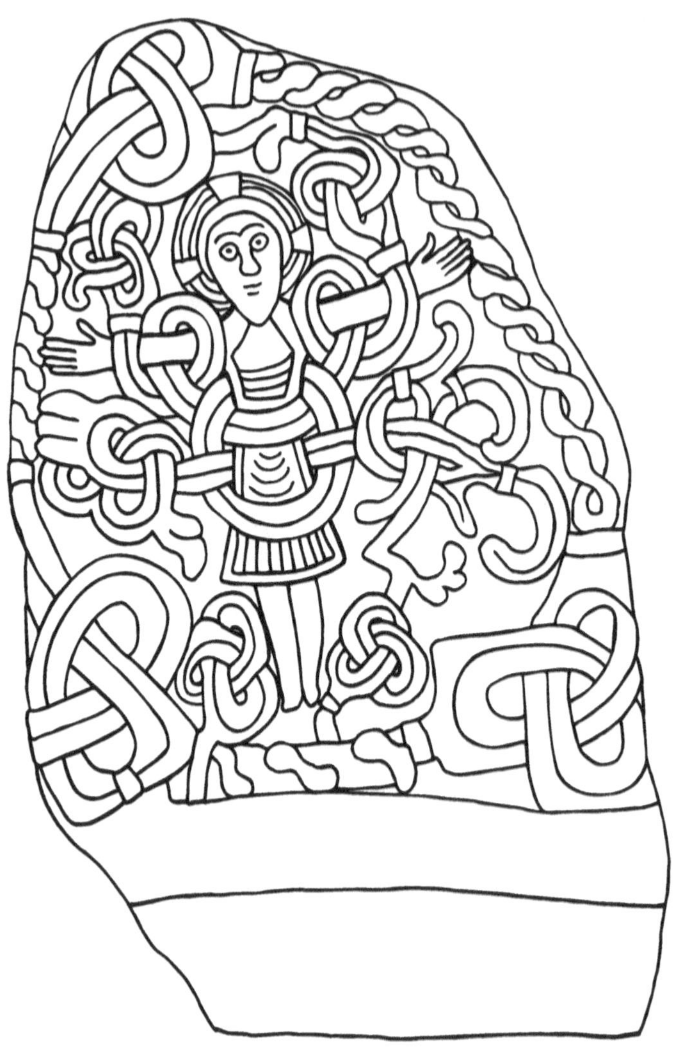

Viking images often show a male figure bound in the curving branches of a tree, the World Tree of Norse mythology. The male figure represented Odin, but the Harald Stone Crucifix shows that Christ has taken the place of Odin. His open arms indicate that unlike Odin, who sacrificed himself for his own purposes, Christ's self-sacrifice was a gift of himself to all people.[262]

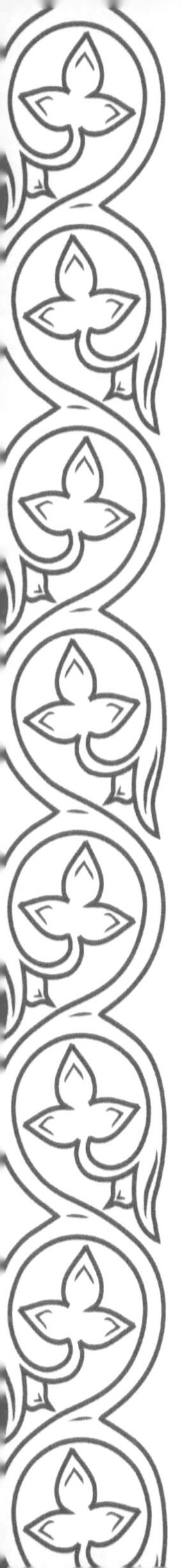

CHAPTER 9

The Fury of the Vikings and the Blessing of Our Enemies

If you love those who love you,
what credit is that to you?
For even sinners love those who love them. . . .
Instead, love your enemies.

Jesus (Luke 6:32, 35)

It is nearly 350 years that we and our fathers
have inhabited this most lovely island,
and never before has such a
terror appeared in Britain
as we have now suffered from a pagan race,
nor was it thought that such an inroad
from the sea could be made.

ENCOUNTER

July 1098: The Anglesey Sound Between Mainland Wales and the Island of Anglesey

Thwack!

An arrow slammed into his shield, the barbs of its iron tip stopping just inches from the king of Norway's shoulder. He spat at it and screamed across the water, "Missed me, ya sons of a Norman whore!" He turned then and shouted down the length of his longship, "Sound for the archers to let loose!"

Deep trumpet tones sounded from ship to ship in a long line of vessels extending down the length of the sound. On each ship, archers huddled behind the round shields that lined the gunwales of their vessels; from the *drakkars* (the dragon-shaped ships), a sky-darkening hail of deadly darts arced into the sky.

On the shore, the Norman forces quickly maneuvered; men-at-arms crouched, their kite-shaped shields held high to guard the archers behind them. Men wielding both longbows and crossbows returned fire against the dragon ships. The din of war settled into a strange orchestration of sounds: the deep reverberation of war trumpets, the whistle of arrows, and the thwack-and-bang of the missiles ending their journeys on wooden shields or steel armor.

Mixed with these—increasingly—came the screams of wounded and dying men.

The king quickly strung his own longbow. He was a hand taller than most men, and his bow was as long as he stood tall; few men other than him could bend the thick yew to full draw-length. He squinted along the arrow at the long line of foes on the shore and then focused on a man on horseback clad in shining brass scales. The king steadied his straining muscles, brought the tip of his arrow into alignment with his target, and loosed the arrow.

"Ha!" He shouted in triumph as the distant figure dropped his lance and fell from the horse. "He'll dine in Valhalla tonight—or wherever Kristens go."

His grin died away as a cry from nearby caught his ear. The king turned and saw, midway down the deck, Svengir, one of his body-guards, curled on the deck, grasping his upper leg. Blood spurted between his fingers, and an arrow impaled his thigh.

"Faster!" the king shouted to his warriors. "More arrows into the air. Make the bastards pay!"

And then—a sight he had never beheld in all his many battles shocked him silent. Magnus Erlendsson, a strong, noble-born man, sat on his oar-bench, eyes closed, face toward the sky, chanting something. As the king watched in amazement, Erlendsson paused, glanced at a book in his hand, then resumed what sounded to the king like an incantation. He had no weapon in his hand.

"Erlendsson!" the king shouted. "Are you bedeviled? Grab a bow, you fool! Our lives are at stake."

"I don't wish to fight." Magnus's voice was calm, matter-of-fact. "I have no quarrel with these men."

"They're giving us a bloody awful contest with their archers and horsemen. What more quarrel do you need, you big nanny goat?"

Magnus shrugged. "We're invading them. They have a right to defend their land."

"But I say it's *our* land!" His Highness was very nearly frothing at his beard.

Magnus shrugged again. "I serve a higher king."

"You worthless fool!" The king's sword flashed from its scabbard and smacked the other man's head with the flat of its blade.

Magnus put a hand up to dab at the stinging, bleeding spot, but otherwise, he appeared unmoved.

"This is because of that accursed God you worship," the king snarled. "That *Kristr*. Does he turn all men who serve him into cowards?"

The younger man sighed. When he got to his feet, he stood almost as tall as the king. "I am no coward," he said. He turned his face toward the attackers, his chest and head exposed above the shield row. "I shall live or die today as my Savior wills it, but I shall not fight. I shall chant the Psalms for the souls of all who suffer in battle today."

As arrows rattled against the deck, the king turned away. "You shall pay for this, Erlendsson," he said over his shoulder. Then he sheathed his sword and picked up his bow to resume the fray.

An arrow whisked past Magnus's ear, but he didn't even flinch. He held his prayerbook and sang the words:

> *In my distress I cry to Yahweh,*
> *that he may answer me:*
> *"Deliver me, O Yahweh, from lying lips,*
> *from a deceitful tongue."*
>
> *Too long have I had my dwelling*
> *among those who hate peace.*
> *I am for peace,*
> *but when I speak,*
> *they are for war.*[264]

The king of Norway did not forget the vow he had made to Magnus Erlendsson: He would make Erlendsson pay for his refusal to fight. After the battle, the king bound and beat Magnus.

But in the middle of the night, Magnus slipped from his bonds and swam ashore. Men with hounds looked for him, but he managed to evade them by hiding in a tall tree. When the search for him was abandoned, Magnus journeyed across Wales into Scotland and up to Orkney.

There, kinsmen made him an earl, with a mandate to rule Orkney jointly with his cousin Haakon. Not content to share the rule of Orkney, however, Haakon surprised Magnus with a sortie of armed warriors. Once again, Magnus refused to fight; instead, he offered to go peacefully into exile.

His cousin would not listen—and either Haakon or someone who served him killed Magnus with an axe. He is still remembered today as Saint Magnus of Orkney.

June 2015: Saint Magnus Cathedral, Kirkwall, Orkney

Orkney is one of the strangest regions of Scotland I've visited—and it's delightful in its uniqueness. The archipelago consists of seventy individual islands that can be reached from a ferry departing John O'Groats at the tip of the Scottish mainland. Orcadians speak of how "the Scots" do things, implying that the people of Orkney consider themselves to be a breed apart. And, in fact, the Orkney Islands are a blend of Gaelic and Scandinavian cultures.

On this cold rainy day in the main Orcadian town of Kirkwall, I am thankful for the vast shelter of Saint Magnus Cathedral. It doesn't feel like other cathedrals I have experienced: the walls and pillars are broader, rougher looking than other great houses of medieval worship.

The building feels cyclopean in its ruggedness, yet Romanesque charm also overlays it. The dark red sandstone spaces of its interior echo the charming tones of Orcadian dialect, a lilting sort of English that's the result of the Norse-Scots cultural fusion.

When I enter the great edifice, I see evidence that this is a temple built by—and in honor of—Norse folk. The Saint Rognvald Chapel, honoring the earl who commissioned this church, features a carved wooden longship and a statue of Rognvald with helm and shield, holding a model of the cathedral in his hands. A stained-glass window in the transept portrays Harold Hardrada, known as "the last Viking," resplendent with winged helmet and battleaxe.

The cathedral's vast stonework honors the memory of the man who would not fight. His remains lie in a column marked with a plaque: "Saint Magnus: Within this pillar lie the remains of Magnus Erlend's Son, Earl of Orkney. . . . Canonised on 13th Dec. 1133. To his memory Rognvald built this cathedral."

In popular culture, Scandinavian people of the Early Middle Ages—Swedes, Danes, Norwegians, and Icelanders—are lumped under the designation *Viking*. But *Viking* does not refer to a cultural, ethnic, or national group; the word is more of a job description. The old Scandinavian sagas say that certain persons would "go viking," which meant they were crossing the oceans to raid and plunder. In the Early Middle Ages, many men and women from the Northern Isles became "Vikings." Sometimes, this was a lifetime career, but more often it was a temporary commitment for farmers, traders, and artisans.

Magnus was a Norseman who refused to be a Viking. Born into a culture that honored raiding, his commitment to Christ changed him from the inside out. He came to prize justice and compassion more than plundered wealth. Saint Magnus reminds us we cannot stereotype groups of people as "bad" and "good."

History has portrayed the early medieval Scandinavians as forces of destruction and nothing else. Closer inspection, however, reveals a more nuanced picture. The artwork on ancient stone reminds us not to be too hasty in declaring the Vikings to be personifications of evil.

DEEPENING

When Jesus told us to love our enemies, he didn't mean we should cultivate an unhealthy attitude of martyrdom. Instead, when we allow love to do its work through us, we may find that even our "enemies" can bring good into our lives.

A Reputation for Violence

The Viking raid on the monastery of Holy Island of Lindisfarne was a catastrophic moment. Historians Hannah and Martyn Whittock explain the impact of that raid:

> Every educated Anglo-Saxon—whether monk, nun, or noble—would probably have been able to recall where they were when they first heard that the monastery of Lindisfarne (Northumberland) had been sacked, in 793. . . . It is often risky to draw parallels between events that occur in different periods of history. . . . But 793 was sure an Anglo-Saxon "9/11 moment." It struck at national security and cultural values in an iconic place and in a brutal and bloody manner.[265]

Christians who lived at the time of the raid saw it as the fulfillment of a biblical prophecy: "The Lord said to me, 'From the north disaster will be poured out on all who live on the land.'"[266] In the twenty-first century, the horrors of the Holy Island raid were republicized on the popular television show *Vikings*.

Holy Island is so named because it has long been especially sacred to Christ-followers in the British Isles. This is the place where Irish-born Saint Aidan arrived from the Holy Island of Iona in the Hebrides in 635, delivering the good news of Jesus to the Anglo-Saxon (now English) people; it is also the place where Aidan's successor Cuthbert became England's first native-born saint.

And today, Lindisfarne is still a special place for many people. More than 600,000 visitors each year drive across the causeway that leads to this tidal island off the Northumberland coast. Many people come because of the picturesque beauty, but many of these travelers also have a sense that the place is still holy, as its name implies. The island is especially significant for those of us who value contemporary expressions of Celtic Christianity.[267]

The Viking raid on Lindisfarne was the beginning of a series of incursions from the north that lasted from 789 to 1098. With their superior sea skills, the Danes, Norwegians, and Swedes raided, traded, and colonized not only the British Isles and Ireland, but also France, Spain, Russia, Turkey, North Africa, and the edge of the North American continent.

What began this explosion of travel, warfare, and cultural exchange? An important element was the shortage of farmland in Scandinavia, coupled with further challenges to political and legal acquisition of such land, which made it difficult to earn a living in the Norse lands. The Norse honored warfare, and they regarded the violent plundering of foreign lands with the same calculated justification that modern corporations pursue profits today. Christian monasteries in Europe and the British Isles, with their treasures and minimal defenses, were easy pickings, a quick way to gain wealth.[268]

History—as most of us learned it anyway—recalls the Norse as a force of raw destruction against so-called civilized lands. Coastal monasteries suffered significantly from the raids, and armies from

Scandinavia colonized entire kingdoms in England, Scotland, Ireland, and France, causing disruption to those realms, especially to the elite classes of their societies. But that is only part of the picture.

Back in the summer of 1993, as residents of Holy Island were commemorating the 1,200th anniversary of the Viking raid, visitors from the Church of Norway arrived at the Church of Saint Mary's—the Lindisfarne's medieval parish church—with two gifts: a letter of reconciliation and a statuary head of Saint Olaf, who was instrumental in bringing Christianity to Norway. A sign in the church today summarizes this encounter: "Peace was definitely declared."[269]

All in the Family

Like most people of Scots ancestry, my DNA includes Scandinavian blood. My mother and my cousin researched our genealogy, enabling me to grasp the names and stories of my Viking-age foremothers and forefathers. On my mother's side, I am descended from members of Clan Gunn, in the northeast of Scotland. The progenitor of that family was Gunni, descended from Swedish and Norwegian Vikings who held power in Orkney. His wife was related to Ragnvald, who ordered the construction of Saint Magnus's cathedral. Some renditions of the Gunn clan crest portray a dragon-prowed longship under sail.

Also on my mother's side, I'm descended from Duncan Donachadh from central Scotland, born in 925, who bore the title "hereditary priest." He was married to Groa Thorsteindottr, the daughter of Thorsteinn "The Red," who was born in Norse-occupied Dublin, Ireland. According to an old saga, Thorsteinn "harried Scotland" but eventually "made peace" by ruling more than half of that country. He had many children and apparently saw fit to marry one of his daughters to a member of the Scots clergy. Their grandchildren ascended to the Scottish throne. I find this fascinating in several ways: first, because it was perfectly acceptable in the Gaelic church of the Early Middle Ages to be a "hereditary" priest, to marry, and to sire children; and second, a Christian priest married the daughter of a Viking chieftain, and that was also seen as a worthy lineage. (I would love to write a novel about their lives and marriage!)

Finally, on my father's side, my English bloodline comes from the Metcalfs in the Lake Region of Northern England. (This was a thousand years before Cumbria would become a prime destination for holiday vacationers.) That family is descended from Arkefrith, born in Denmark in 990, who sailed to England with Canute in 1016; Canute conquered the Anglo-Saxons, married the English king Aethelred's widow, and took the English throne in 1017. Canute rewarded Arkefrith's service in the conquest by deeding him the entire Lake Region of England. The following year, Canute's brother, king of Denmark, died, and Canute inherited Denmark's throne. Nine years later, after some warring, he added Norway to his list of royal rulership: He was now "Canute the Great, Ruler of the North Sea Empire."

Canute then fostered a revitalization of the Christian church in England. In a document sent from Denmark, he promised he "would be a good Christian king," and he "exhorted the recipients of the letter to keep the Sunday fast, honour the saints, confess their sins, and look forward to attaining 'the bliss of the heavenly kingdom.'"[270]

According to an old story, when Canute's underlings praised him to the heavens, he decided to give them a lesson about humility. He ordered his throne to be set on a beach at the edge of the incoming ocean tide, and then he commanded the waves, "Stop! Come no further!" When that—obviously—didn't work, he told his subjects to remember that only God is truly great. He hung his golden crown on Christ's head on a life-size crucifix.[271]

Much More Than Raiders

Books on the history of Ireland and Britain tend to blame Viking raids for the demise of a distinctly Celtic Christianity, but according to current scholarship and archaeology, this damaging impact is exaggerated. While the Scandinavian raiders were violent, their contemporaries in Europe and the British Isles had much the same views toward warfare and the violent taking of goods. A study of raids in Ireland indicates that out of 113 attacks on monasteries between 795 and 820, Vikings were responsible for only twenty-six; Irish rulers or even competing monasteries conducted three-fourths of the raids. The Christian Anglo-Saxons also sailed to Ireland and raided monasteries. Furthermore, when the sea raiders appeared on their coasts, various rulers in the British Isles jumped to make alliances with the Vikings and joined in attacking regional rivals.[272]

For most ordinary people, the impact of Viking colonization was relatively benign, for several reasons. The Vikings were great cultural chameleons who adopted the characteristics of the dominant social structures of the kingdoms they conquered.[273] Many Viking overlords forced local rulers to give them a significant share of the money they levied against their vassals. Meanwhile, commoners—including most of the clergy and members of monastic communities—could carry on with their lives much as they had before. As the Scandinavian colonizers adapted to the languages, farming techniques, trade practices, and cultural customs where they settled, they themselves changed far more than they changed the people they conquered.

Christian faith was one element that changed the lives of the Norse who left their homelands. King Haakon the Good, for example, was raised at the court of King Athelston of England, and there Haakon embraced the faith of Christ. When he gained the throne of Norway in 934, he promoted the Christ-way among his subjects.

Another tenth-century Norse ruler, King Harald Bluetooth, led the conversion of his kingdom. The Jelling Stone crucifix (illustrated at the beginning of this chapter) bears the inscription: "Harald commanded these memorials to be raised . . . Harald who made the Danes Christian."[274]

The story of Iceland's conversion indicates a creative and peaceful process. By the summer of 1000, at least half of the island's Norse population were Christian, and followers of the Christ-way and those who worshipped the older Gods and Goddesses were in conflict. They all agreed that Iceland must have a single religious path—but which one, and how could the issue be settled amicably? Both Christians and Pagans respected a seer named Thorgeir, and they decided to entrust the matter to his hands. He isolated himself in a shelter for three days of vision-seeking, after which he emerged and declared that the Icelanders would all outwardly worship Christ, while allowing individuals and families—if they wished—to continue their worship of their former deities, but only in private.[275]

While the Viking raids of the 800s put fear into the hearts of clergy and monks, two centuries later, converted Scandinavian rulers strengthened Christian faith in Anglo-Celtic kingdoms. Viking rulers played a major role in the so-called Tenth-Century Reformation and in the expansion of church-building in the following century.[276]

The Celtic-Scandinavian Crosses Still Speak Today

Some of the largest and most beautiful "Celtic" crosses in Ireland and the British Isles are infused with Scandinavian artistry. They remind us not to be too quick to label the Norse as historical enemies, when in fact they became fellow Christians and sacred artists.

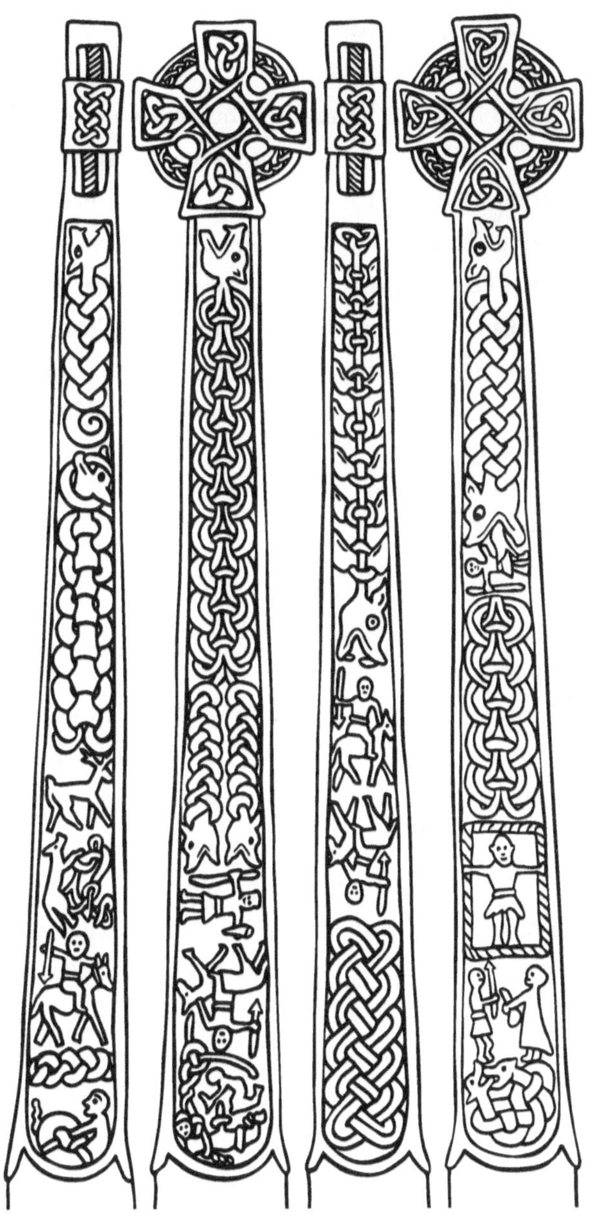

*The Gosforth Cross has scenes that combine images from
Norse mythology with Christian imagery.*

Norse influence on Celtic crosses may extend beyond those with obvious Viking artistic elements in their design. In chapter 7, I noted the anonymous Irish "Michelangelo" who carved one of the greatest masterpieces of Irish stone art, the scripture cross at Monasterboice. Irish historian Máire de Paor notes: "Monasterboice apparently escaped Viking plunder, though it was near Viking encampments; it has sometimes been suggested that in some way it was under Norse protection or had a special relationship with the East Coast Vikings."[277] Wealth made by alliances with the colonizing Scandinavians may have allowed that monastery to commission this outstanding artist to create such an extraordinary high cross.

The Gosforth Cross

The tenth-century Gosforth Cross, standing tall and thin, is one of the finest high crosses in England. At first glance, it seems a typical Celtic cross, with encircled cross-arms and knotwork. The horizontal and vertical arms of the cross display typical Celtic triquetra designs.

If we look more closely, however, we can see abundant evidence of Scandinavian craftsmanship. The knotwork up and down the length of the shaft is in the Ringerike Norse style, where the knots are made of serpents wrapping around one another. The pictorial presentations seem double-coded: Christian motifs that could also be scenes from Norse mythology. The east side seems like the crucifixion of Christ, complete with Longinus spearing Christ's side—but is that a Valkyrie below the cross? Could the image also represent the death of the God Baldr? On the west side, do we see the binding of Satan? Or is it the binding of Loki, when the Gods could stand no more of his troublemaking?[278]

Lacking a time machine, we're unlikely to fully grasp either the artist's motivations or the original viewers' understanding. Did the stone carver seek to draw people to the new faith by illustrating similarities to their Pagan tales? Or did the sponsor of the Gosforth Cross think they could play both sides, shaping a monument to satisfy both Pagan and Christian community members? All we can say with certainty is that this encircled cross was hewn from stone at a time when members of the local community still recalled the tales of the Gods and Goddesses, while also being familiar with the Gospels. The result of the blended artistic and conceptual forms is a unique work of art that (literally and figuratively) stands above other works of the same time.

The Maen Achwyfan Cross

The Maen Achwyfan wheel cross, one of the most impressive in Wales, is another example of Viking influence on ancient stone carvings. The cross is located outdoors, in what experts believe is likely its original location, near the village of Whitford in Flintshire. Carved from a single piece of stone, the cross stands eleven feet tall and is entirely covered with elaborate designs. Experts date it from the late tenth to early eleventh century, a time when the Norse colonized the local area, and its distinctively Scandinavian artistic elements have been recognized for centuries.[279] The shaft's central part seems to me to be patterned in the Jellinge style that originated in Denmark.

On the bottom portion of the cross's east face is its most intriguing figure: a naked male holding a spear in one hand and a distinctively Viking "bearded"-style axe in the other. He is surrounded by a great writhing serpent, indicating he may represent Sigurd, the dragon slayer of the Nibelung saga.[280]

This cross raises more questions than it answers. Why would a Norse monster-killing hero be carved onto a cross, a Christian symbol? Is it Sigurd—or the Archangel Michael slaying the great dragon, "that ancient serpent called the devil or Satan"?[281] Or is it Christ "who came to destroy the devil's work"?[282] You or I might be surprised to see Saint Michael or Christ portrayed like a Viking berserker, but a tenth-century recently converted Norse artist would not share these scruples. This may be another example of the artist using contemporary imagery to bring the Bible alive. Whatever the original meaning, the Maen Achwyfan cross is a splendid and impressive product of the encounters between Welsh and Scandinavian societies.

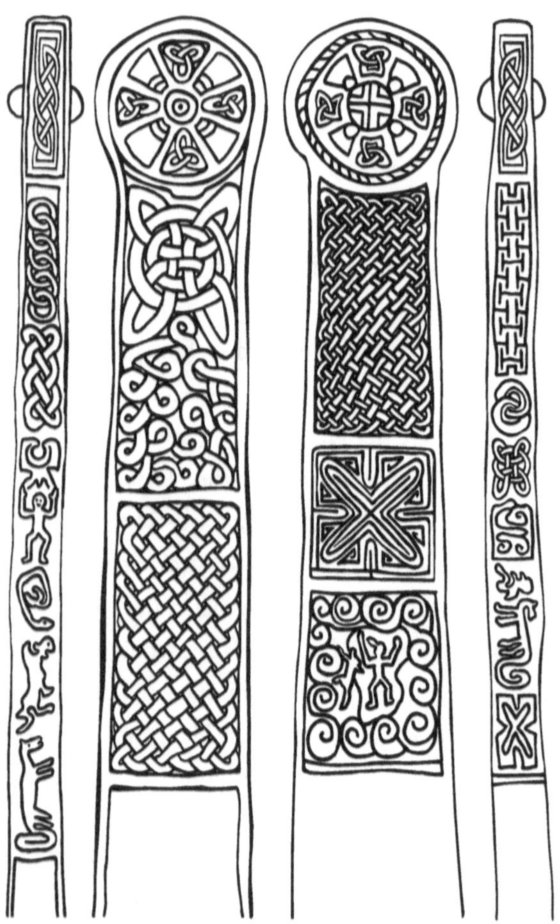

Experts believe Maen Achwyfan *means "Stone of Saint Cwyfan" and link the stone to a 7th-century Welsh saint. Although the Norse imagery is clear on the stone today, the stone itself may predate the Vikings.*[283]

Viking Influence on the Isle of Man

The Isle of Man, which lies between Ireland and Britain, is a relatively small land mass with an outsized cultural history. A stopping point in the maritime crossroads, the isle was successively utilized and colonized by various Celtic people, the Romans, and—after 820—the Norse.

Nigel Pennick, an authority on ancient belief systems, explains: "Under Norse rulership, which initially was Pagan, syncretic religious practices evolved, in which Christian and Pagan elements which had the same symbolic meaning co-existed alongside one another."[284] On Thor's Cross, the Norse Gods mingle with Christian figures, along with Earth spirits (dwarfs, gnomes, trolls, giants, and dragons).

Thor's Cross, as well as other stone crosses on the Isle of Man, represent the comparatively peaceful interweaving of Norse mythology with Christian scripture. "A violent conversion to the new religion was unnecessary," states historian W. A. Chaney, "when the old provided so many parallelisms that the tribal culture could absorb the conquering God without disrupting many of its basic preconceptions."[285] This was as true for the Norse as it had been for the Celts and the Anglo-Saxons.

Today, we often think of "conversion" as the total replacement of old belief systems with new religious beliefs, but in the Early Middle Ages, people saw things differently. Rather than replacing Pagan myth, Christian stories intermingled with them, adding to their meaning while enriching Christianity with new imagery. As twentieth-century archeologist T. C. Lethbridge notes, this combination of beliefs did not negate the reality of conversion; it only meant that the Celts, the Anglo-Saxons, and the Norse could still "see a lot of sense in the old beliefs also."[286] At first glance,

Christians may find this syncretism startling—but it's a process that's been going on since the very beginning of Christianity, when the early Christ-followers absorbed many of the classical Greco-Roman ideas.

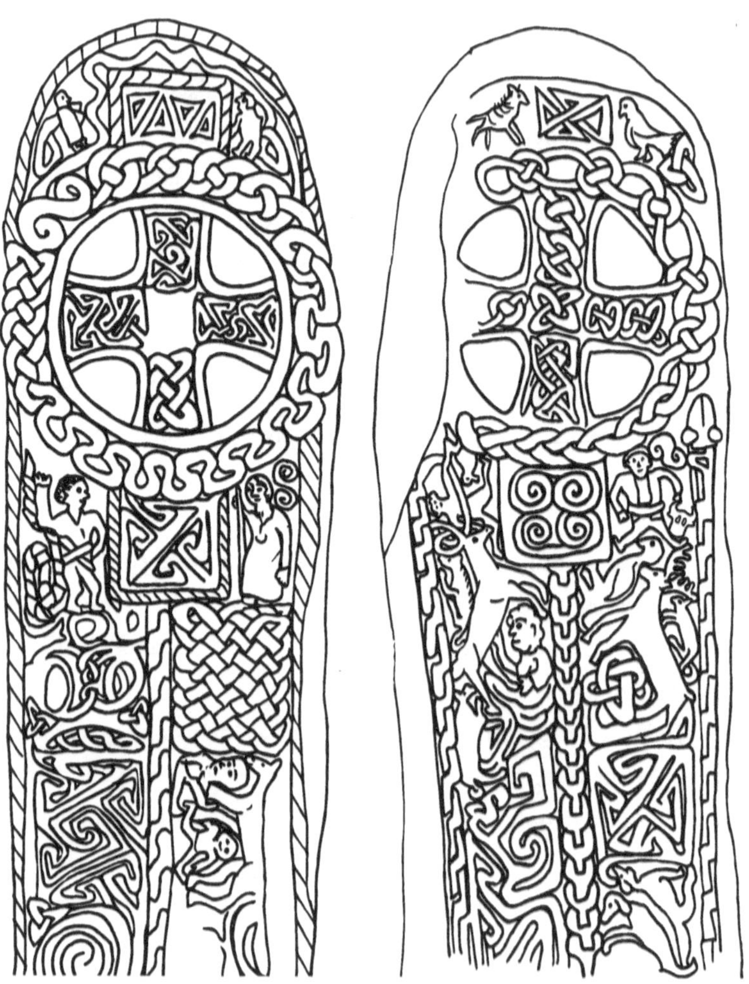

Thor's Cross got its name because it bears a carving of a man carrying something thought to be the head of an ox (see the middle right of the image on the right), which, according to Norse mythology, Thor used as bait to catch a huge serpent.

The Litmus Test of Christian Faith

The Vikings—who certainly inflicted suffering upon Christians in the Celtic lands—also made significant economic, artistic, and social contributions to those lands. The Scandinavians who came to Europe and the Isles were not all Vikings (raiders); many of them lived alongside their Irish, Scots, Welsh, and English neighbors as fellow subjects with a shared devotion to Christ.

British essayist G. K. Chesterton writes: "The Christian ideal has not been tried and found wanting. It has been found difficult; and left untried."[287] This may especially be true of Christ's teaching about loving one's enemies. The most recent American presidential election is an example of many Christians' failure to love those on the opposite side.

This is normal human nature, of course. Most of us like to show kindness to our friends, and many of us wish vengeance on our enemies (even if we won't go so far as to carry that out with physical violence). Countless tales across cultures and centuries glorify the taking of revenge, the exercise of tit-for-tat even to the death, but the earliest followers of the risen Christ demonstrated a different way, insisting on love for everyone, even the people who threatened their lives. They were following Jesus' teaching when he said, "If you love those who love you, what credit is that to you? Even 'bad' people—people whose lives fall wide from the mark God desires—love the people who love them. . . . But I say, love the people who wish you harm."[288] Distinguishing between ordinary (and conditional) love and his own prescription for unconditional love, Jesus calls his followers to a hard reckoning: Love-for-enemies may be the litmus test of a genuine faith in Christ.

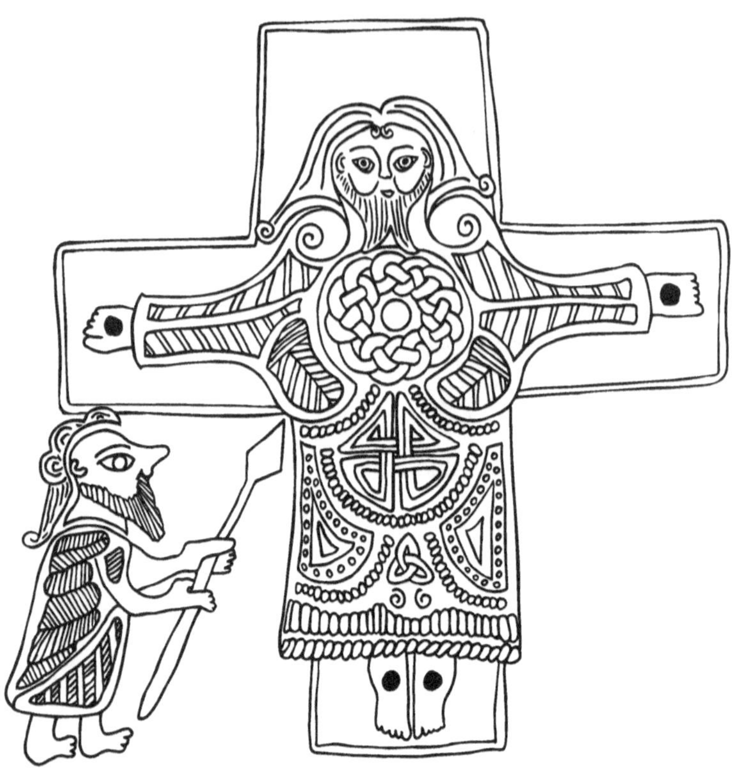

This cross slab from the Calf of Man (a smaller island off the coast of the Isle of Man) is an example of a medieval depiction of Christ and Longinus, illustrating the power of unconditional love and forgiveness.

The energy of enemy-love is most concentrated at Christ's crucifixion. Out of his agony, Jesus cried, "Father, forgive them."[289] The imperfect tense of the original Greek verb indicates that Jesus did not say this only once from the cross; he kept on saying this prayer repeatedly.

John's Gospel tells of Christ's fifth wound, when a legionnaire—Longinus, according to tradition—pierced his side with a spear, letting out a flow of blood and water.[290] Numerous Celtic scripture crosses and other early medieval crucifixion depictions prominently portray the Roman soldier, a popular visual illustration of Christ forgiving his enemies.

Early Christ-teachers interpreted this act metaphorically: For them, the flow of water and blood indicated new birth, mingling the water and blood of natural human birth with Christ's spiritual power of regeneration. From Christ's pierced side, God was re-birthing the world.

The soldier who speared Jesus is often associated with the centurion in Mark's Gospel who testified at the crucifixion, "Truly this man was God's son!"[291] This individual is given no name in the canonical Gospels, but the Gospel of Nicodemus (also known as the Acts of Pilate), a fourth- or fifth-century noncanonical writing, gives him the name *Longinus,* and thus he has been know ever since. According to a still-later medieval legend, Longinus suffered from an eye malady that was miraculously healed by the water and blood that fell from Jesus' side. This cure was the cause of Longinus's conversion, and medieval Christ-followers clearly perceived the symbolism at work in the story, where spiritual illumination enlightened even the man who sought to ensure Christ's death.

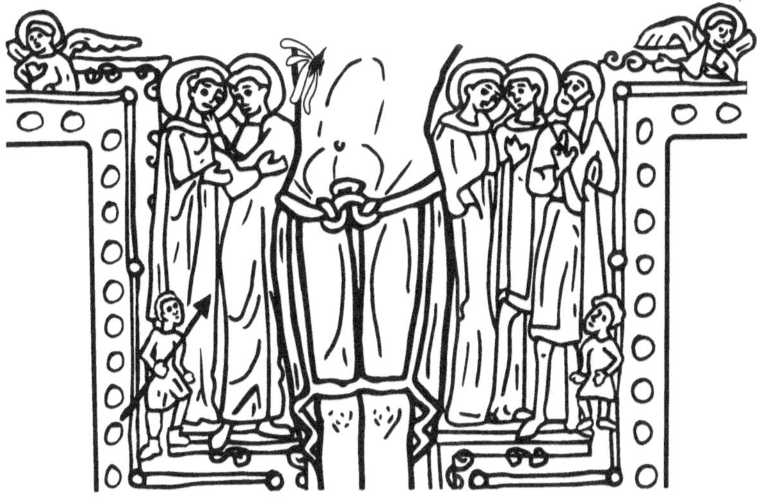

A detail from the San Damiano Cross, showing Longinus with his spear.

The Cross of San Damiano

The twelfth-century cross at San Damiano, Italy (the same cross that would speak to Saint Francis a century later, calling him to rebuild the church), illustrates Christ's forgiveness. In the southwest corner of the central panel, Longinus holds his spear and gazes upward at Christ; the life-giving blood of the savior arcs out from the wound in his side, on a trajectory that will wash away Longinus's malady and sin. Historians believe this cross was created by a Syrian monk, one of the many Syrian Christ-followers who brought their desert spirituality to this region of Italy, just as they had to Celtic lands, creating a spiritual community much like the Celts'.[292]

Considering Francis's focused devotion to this cross, I believe he would have noted this image of forgiveness. Perhaps it helped convert him to the extraordinary faith that inspired him to cross enemy lines to talk peace with the Muslim sultan during the Crusades.

Saint Clare, Francis's friend and spiritual companion, advised her followers to spend time in meditation gazing at this same cross. She writes:

> *Look into this mirror every day,*
> *. . . And continually examine your face in it,*
> *So that in this way you may adorn yourself completely,*
> *Inwardly and outwardly. . . .*[293]

In other words, Clare recommends we use the meaning of the San Damiano Cross—its symbolism—as a "mirror," the standard against which we measure ourselves, "inwardly and outwardly." Today, we can offer the same challenge to ourselves: *How well do we live up to the mercy and unconditional love of Christ as demonstrated from the cross?*

Maghera Crucifixion

The old church of St. Lurach, in County Derry, Ireland, contains another artistic portrayal of Christ extending forgiveness from the cross. On the Maghera Crucifixion, Jesus is dressed in the vestments of a priest, reminding the viewer that the same Christ who was crucified was then resurrected and still lives; his role as intercessor and shepherd for God's people continues on throughout eternity.

Christ's arms are unnaturally extended in the carving, so that they hover over the gathered onlookers, including disciples and Romans, gathering them into one company of the forgiven. Blood from Christ's side sprays out like rays of sunshine falling on Longinus, a reminder that this atonement covers even the enemy.

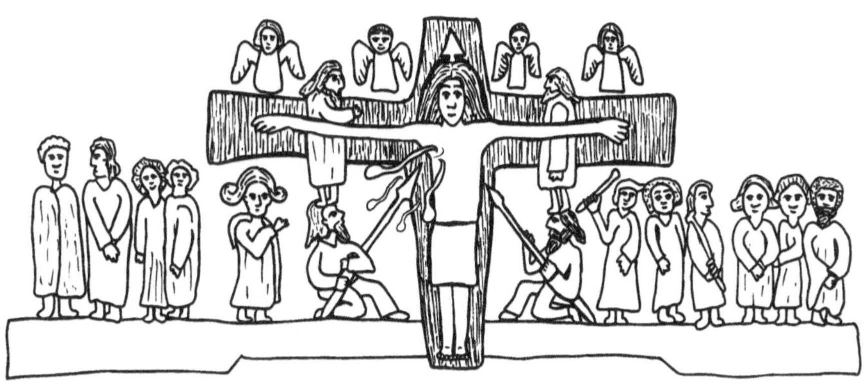

St. Lurach's Church, where the Maghera Crucifixion stands, dates back to the 10th century; it was built on the site of a 6th-century monastery founded by St. Lurach. Contained within the ruins is this sculpture of the crucifixion, thought to date from the 10th century, making it one of the oldest in Ireland.

APPLICATIONS FOR TODAY

A closer look at history challenges our ideas of who are enemies and who are kindred. This in turn should draw us to reconsider whom we label "enemies"—and whether we love these people as Christ commanded.

As I write this book, violence and conflict are everywhere. Wars in the Middle East and Europe escalate; in the United States and many other countries, differing political beliefs sever families and communities. This reality may trouble us, but we feel powerless to lessen the aggression around us. And yet the still, small voice of Jesus calls through the world's angry noise, asking us to practice unconditional love. The more we answer that call, the more peaceful actions will ripple out, gaining momentum.

In the Gospels, the cross is the ultimate demonstration of yielding power and privilege. Ironically, over the centuries, the cross has become a symbol of dominance. It is the mark Christians stamp to assert their right to dictate the behaviors and beliefs of other members of their society.

Jesus of Nazareth could have led an armed revolt against his people's oppressors; many of his fellow Jews worked for their liberation in that way. Instead, Jesus chose to live as a servant, someone who spoke truth to power while insisting on love of enemy. The instrument of his torture and death became the ultimate statement of unconditional forgiveness for all (no exceptions). As we use him as our role model, we can become walking epicenters of reconciliation, little christs radiating redemption.

LECTIO DIVINA

You may already be familiar with this well-known form of Christian meditation, which helps to get the truths of scripture traveling from the mind to the heart. As you engage in the following four steps, I suggest that you also keep a cross as your companion (either in visual or tactile form or both), imagining that Christ's arms on the cross are embracing your meditation time.

1. READ the selected passage, preferably out loud. In this first reading, just let the words soak in, hearing their sound, noting their meaning but only in a general way.

2. REFLECT as you read the selected passage again and be alert for an element that seems directed toward you, personally and directly. This could be a word, phrase, or mental image. See whatever element of the scripture that stands out as God addressing you.

3. RESPOND by reading the selected passage a third time, focusing attention on the element of the text that stood out for you in the second reading, above. After you have finished the third reading, utter your response to that message, in prayer. Does this scripture call you to be thankful? To change some aspect of life to live

more skillfully? To commit yourself to a specific action? Converse with the One who gave himself wholly for you.

4. REST after reading the text for a fourth and final time, receiving it as a gift from your Beloved. Imagine yourself as a child sitting in the lap of the Divine, listening to the Life Giver's words of love. Take a moment to be aware of your feelings. Say a short final utterance connecting what you just received with what lies ahead in your day.

Suggested scriptures: Psalm 46, Psalm 131, Matthew 5:43–48, Romans 12:14–21. These readings will point you toward reconciliation and peace.

Loving Friendliness

In Marcus Borg's book titled *Jesus and Buddha: The Parallel Sayings*, Jack Kornfield shares an experience that speaks to the Divine truth that reaches past the boundaries of nationality and religion, empowering us to forgive even our enemies. In the middle of the Vietnam War, when Kornfield visited a monastery in the Mekong Delta, he came across two statues, both fifty feet high. One statue portrayed Buddha, the other, Christ—and the two were arm in arm. Kornfield recalls, "While helicopter gunships flew by overhead and war raged around us, Buddha and Jesus stood there like brothers, expressing compassion and healing for all who would follow their way."[294]

Given the similar peace teachings of Gautama Buddha and Jesus Christ, it is unsurprising that some Christ-followers find Buddhist practices helpful in living out Christ's teachings. One helpful practice is the metta (usually translated as "loving kindness," though "loving friendliness" may be more accurate[295]) meditation. The boxed exercise is an adaptation of this practice, as seen through the lens of Celtic Christianity. (In adapting the words of the original metta meditation, I do not mean to imply any lack in the original Buddhist practice. In its original form, it is elegant and goes straight to the heart.)

LOVING FRIENDLINESS MEDITATION

Begin by sitting comfortably, and take a series of slow, calming breaths. Let your gaze soften. If you ponder Christ's words, "Love your enemy," you may discover the worst enemy is yourself. We each have a tragic ability to torment ourselves with painful memories, regret, and shame. But we cannot love others unconditionally if we refuse to offer the same kindness to our own souls.

Imagine you are looking at yourself through the eyes of someone who loves you (a person or an animal). What does this being love about you? Why do they enjoy spending time with you? Now, think of Christ with his arms extended on the cross-beam; he is reaching out to welcome you, to hug you. He feels nothing but delight in your presence. He knows your every thought in every moment, and with that complete knowledge, he wishes nothing more than your friendship and the pleasure of being with you. Sit with this feeling of absolute love for a minute. Then repeat these lines, slowly, allowing them to sink into your mind and heart. Spend as long as you need to with them.

May I be held in loving kindness.
May I feel connected and calm.
May I accept myself just as I am.
May I be happy.

Now expand your contemplation by imagining someone dear to you, a person you care about who has always been there for you. Think about this person's goodness; consider what you love about them. As you again turn your attention to the cross, imagine Christ's delight in this dear one. He cares about them even more deeply than you do. Sit with your feeling—and Christ's feeling—of absolute love toward this individual. Then pray:

May you be held in lovingkindness.
May you feel absolute love now.
May you accept yourself just as you are.
May you be happy.

Next, think of an acquaintance, someone who gives you feelings that are neither good nor bad. It might be a neighbor, a cashier where you shop, a co-worker you don't know well. Though this person is mostly a mystery to you, Christ knows them; they are the object of his self-giving and unconditional love on the cross. As you bring this person to mind, pray for them:

May you be held in lovingkindness.
May you feel absolute love now.
May you accept yourself just as you are.
May you be happy.

Finally, I invite you to expand your heart. Imagine someone with whom you've had a difficult relationship—or someone you don't know personally who nevertheless triggers in you feelings of anger, dislike, or fear. Consider the humanity you have in common with this person. Like you, they experience physical and emotional pain and happiness. Like you, they were once a child, a pure and innocent baby. As you turn your attention again to the cross, hear Christ saying, "Forgive them." Jesus welcomes this person you find so unlikeable in the same affectionate way he embraces your most beloved person. Apply to this person the words of loving friendliness:

> *May you be held in lovingkindness.*
> *May you feel absolute love now.*
> *May you accept yourself just as you are.*
> *May you be happy.*

If you've been blessed by this adapted metta practice below, I suggest you seek out the authentic Buddhist practice online.[296]

The apostle Paul told the Christ-followers in the Greek city of Philippi, "Whatever is true, whatever is honorable, whatever is just, whatever is pure, whatever is pleasing, whatever is commendable, if there is any excellence and if there is anything worthy of praise, think about these things."[297] All truth is God's truth, so Paul's "whatever" must include things that are true (honorable, just, pure, pleasing, and commendable) when they come from people or groups who are very different from ourselves—even the people we may consider to be enemies!

God,

enkindle in my inmost heart

the flaming spark of love for my enemy,

for my relative,

for my friend,

for the wise person,

for the foolish person,

for the unfortunate person,

O son of gentle shining Mary,

from the lowest

most perverse person

to the one of highest fame.

CALVIN MILLER[298]

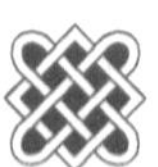

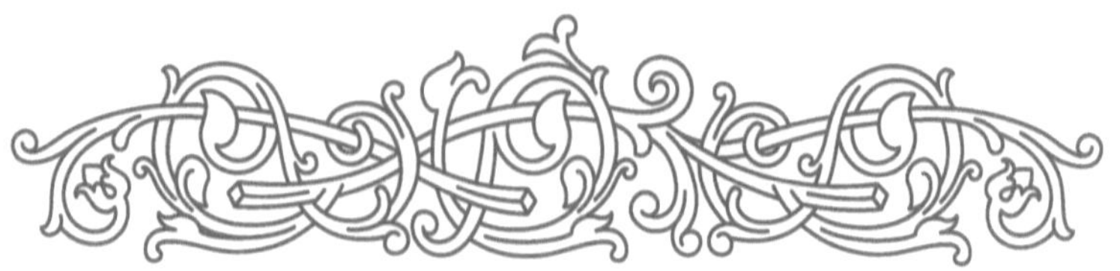

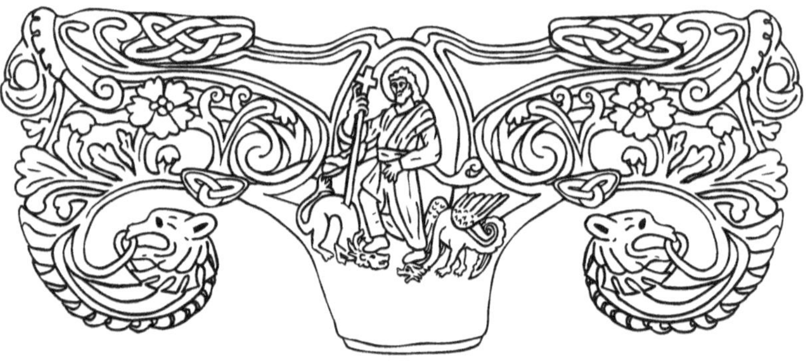

*This early Saxon carving from the head of a tau-shaped cross
shows Christ as a strong hero, treading boldly over his enemies.*

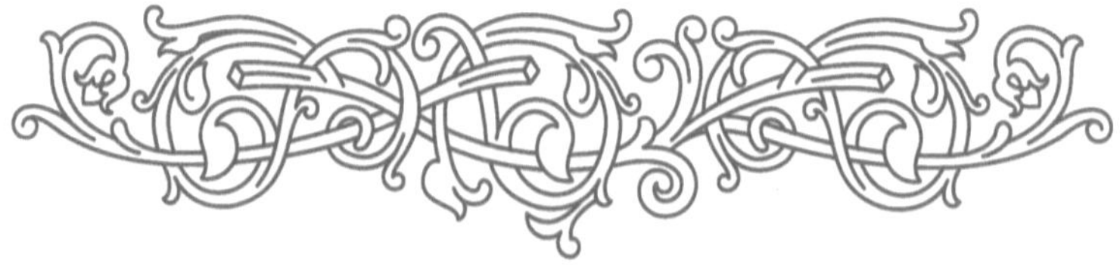

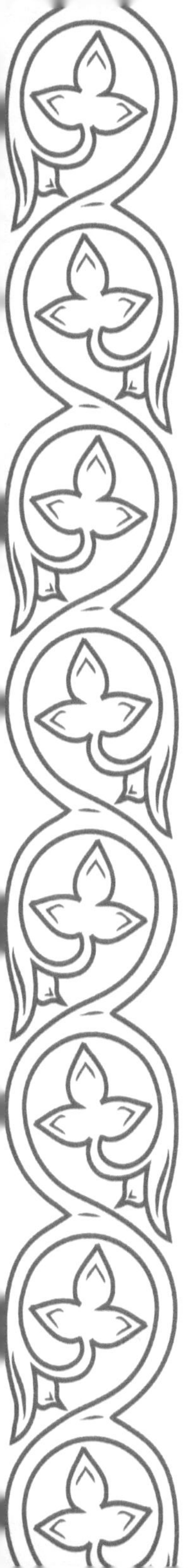

CHAPTER 10

Christ the Hero

And the Word became flesh and lived among us,
and we have seen his glory . . .
full of grace and truth.

John 1:14

The journey of the hero
is about the courage to seek the depths;
the image of creative rebirth;
the eternal cycle of change within us;
the uncanny discovery that the seeker
is the mystery which the seeker seeks to know.
The hero journey is a symbol that binds,
in the original sense of the word,
two distant ideas, the spiritual
quest of the ancients
with the modern search for identity.

Joseph Campbell

ENCOUNTER

15 January III 3019 (according to the calendar of Middle Earth): Moria[299]

Deep in the underground realm beneath the Misty Mountains, the wizard Gandalf stands firm on a stone bridge that spans a still deeper chasm. He leans on his staff, the way any gray-haired older man might—but his other hand brandishes a gleaming sword. A fearsome monster emerges from the chasm, blowing flames from its nostrils. Immense shadowy wings reach out for Gandalf.

Gandalf is undaunted. "You cannot pass!" he thunders. "I am a servant of the Secret Fire. Go back to the Shadow! You cannot pass."

The monster makes no answer. As it moves closer to Gandalf, it expands. Its wings now fill the entire cavern, and it holds high a whip, ready to strike. Gandalf's light still glimmers, like an ember in the night, but he seems so small in comparison to the evil being that's looming over him.

The monster's flaming sword stabs the air. The wizard's blade answers, and the enemy's weapon splinters into burning fragments.

The mighty blow takes its toll on Gandalf; he staggers, takes a step backward—but then he plants his feet firmly on the bridge once more. "You cannot pass!" he shouts again.

But the monster does not obey. Instead, it leaps closer to Gandalf, its full weight on the narrow span of stone beneath their feet. Gandalf lifts his staff—

And slams it down on the bridge. White flame fills the air. The bridge collapses.

The monster screams as it plummets into the abyss. Even as it falls, it snaps its whip. The thongs hiss through the air and twist around Gandalf's legs; the wizard loses his footing. He too falls, down, down, down . . .

 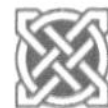 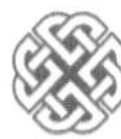

Gandalf's steadfast defiance of the monster allows his friends to escape. But it will be a considerable time before (*spoiler alert!*) we learn Gandalf has survived his descent into the underworld. He pursues the monster (the Balrog), and after days of battle, Gandalf triumphs. He returns to his friends, transformed, shining white.

This whole sequence is my favorite analogy of Christ's equally heroic death. There are many other similar hero stories, though, both ancient and modern.

DEEPENING

The Hero's Journey

The *Epic of Gilgamesh*—some of which was written some four thousand years ago, making it the oldest known work of written literature—recounts the exploits of Gilgamesh, king of Uruk, who possesses extraordinary strength, wisdom, and courage; he is the archetypal hero.

While Gilgamesh may be the first written hero, he cannot be the first. The desire for a hero is as old as humanity.

Joseph Campbell

In the late nineteenth century and in the first half of the twentieth, scholars began to notice that many hero stories follow a common pattern. Various psychologists and anthropologists wrote about it, including Carl Jung, but Joseph Campbell was the one who made this idea famous.

Campbell identifies seventeen stages of the hero's journey, but he summarizes them all as following this overall narrative pattern:

A hero ventures forth from the world of common day into
a region of supernatural wonder: fabulous forces are there
encountered and a decisive victory is won: the hero comes
back from this mysterious adventure with the power to
bestow boons on his fellow [humanity].[300]

The "region of supernatural wonder" that Campbell describes
is very often an underground realm. As Jungian mythologist Jean
Shinoda Bolen writes: "Most heroic journeys involve going through
a dark place—through mountain caverns, the underworld, or laby-
rinthine passages to emerge, finally, into the light."[301]

The Descent of the Hero

Stories of descent into the realm of the dead come from every continent, down through the ages. The earliest known tales of descent to
the land of departed souls are accounts of the Mesopotamian Goddess
Inanna (later known as Ishtar) who seeks to extend her power into
the under-realm.

Our modern hero stories contain similar scenes. In *Star Wars: A
New Hope*, for instance, when Luke, Han, Chewbacca, and Princess
Lei fall into Darth Vader's clutches, they descend together into a
garbage compactor, before, eventually, being delivered. There are
countless other examples: The TV series *Stranger Things* is based
on the existence of an underworld; the hero in *Doctor Strange* has
to enter the Dark Realm and fight Dormammu, ruler of the Dark
Dimension; in *Thor*, the god-hero descends to battle frost giants in
the shadowed world of Jotunheim; *Alien*'s Ripley goes down into
the alien queen's lair to rescue Newt from an inferno filled with
otherworldly monsters.

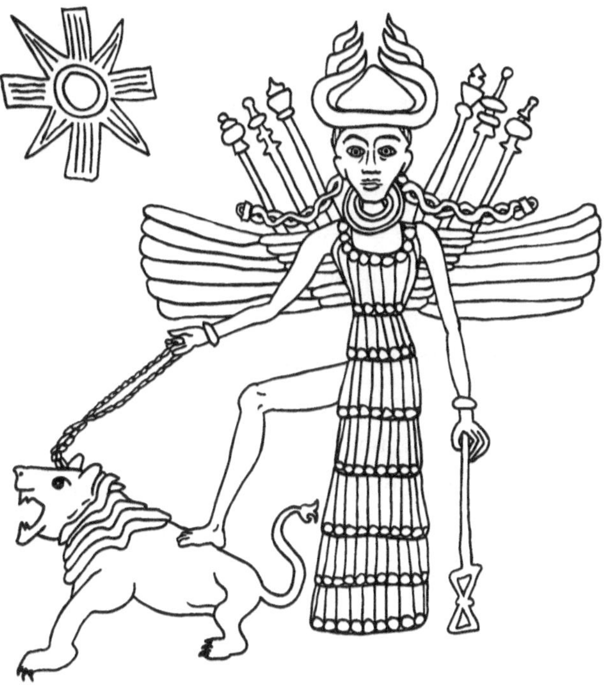

This drawing shows the imagery on an ancient seal (created more than 2,000 years before the Common Era). The Goddess Inanna carries weapons on her back and rests her foot on her pet lion. Her most famous myth tells of her descent into the underworld. She lies there dead for three days until she is brought back to life and rescued.

In some descent myths, the person descending to the underworld fails to observe strict underworld protocols, resulting in the loss of their loved one. In a Wyandot First Nations tale, for example, a warrior goes down to the Land of Souls to recover his sister; he places her soul in a hollowed gourd, but her soul spills out on the ground before he can return to the mortal realm. Likewise, Orpheus cannot obey the strict dictate not to look behind him as he and his wife Eurydice ascend back to mortal lands, and Eurydice's return to life is negated. These myths reinforce the finality of death.[302]

Other myths tell about divine or semi-divine heroes who succeed after superhuman effort in the under realms. In one Buddhist legend, Miaoshan (also known as Kwan Yin, the Boddhisatva of Compassion) dies by taking within herself the negative karma of her executioner. Weighted by the bad karma, she sinks into the lower realms of the dead. There, she releases the good karma she attained by her own efforts during mortal life and turns the eternal realm of suffering into a paradise.[303]

A very old Welsh legend, attributed to the legendary bard Taliesin, recounts the descent of Arthur into the subterranean world of Annwn. Annwn is part of the primordial stuff of the universe, the force of nothingness that exists outside the energy of the All-Creator; today, we might refer to it as the abyss or chaos.[304] Arthur goes down into Annwn with three shiploads of warriors, determined to take away a magical diamond-studded cauldron.[305] (The Arthur of this Celtic myth differs from the monarch of courtly romances popularized much later by Mallory and others; this Arthur is a remembrance of the Breton deity Artaius, who is both god and man.) Arthur's raid succeeds, but at tremendous cost: Only nine warriors out of his vast company survive the combat.

The Christ story can also be seen as a heroic descent from the realm of mortal life to the realm of the dead. Does that surprise you? If you profess to be a Christ-follower, what do you make of the abundance of similar legends, some far older than the Gospels? These tales clearly parallel Jesus' story, and yet they belong to other cultures' belief systems and mythology.

The wisdom of C. S. Lewis may be helpful to you if you're a Christian with these concerns. In his book *Miracles*, Lewis says all myth is, "at its best, a real though unfocused gleam of divine truth falling on human imagination."[306] Lewis also wrote an essay titled "Myth Become Fact," in which he explains:

The heart of Christianity is a myth which is also a fact. The old myth of the Dying God, *without ceasing to be myth,* comes down from the heaven of legend and imagination to the earth of history. It *happens*—at a particular date, in a particular place, followed by definable historical consequences. We pass from a Balder or an Osiris, dying nobody knows when or where, to a historical Person crucified (it is all in order) *under Pontius Pilate.* By becoming fact it does not cease to be myth: that is the miracle.

Lewis concludes, "We must not be ashamed of the mythical radiance resting on our theology. We must not be nervous about 'parallels' and 'Pagan Christs': they *ought to be there—it would be a stumbling block if they weren't.*"[307]

The Celtic Hero

Christ's early followers in the British Isles and Ireland thought of Christ's death as the act of an epic hero. In fact, he became the ultimate hero, whose bravery, strength, and wisdom were displayed most mightily in his crucifixion and its aftermath. This made sense to people whose lives were shaped by their fierce battle-heroes. (They also understood Christ to be a seer, sage, and king, other roles of importance in Celtic society.) Theological understanding is always shaped by the theologians' cultural background.

The Anglo-Saxon *Dream of the Rood,* among the earliest works in the English language, depicts Christ on the cross:

> *Almighty God stripped himself.*
> *When he willed to mount the gallows.*
> *Courageous before all men . . .*
> *A powerful king . . .*
> *The Lord of Heaven.*[308]

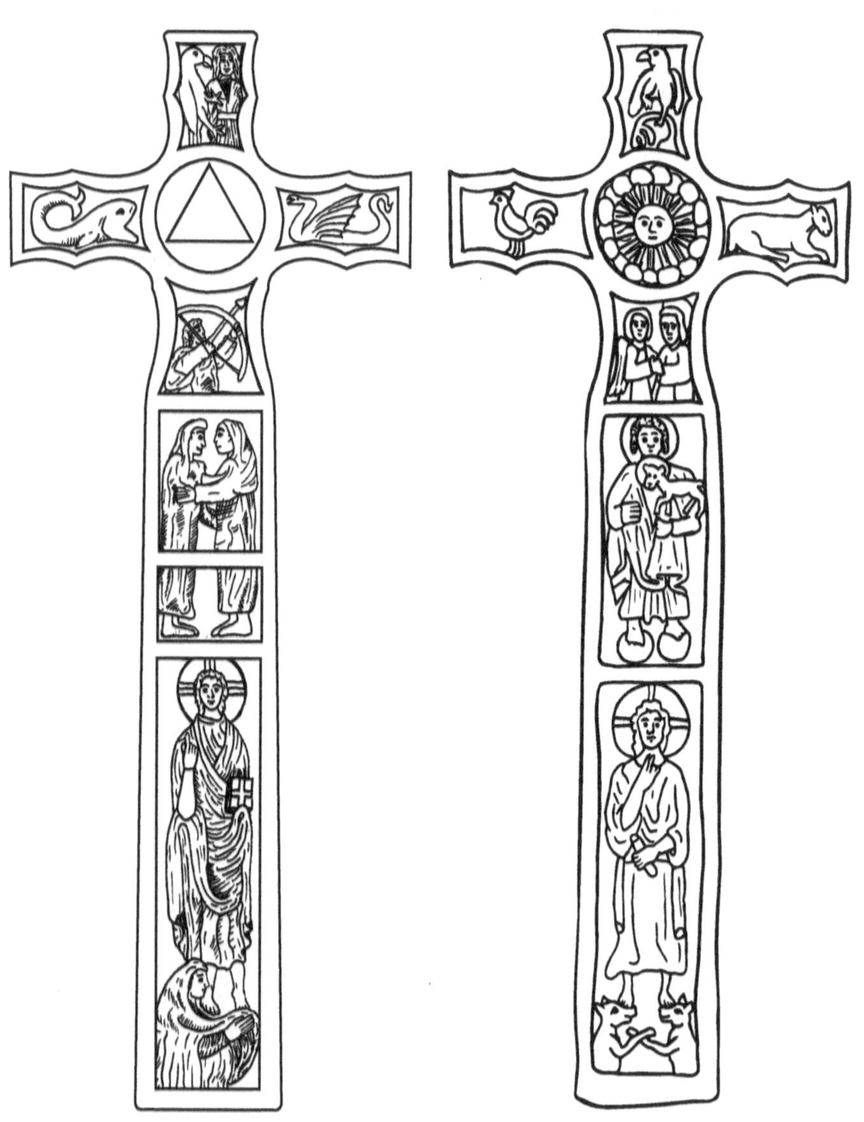

The artist who sculpted the Ruthwell Cross (also featured in chapter 1) portrayed Christ on both front and back of the shaft. On one side, Christ stands, blessing Mary Magdalene as she anoints his feet; on the other side, he is the King of Creation standing in majesty atop two beasts. Runic lettering on the cross's sides spells out portions of the Dream of the Rood.

In the poem, Christ journeys to the cross as though to a battlefield. The poem describes Christ's "foes" as the Roman guards who presided over the crucifixion, and the cross is their battleground. The poem's words do not indicate that Christ is a victim in any way; instead, as scholar Carol Jean Wolf notes, Christ "is an active, even eager agent."[309] He purposefully, willingly climbs the cross, demonstrating a hero's courage, resolution, and strength. The words that describe Christ's actions all parallel the language used in Pagan hero tales.[310]

The poet writes that all Creation weeps at Christ's death, yet at the same time, the poem says, when the apostles remove Christ from the cross, he is not really dead, only "limb-weary"; he must rest before he undertakes the next phase of his heroic battle to free all humanity.

The Athlone Crucifix is another ancient portrayal of Christ as the hero of the cross. In this Celtic copper sculpture, originally used either for an altar or the cover of a sacred book, Christ stands fully upright, massive, strong, apparently unbroken, facing the viewer directly. On his head is a triskele, symbol of the Trinity, and perhaps a crown, reminding us of his Divinity. He wears a full-length priest's robe like a stole, its material adorned with vertical knotwork patterns and horizontal wave-like spirals along the bottom hem. On his chest, he wears a breastplate decorated with six spirals, an ancient symbol that dates back to prehistoric times; the breastplate itself is a reminder of Christ's unvanquishable power and his warrior-courage.

This is the same image of Christ we find in *The Dream of the Rood*: courageous, powerful, the Lord of Heaven. He is the "King of glory, Yahweh, strong and mighty, Yahweh, mighty in battle," the same one who will descend to Hades and command, "Lift up your heads, O Gates, and be lifted up, O ancient doors,"[311] for he "shatters the doors of bronze and cuts in two the bars of iron"[312] as he demolishes the entrance to the underworld.

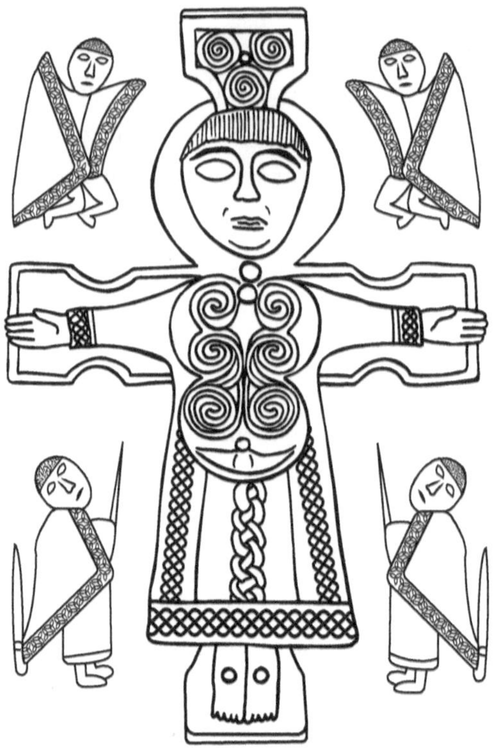

The Athlone Crucifix's similarity to Syrian illuminations suggests it may date to the seventh or eighth century. Christ's body takes the shape of the cross, making the instrument of crucifixion and the crucified body into one.

Holy Storytelling

The Irish, Picts, Welsh, and Britons were great storytellers, their bards noted for their emotional depth, wordcraft, and musical skill. In fact, storytellers, often working in song, were the most important members of ancient Celtic society, the influencers of their time. Their words could elevate a woman or man to the highest levels of society, and if the bards made someone the butt of their jokes, that person would likely topple from power to disgrace. Bards such as Taliesin became legends, as important in their own right as the heroes in their poems.

When the gospel came to Ireland and the British Isles, Christian clerics assumed the vital role of storytellers; this was in stark contrast to the attitudes prevailing elsewhere in the Christian world at the time, which denigrated poetry, especially in vernacular languages.[313] Celtic Christians "assimilated and adapted the druidic, bardic approach," creating the unique role of "poet-priest."[314]

The Celts knew that stories are important vehicles for deep truth. Ancient people were not immune to many of the same anxieties we face today—but as they listened to their storytellers, they were comforted.

The Light of Story

The fear of death has likely been present with humanity as long as we have had consciousness. We dread the loss of our bodies, the separation from friends and family. We hate the darkness of the unknown. We wonder how our lives will be judged when we enter the next life.

This Old Irish piece of writing, attributed to the great Saint Brendan, expresses these worries:

> *"Do you fear death, Brendan?" said the bishop. . . .*
> *"I do indeed," said Brendan.*
> *"Death, certain, the time uncertain.*
> *Leaving friends, the presence of foes.*
> *An unknown journey, an unfamiliar land.*
> *A dark way, lingering without return.*
> *Fright of wrath, horror of monsters.*
> *A terrible valley, whose bottom human sight does not reach,*
> *which is full of fire and monsters.*
> *A crooked unsteady bridge across it,*
> *unless your good deeds support you.*
> *A King certainly awaiting you,*
> *Uncertain the judgement at his hand. . . .*

When the ancient Celts (and their neighbors the Saxons) felt these fears, they turned to story, both written and visual (as in the case of the scripture crosses). Creative imagery revealed to them the truth that shines even in the midst of death.

The Celts were warriors, and many of their written and visual stories were filled with violence and action. But not always. Sometimes, they portrayed their heroes in gentler ways, creating a calm and reassuring narrative to comfort the anxious heart.

A good example of this is a stone slab, now housed in Bristol Cathedral, that shows Jesus in the underworld. Here, he is not a warrior. Instead, he appears to stand quietly, his bare feet resting almost gently

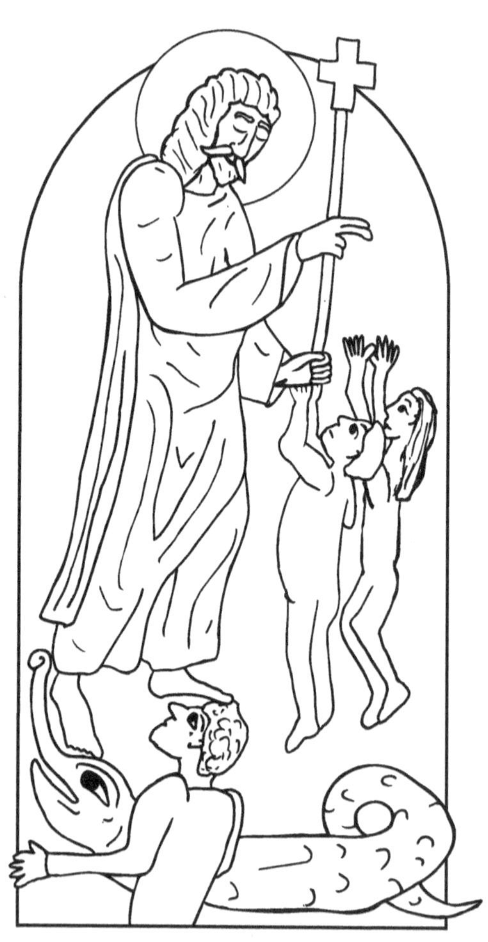

This stone slab, showing Christ rescuing Adam and Eve from Sheol, was discovered in the 19th century in a pile of post-riot rubble from a 12th-century chapel.

on the devil and a demonic creature. Christ has one hand outstretched, as though he is gesturing while in speech; with his other hand, he grasps a simple cross. He looks down kindly at two human children, Adam and Eve, as they stand on tiptoe to grasp the hand that holds the cross.

Because of holes drilled in the stone, as though it had originally attached to hinges, scholars speculate its artist, perhaps a Saxon working in the eleventh or twelfth century, created this image for a portable Celtic shrine or reliquary. The shrine would have held a holy relic, allowing it to be carried from community to community, and perhaps this is how a Celtic shrine ended up in Bristol.[316] Archeologists and historians have various theories, but no one knows for certain.

In any case, the story in stone can still speak to us today, reminding us of Christ's reassuring presence even in the murky depths of our lives. That is the genius of good artwork: It speaks with a timeless voice, a voice that breathes Spirit messages directly into our souls.

Where did these powerful stories come from? How did they spring to life here on these remote Celtic islands? The Welsh attributed artistic inspiration—the breath of creativity—to something they called *awen*.

Awen

Awen was the gift of inspiration that gave magical power to the Pagan singers of tales, as well as to their successors, the Christian poet-priests who invoked the same power for their compositions:

> *The Lord God will give me sweet awen*
> *Like that from the Cauldron of Ceridwen.*[317]

Note that the composer equates God's awen with that given by Ceridwen, the Pagan Goddess whose cauldron gave the gift of poetic inspiration.

In the late twelfth century, another poet began his *Ode to St David* with this invocation:

> *May the blessed Lord in the midst of the night grant me*
> *Awen with the breath on the rising dawn.*[318]

Awen is akin to Spirit's creative movement within us and through the world around us.

While later forms of Christianity often were skeptical of the imagination, believing it might all too easily lead us astray, the Celts honored it as a holy gift. They knew our powers of imagination allow us to see truth more clearly, bringing to life new possibilities in the real world.

Not Fantasy!

When the Welsh and other Celts brought the powers of their imagination to the Christ story, they were not relegating it to the hazy world of fantasy. For them, awen was grounded in the practical world of relationships and daily work, expressed in the ordinary actions of life. And, since they were already steeped in stories of heroes whose quests led them into the under-realms, the story of Christ's descent made perfect sense to them.

Some modern-day Christians, however, may have more trouble accepting this story. If you're an Evangelical Christian, you may believe the justice and purity of God would never allow Jesus to descend into the underworld. To you, this may indeed seem like pure fantasy, a made-up story. But this story is not the product of whimsy; it's simply based on an earlier understanding of Christ's saving work, one that also remained faithful to the teachings of scripture.

The early Celtic Christians saw Christ's descent foretold in passages in the Hebrew scriptures. *Sheol* was the Hebrew term for the underworld (we'll talk about that more in the next chapter), and Hannah, for example, prophesies at the birth of her son the Prophet

Samuel: "The Lord . . . brings down to Sheol and he raises up."[319] The psalmist writes: "If I make my bed in Sheol, you are there,"[320] which likewise suggests the Divine descent to the lower world.

Jesus declares the soon-to-come fulfillment of these older promises: "Very truly, I tell you, the hour is coming and is now here when the dead will hear the voice of the Son of God, and those who hear will live."[321] Then, after Christ leaves the disciples and returns to Heaven, Peter addresses the crowd on the Feast of Pentecost, speaking about Christ's recent descent to Hades: "For David says concerning [Christ] . . . you will not abandon my soul to Hades or let your holy one see corruption."[322]

Prophetic passages in the Hebrew Bible, Jesus' own words as recorded by John, and the testimony of the apostle Peter all indicate Christ's saving mission involved a descent into the realm of death. We may not know the exact details—but according to scripture, this story really happened!

Justice and Mercy

The early theology built around this story did not dismiss sin lightly. Christianity and Judaism are both founded on belief in a moral God, a Creator who sets behavioral boundaries and then covenants to guard those boundaries. God cares if people treat each other kindly or cruelly. According to Jesus, behaviors have consequences.

Nevertheless, God is not interested in a Victorian sort of morality built on false prohibitions, nor does God think of morality in abstract or dualistic terms of "good" and "bad." Instead, Divine morality is an expression of the Creator's passionate concern for the well-being of every part of Creation.

Today, however, we often think of justice in terms of *punishment.* Justice is done, we may believe, when the murderer is executed and the backstabbing co-worker gets fired from the job. This sense of "I will feel better when the offending party has suffered" is *retributive* justice.

But is the world better because the criminal has suffered—or would it be more beneficial if the criminal could be changed into an agent of good? Does it really help to see a co-worker fired—or does their misfortune diminish the common good? If God's endgame is redemption, as scripture says, then retribution falls short of the Divine kin-dom. God's justice may better be understood as *restorative* justice.

In the second century, Clement of Alexandria saw justice and mercy as mirrored virtues. "The chastisements of God are salvific and pedagogic," he wrote, "leading to conversion and preferring the salvation of the sinner to his death."[323] Even God's apparent punishments are a means to restoration.

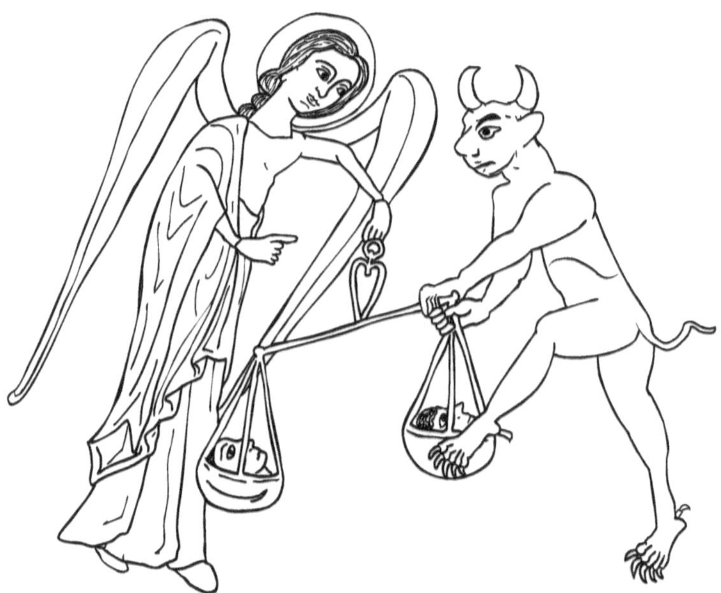

The weighing of souls portrayed on the Cross of the Scriptures was a common theme in medieval artwork. This image, taken from a late 12th- or early 13th-century altarpiece, portrays the same meaning as the carving on the stone cross: Although the powers of evil try to weigh down the soul, the forces of good (represented here by the Archangel Michael) ensure that the soul's essential goodness outweighs the evil.

God as Abba

Jesus speaks of the Creator as "Father"—*Abba*—a loving parent whose forgiveness is the basis for the radical love Jesus conveys when he says,

> Love your enemies, do good, and lend, expecting nothing in return. Your reward will be great, and you will be children of the Most High, for he himself is kind to the ungrateful and the wicked. Be merciful, just as your Father is merciful.[324]

Notice Jesus puts no boundaries around this commandment; he doesn't say, "Love all your enemies except people who aren't Christians," nor does he say, "Do good and lend, but not to people who exhibit certain behaviors you don't approve of." When it comes to forgiveness, Jesus indicates God has no limits—and we are to carry that same unconditional love to the people around us.

The concept of God-as-Abba was at the heart of Jesus' relationship with Divinity, and it's made me also better understand God's identity. As a father, I would do anything for my children. If they made unwise choices, I would *never* wish them to suffer; I'd only want them to be restored to happiness. If we were separated by hurt or misunderstanding, I would want the breach mended as quickly as possible, and I'd do whatever I could to reach out to them. I cannot imagine any point where I would ever say, "You can never come home."

As Jesus reminded us, God is a better father than any human[325]—and so, I cannot believe Abba-God would ever close the door to reconciliation with any part of Creation, in this life or beyond. Christ's descent to Hades is visible proof that Abba's love for prodigal children extends beyond the short span of human life.

Ancient Christians were as troubled as we are at the apparent unfairness of a limited view of God's mercy, and they recognized that Christ's underworld actions addressed this concern. Clement of Alexandria, the leading second-century theologian, wrote:

> It is not right that these [souls who departed from life without hearing or believing the gospel] should be condemned. . . . How is it possible that Christ did not for this cause preach the Gospel to those who had departed this life before his coming?"[326]

(We'll discuss these ideas more in the next chapter.)

The Hero's Return

The final component of Joseph Campbell's hero journey is the return home. The hero does not return unchanged to her old life; instead, she becomes a catalyst that transforms the familiar world from which she came. She brings with her gifts from her journey, gifts that will heal and restore the ordinary realm. The Gospel accounts also end with the hero's return: Christ's descent into the underworld morphs into the triumph of his exaltation.

The Dream of the Rood also makes clear that Christ's battle-victory is not the end of the story. Instead, the speaking Cross indicates it has an eternal purpose that extends throughout time and space. The Cross has now become "a cosmic sign, comprehending all space, visible and invisible."[327] But, the Cross implies, this immense and universal symbol is also intimate. It points to the union of our inmost being with the Divine. This is one of the gifts the Christ-Hero brings.

Robert B. Burlin, a professor of Old English, believes the Ruthwell Cross, with its inscription from *The Dream of the Rood,* also indicates a vision of the restoration Christ brought with him from the underrealm. On one of the main panels of that cross, Jesus is shown standing above the heads of beasts (as you'll see in the illustration on page 25).

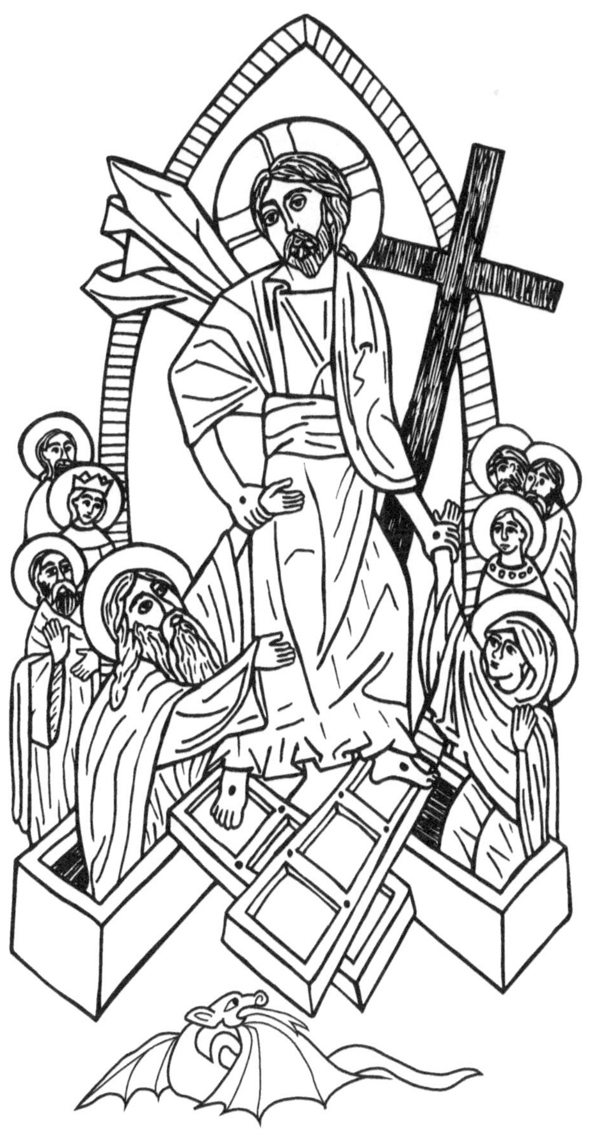

In Eastern Orthodox icons like this one, the descent to Hades is illustrated as simultaneous with Christ's resurrection. Beneath Christ are the smashed gates of Hades and the defeated devil, in Christ's hands are the delivered souls, and he is rising in the exaltation of his resurrection. Western depictions of Christ's resurrection usually show him alone as he rises from the tomb, but in Eastern iconography, he is almost always portrayed as rising with a crowd of the redeemed.

Although some scholars believe this is a portrayal of Christ treading on the powers of evil, Burlin believes it actually illustrates Christ's time in the desert (as told by Mark in his Gospel), when Jesus' only companions were wild animals; in fact, a Latin inscription on the panel explicitly states that the beasts of the desert recognize Christ. The carving gives us a vision of God's peaceable kin-dom, a place where Christ restores humanity's harmony with Nature.[328]

Burlin also believes the later portions of *The Dream of the Rood* describe an ongoing "communion between the natural and supernatural worlds." The implication is that when Christ returned from the underworld, he did not isolate himself in Heaven. The gifts he brought with him are ours to enjoy in the here and now; we do not have to wait for the afterlife. The vision of the Rood, Burlin says, is both "a way to Life and a way of life," opening the spiritual world to the experience of ordinary humans.[329]

What Burlin sees in both the verbal and visual ancient artwork is what I would call the Celtic vision of the world. "Spiritual" and "physical" are not separated in this vision, nor are humans isolated any longer from the biological world. All is united in harmony.

APPLICATIONS FOR TODAY

A Strong Sanctuary

When I visited the monastery of Glendalough in Ireland, I realized what the protection of the cross looked like back in the Early Middle Ages in practical terms. The monastery's outer walls, entrances, high crosses, towers, chapels, and monastic quarters still stand (though now roofless). When I stepped through the main entrance, I saw on the wall just within the outer portal a deeply etched cross, about the height of a person, its outline sharp even after 1,100 years. This cross was literally life-saving (and not only in a spiritual sense).

The law of sanctuary was simple: If a man or woman fleeing enemies or authorities placed their hand on the sanctuary cross—the carved cross set within the gate—their life would be spared and retribution canceled. The monks of Glendalough asked no questions; the safe refuge they offered was unconditional. The cross literally offered protection and new life.

While ancient tales describe Christ as a warrior whose victory standard is the cross, today we might think of the cross's power as a force that strengthens our inner resolve against the powers of personal and global destruction. We might also see the cross as a sanctuary, a place of safety where no enemy can reach us.

MYTHOLOGY AND HEROES

Joseph Campbell writes, "Mythologies are in fact the public dreams that move and shape societies." Think of your favorite television shows and movies; think of the current political situation. Can you describe the mythologies they each reflect? Do these "public dreams" reflect hope—or despair?

Celtic lore focused on the people's heroes. From the late Bronze Age to the Early Iron Age, Gaelic singer-sages retold tales of their heroes and demigods, Maeb, Cuchulain, Finn, Arthur, Brigid, and others. The heroes of the past were as real and present as their neighbors: The Celtic mind could not imagine a world that was not defined by larger-than-life heroes.

As individuals, we cannot choose the mythologies our society believes—but we *can* choose to honor and celebrate our own heroes, whether they are fictional or real-life. As you think of your favorite heroes—two of mine are Jean Luc Picard and Doctor. Who—can you see Jesus reflected in them? Can you allow these individuals to give you a new glimpse of Jesus, perhaps one you've never seen before? Are you surprised by what you see?

As you leave this exercise and go about your life, mentally bring your heroes—whoever they are—with you. Picture them as Jesus, holding high a cross. Turn to them whenever you encounter hopelessness and injustice in the world around you. Allow the cross to strengthen your resolve as you work to share Divine love with people and circumstances in your life.

Descending to the Inner Abyss

Swiss psychiatrist Carl Jung developed the concept of the shadow self, which he defined as the hidden, unconscious, and sometimes negative aspects of our being that we repress or deny. Jung taught that each person must confront their shadow self if they seek to grow, both in self-understanding and in their relationships with others.

As we come to understand the shadow, we don't defeat it or destroy it. "What if I should discover that the poorest of the beggars and the most impudent of offenders are all within me," wrote Jung. "And that I stand in need of the alms of my own kindness. That I, myself, am the enemy who must be loved—what then?"[330] To confront our shadow, we need to acknowledge its existence, become aware of its power, and then fully and lovingly engage with it.

The shadow self is not what Christians might call the "sinful man" that lives within us, despite our faith in Christ. Jung's shadow concept, since it holds *everything* we have rejected about ourselves, can also be a source of creativity, freedom, and empowerment; we not only face it but befriend it, and in doing so, we gain access to the shadow's power and potential. This process can be challenging and painful. We don't like to face unpleasant truths and emotions we've avoided, possibly for a lifetime, or projected onto others. Interacting with our shadow requires humility and perseverance; it's not easy, but more skillful living can be the result.

Jung suggested various methods and techniques for confronting our shadow selves, including dream analysis, active imagination, art therapy, and psychotherapy. These practices had ancient antecedents; more than a thousand years before Jung, the Desert Mothers and Fathers of the Middle East were already thinking deeply about soul healing, developing processes for psychic therapy. (The Greek word for "soul," *psyche,* is also our word for the inner self). These men and women, as they sought the Divine presence in the desert, far from society's distractions, understood that Christ's descent to Sheol mirrors the inward journey of descent into the shadow realms of the soul.

Saint Macarius the Great, one of the Desert Fathers, writes:

When you hear that the Lord in the old days . . . descended into Hell and performed a glorious deed, do not think that all these events are far from your soul. . . . The Lord comes into the souls that seek Him, into the depth of the heart's Hell, and there commands death, saying: "Release the imprisoned souls which have sought Me and which you hold by force." . . . God the Lord of everything enters caves and abodes in which death has settled . . . [just as] rain coming down from the sky reaches the nethermost parts of the earth, moistens and renews the roots there and gives birth to new shoots.[331]

A JOURNEY OF THE IMAGINATION

Allow me to suggest that the strength of the cross coupled with the imagery of Christ's descent may aid you should you dare to descend to those dark places within you. I will sketch out the bare bones of this exercise and leave room for you to flesh out your individual practice.

Hold on to a cross, literally, one that is easy to grip with rounded edges. I suggest wood rather than metal, since wood was once living tissue, while the cold weight of metal may imply that you're still holding a burden. For this exercise, the cross is a tangible companion, the comforting presence of Christ who descends with you, hand-in-hand.

While holding the cross, close your eyes and imagine the drama of Christ's descent:

his soul downward going, smashing the gates of the under-realm,
binding the enemy of Creation,
urging all the souls of departed humanity
to join him in glorious joy,
and leading the multitudes upward into
the all-healing light of God.

Then, in the cinema of your mind, replay this drama—but this time, see yourself alongside Christ, as you descend together into the hidden depths of your private consciousness. Imagine you find there the ancient souls of countless eons; look more closely and see that each soul carries an aspect of your self—and not just the parts you parade and prefer, but the hidden, the shameful, the less-than-glorious aspects of who you are. Look how your Companion gazes at these ashamed faces: Do you see his immense joy that he can set them each free? Watch, as Christ embraces each sad soul. Listen as whispers, "I love you so much," to each one of them.

Now, imagine that most of those trapped souls have slipped free into the open air; only a few remain, hanging back, lingering in the shadows. Can you give each soul a name, recognizing that each one is an aspect of you? You might give your lifelong belief that you're too fat the name of *Lotus* (someone lovely and perfect), or you could name the shame you feel over certain memories from your childhood *Michael* (someone valiant and strong).

Christ goes to each of these shadowed souls, and one by one, and puts his hands on their shoulders. He speaks for a few moments to each of them. Only you know what he says. Spend a moment here, listening to his words to each aspect of your shadow-self.

And finally, as you can in dreams, shift your consciousness from one character to another: Now you are Christ. You are breathing with his lungs, seeing what he sees, feeling what he feels. Can you sense the breath of Spirit affirming your worth? Can you see how beautiful you are in his eyes? Can you feel how much he loves you?

Take your time as you work through this exercise. Continue to think about it when you are done, perhaps journaling your insights and discoveries as they unfold. You can also return to it as many times as you need.

As Joseph Campbell knew, the shadowy secret caves within us may be the very places where "the treasures of life" are hidden. When we think we are stumbling, falling into times of confusion and suffering, in reality, we may be on the verge of discovering new light, new insight, new joy. "The very cave you are afraid to enter turns out to be the source of what you were looking for."[332]

Remember, Christ says to you, including your shadow:

You are beloved!
You are a valued part of me!
Arise now—for you are an inseparable part
of my reunited self—upward
into the all-encompassing embrace
of the most Holy and Passionate God,
the Life-Giver.

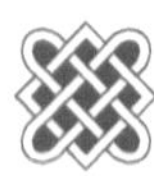

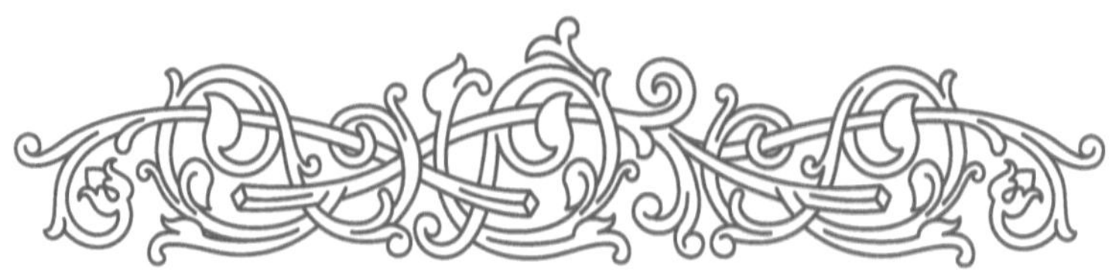

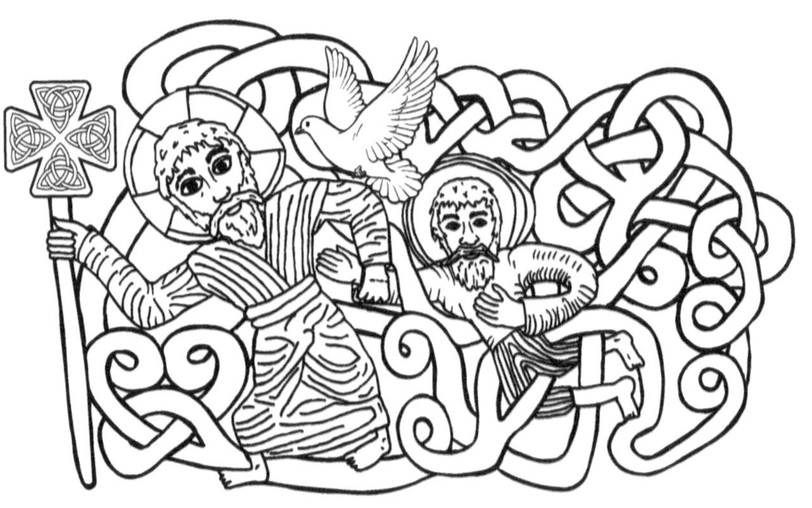

The Eardisley baptismal font shows Christ pulling Adam out of Hades.

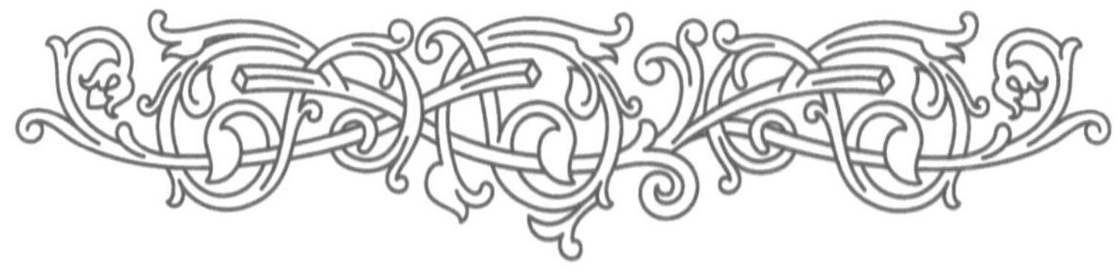

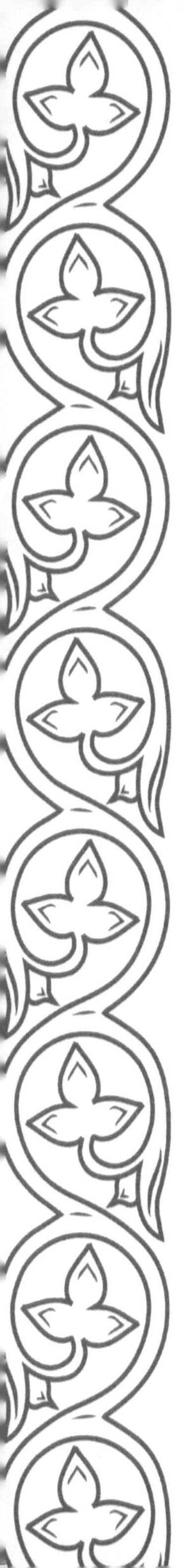

CHAPTER 11

Divine Love Sets Us Free

Some sat in darkness and in gloom,
prisoners in misery and in irons,
for they had rebelled against the words of God
and spurned the counsel of the Most High.
Their hearts were bowed down with hard labor;
they fell down, with no one to help.
Then they cried to Yahweh in their trouble,
and he saved them from their distress;
he brought them out of darkness and gloom,
and broke their bonds apart . . .
shatters the doors of bronze
and cuts in two the bars of iron.

PSALM 107:10–17

GOSPEL OF NICODEMUS[333]

ENCOUNTER

May 30, 2023:
Between Rabanal del Camino and
El Acebo on the Camino de Santiago

After walking for forty days and 600 kilometers on the Camino de Santiago, from France across the north of Spain, my wife Marsha and I came to the Cruz de Ferro (Iron Cross). It stood on a hilltop, surrounded by forests; God's presence there was palpable.

The Cruz de Ferro is one of the most ancient monuments on the Camino. The site on which it's built was likely a holy place, first for Iron Age Celts and then for Romans,[334] and then medieval Christians placed a wrought-iron cross high atop an ancient oak trunk. For centuries, pilgrims have carried stones from their homes to this place; they leave their stones at the foot of the cross to signify some form of inner release. Today, the cross is surrounded by a hill of stones that's some 23 feet high and 100 feet in diameter.[335]

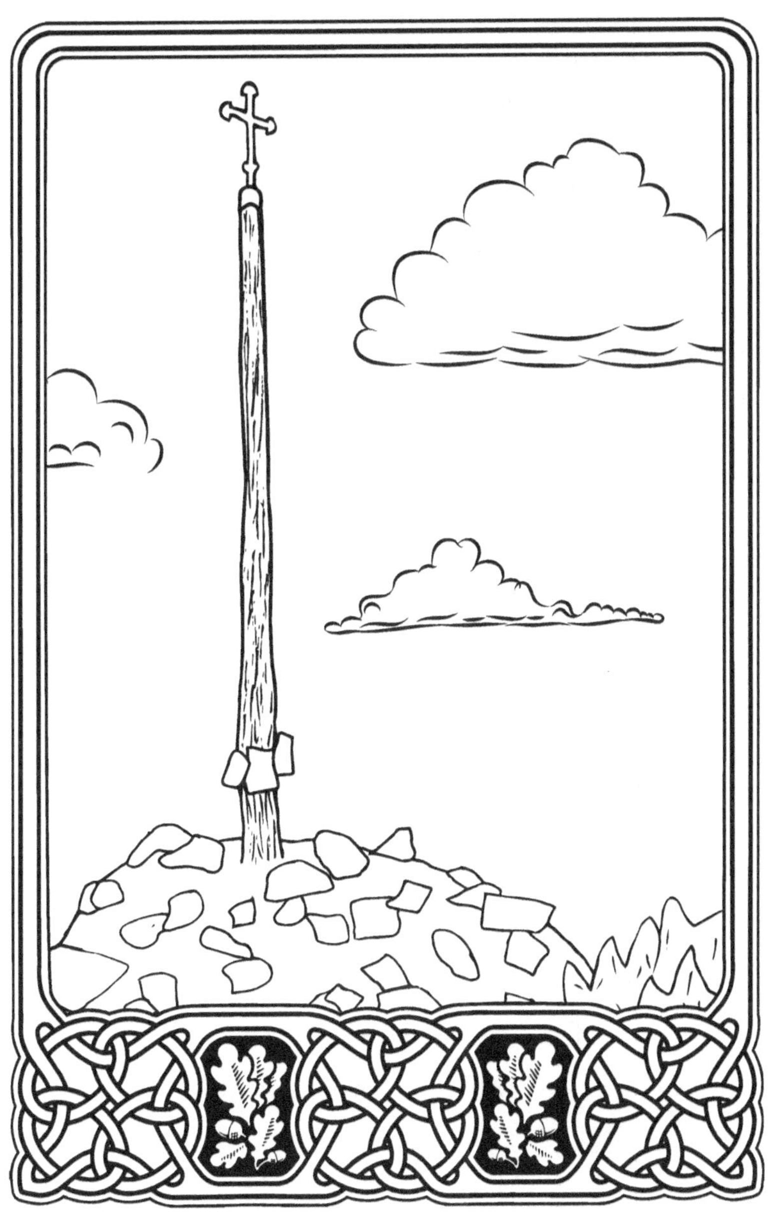

Months before, back in New York State, I had placed a smooth black stone from the Hudson River in my pack. As I walked the footsore miles, I pared off every ounce of weight from my pack that I did not need—but I kept that stone. The weight of the pack reminded me of *Pilgrim's Progress* and its hero, Christian, carrying the huge bundle of his sins as he journeyed toward the heavenly land.

Over the course of thirty years serving as a minister, I had internalized a load of hurt, bitterness, and anger over various conflicts and mistreatments. This was what the stone I carried represented to me. I knew that to continue serving God's people with a loving heart I needed to be freed from that baggage. On the stone, I had written 1 Peter 5:7, "Cast all your anxieties upon him for he cares for you."

I reached the hilltop and pulled the burden-stone from my pack. I found myself crying as I dropped onto my knees, praying silently: "Jesus, for thirty years I've taken things personally, carrying hurts and criticism on my shoulders and forgetting that it is *your* church, and you can take care of the conflicts. I choose to leave my anxieties here. I release the hurts of the past and leave them behind."

At last, I stood up and descended the hill of stones. I sank onto a nearby bench as I was again overcome by weeping. Then, as I sat there, I realized I felt inwardly lightened. In the following months, I returned to my pastoral duties with a markedly more carefree attitude. In a very real way, God had set me free.

Twentieth-Century United States: Imprisonment and Redemption

Rubin "Hurricane" Carter was a successful professional boxer when, on June 17, 1966, his life took a catastrophic turn. Two white men and a white woman were shot at a New Jersey bar—and Carter and another man, John Artis, were falsely accused and then convicted of the crimes, based on the testimony of two known criminals. They were each sentenced to life in prison.

From prison, Carter wrote his memoir and sent a copy to rock star Bob Dylan; in response, Dylan wrote a hit song that generated awareness of the injustice done to Carter. Finally, after two decades in prison, Carter and Artis were both released when a judge determined their convictions were based on racism rather than reason.

A few years later, the former boxer moved to Canada, where he lived with a group of people who had been activists for his freedom. With them, he worked as an advocate for others who were unjustly incarcerated. Doctors diagnosed Carter with prostate cancer in 2011, and Artis, who had remained friends with him for nearly fifty years, cared for him until he died in 2014.

In 1999, the film *The Hurricane*, starring Denzel Washington as Carter, dramatized the events of his life. That movie included a now-famous line: "Hate put me in prison. Love's gonna bust me out."[336]

DEEPENING

Love Busts Us Out

The great high crosses, covered with illustrations of biblical scenes, show surprisingly few portrayals of Christ's resurrection. Why? Because the real action of Christ's atonement—for Celtic Christians—took place not on Easter but on Holy Saturday.[337] These crosses obviously symbolize Christ and his saving work at Calvary, but they also pointed to an often hidden—though tremendously important—aspect of Christ's work. His descent into the underworld had a purpose. He was not only a warrior, come to defeat the forces of evil. Jesus was also a jailbreaker.

"Love's gonna bust me out" would be a great tagline to describe this event, which Christians, for the first 1,500 years of their faith, regarded as the turning point of history: the Harrowing of Hell. On Holy Saturday, Love busted out the souls the devil's hatred had imprisoned.

Then, according to this Old English poem,

> *The exiled wretches thronged, every one of them*
> *who were allowed to see that Victory-Child,*
> *Adam and Abraham, Isaac and Jacob,*
> *. . . Moses and David, Isaiah and Zacharias—*
> *many of the high-fathers, likewise an assembly of heroes,*
> *an army of wise men, a company of women,*
> *many, many women, an uncountable people.*[338]

The Harrowing of Hades—also known as the Descent into Hell, Holy Saturday, and the Conquest of Hell—is the belief that between the Saturday of Christ's death on the cross and the Sunday of his resurrection, when Christ descended into Sheol, he not only defeated death and the forces of evil; he also freed the souls languishing there. Even in churches that deny belief in the Harrowing of Hades, worshipers commonly repeat the Apostles' Creed's phrase, "he descended into hell."

Christ's descent into Hades took place on Saturday (the Jewish Sabbath). In some traditions—both Jewish and Christian—the Sabbath Day is very literally a day of rest (as in, *do nothing but sit around*), but the seventh day is also a day of *completion*, the day when God finished the work of Creation. Jews understand the Sabbath as a promise of Shalom, God's restored kin-dom, when damaged Creation has been repaired. When Jesus' soul journeyed down into the land of the dead on the Sabbath Day, he did what he had been doing all along in his earthly ministry: He set people free from their suffering. This is the meaning of the Harrowing of Hades.

In Middle English, a *harrow* (or *haru*) was a heavy wooden rake used both for harvesting and to turn over soil in preparation for planting new seed. Just as a farmer overturns soil for new life to grow, so Christ overturned Hades—and just as the farmer harvests the fruit of her labor, so Christ brings home souls.

Ancient Harrowing Accounts

This passage from one of Peter's epistles is the most extensive description of the Harrowing in the Christian scriptures:

> Christ also suffered for sins once for all, the righteous for the unrighteous, in order to bring you to God. He was put to death in the flesh but made alive in the spirit, in which also he went and made a proclamation to the spirits in prison, who in former times did not obey, when God waited patiently in the days of Noah, during the building of the ark.[339]

Note what Peter emphasizes: Christ preaches to those who "in former times did not obey." Later accounts of the descent imagine Christ addressing *righteous* souls in Hades—the saints and prophets of the Hebrew scriptures—but here, Peter spotlights the *unrighteous* nature of Christ's underworld audience and indicates they have the opportunity to accept Christ's invitation *after* earthly life has ended. As Jesus said during his earthly ministry, "I have not come to call the righteous, but sinners, to repentance."[340] Apparently, his mission extends into the afterlife.

Peter includes another description of the Harrowing in his epistle: "For this is the reason the gospel was proclaimed even to the dead, so that, though they had been judged in the flesh as everyone is judged, they might live in the spirit as God does."[341] Again, Peter emphasizes the opportunity for after-death conversion.

In the century before Christ, hope for deliverance from Sheol was strong, as indicated in 2 Esdras (an "apocryphal book" included in most Catholic Bibles but not Protestant), where the angel Uriel declares: "In Hades the chambers of the souls are like the womb. For just as a woman who is in labor makes haste to escape the pangs of birth, so also do these places hasten to give back those things who were committed to them."[342] Sheol—the common domain of all the dead, whether saints or sinners—was a womb waiting to deliver its inhabitants to a new quality of life!

For Christ's followers in the early centuries after his death and resurrection, this was too good a story to let it stop there; it was a drama that begged to be more fully scripted. Sculptors, poets, musicians, and writers applied their skills to the story. Within about a century after the event occurred, elaborations of the Harrowing were written in Hebrew, Ethiopic, Syriac, and Greek languages.[343]

The most detailed and important Harrowing account comes from the Gospel of Nicodemus, a document that was widely translated, copied, read, quoted, and artistically portrayed throughout the Christian world in the Early Middle Ages. Much of the medieval understanding of the Harrowing comes from this work.

In the Gospel of Nicodemus, Jesus appears at the gates of Hades, and a voice rings out: "Lift up, O Princes, your gates, and be ye lifted up ye doors of hell, and the King of Glory shall come in."[344] The gates break open, and the "King of Glory trampled upon death, and laid hold on Satan the prince and delivered him unto the power of Hell, and drew Adam to him in his own brightness."[345]

And now, the prison break commences. Christ takes Adam by the hand, leads him out of Hades—with all the souls following—and then delivers them all into the care of the Archangel Michael for safe passage to Heaven.

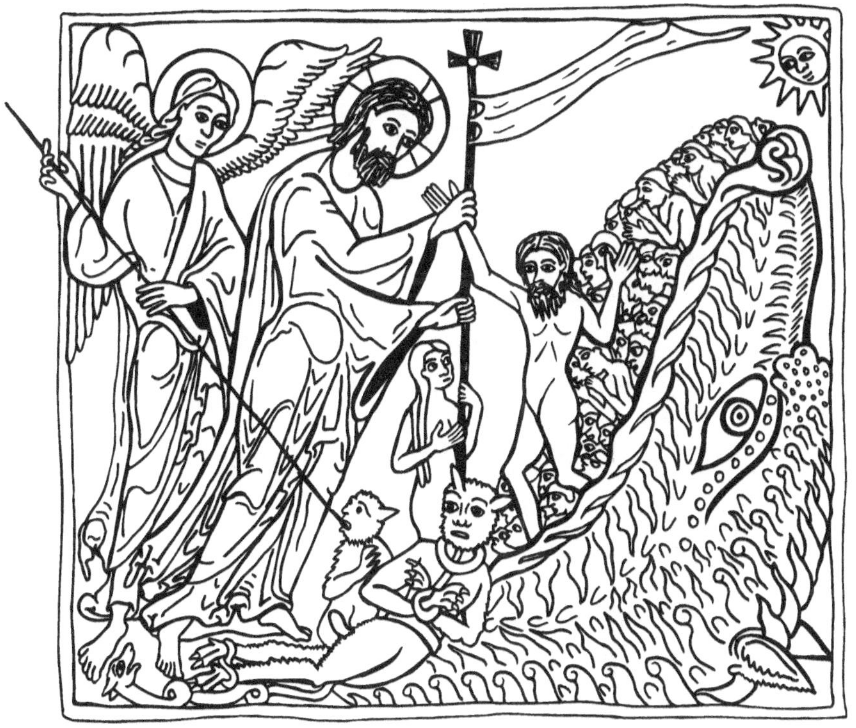

The 11th-century Harley Psalter contains this image of the Harrowing of Hades.

The Harrowing inspired other retellings, especially in the Early Middle Ages. The Irish poet Blathmac, for instance, writing between 750 and 770, retells Christ's descent as a combat with Satan:

It is he who suffered on the cross, who was buried beneath cold stone, and who went after that on a visit to Hell. He was victorious from fighting that, his battle with the devil. Miserable devil, his strength was crushed; a great prey was taken from him. It is your son, Jesus, who cast seven chains about his neck and bound him (no falsehood!) in the depths of his dwelling. He then returned to his body when he cast off the great attack, and he arose (bright tidings!) on Easter after three days.[346]

John Scotus Eriugena also describes Christ's conquest of Satan and Hades:

> *The great light of the world flashes triumphant out of Hell;*
> *dying death is dumbfounded by the beginnings of life.*
> *The furies bound, the fates gather round from all sides,*
> *astonished by the doleful moans of the Styx.*
> *Then the prince of the abyss seeks the accustomed arms*
> *by which he subdued the human race to his power.*
> *But as soon as he sees the broken threshold in crumbling ruins*
> *he flees in shock and terror to the ruins of his house.*

As Satan runs through subterranean corridors, Christ seizes him, chains him, and then "dashed him completely and crushed his head." For Eriugena, Christ is an action hero, demolishing the gates, running down the devil, and giving him a smashing blow.

A less violent account of the Harrowing comes from the seventh-century Pseudo-Epiphanius. His homily "On the Great and Holy Saturday" contains this dialogue between Christ and Adam, which takes place after Christ entered Sheol:

> The Lord enters among them bearing his conquering
> cross . . . [and] taking Adam by the hand, he says: "Rise up,
> you who sleep, and Christ will enlighten you. I am your God

but, because of you, I became your son; because of you, *and
all those descended from you*, I now speak with authoritative
command: To the prisoners, Depart; To those in darkness,
Be enlightened; To those who are asleep, Awaken.

I command you: Awake sleeper! I did not create you for
this, that you remain dead. Arise my likeness, made in my
own image. Arise, let us leave here. For you are in me and I
in you, we are but one undivided person.[347]

The Harrowing of Hades also inspired visual art in a variety of
mediums. My personal favorite is the twelfth-century carving on the
baptismal font of the Church of Saint Mary Magdalene on the Welsh
border. (The drawing at the beginning of this chapter is based on this
carving.) It shows Christ, with the cross in his right hand and the Holy
Spirit nestled on his shoulder, grabbing Adam by the wrist and pulling
him forcefully from the netherworld's clutches. Vines (or tentacles)
wrap around Adam's legs to hold him back, but the size and stance of
the Christ figure leave no doubt in the viewer's mind that Christ will
indeed pull him free.

You may be asking: What happened to the people who arrived
in Sheol *after* the Harrowing? Was this a "one-and-done" deal? What
if some poor soul arrived in the afterlife just after Christ ascended?
Would she ask a nearby demon, "Why is this enormous place empty?"
And would the sniggering devil tell her, "You're just a minute late I'm
afraid. The Son of God came down and busted everyone out—millions of captives—and they're all gone up to heaven now. Too bad for
you, Missy. You missed out!"

The fourteenth-century mystic Julian of Norwich was definite in
her answer to this concern: The Harrowing is ongoing, "for as long
as it is needed."[348] The Gospel of Nicodemus also addresses this issue,
saying that, as Christ is about to leave Hades,

all the saints of God asked the Lord to leave as a sign of victory the sign of His holy cross in the lower world, that its most impious officers might not retain as an offender any one whom the Lord had absolved. And so it was done. And the Lord set His cross in the midst of Hades, which is the sign of victory, and which will remain even to eternity.[349]

Based on this, the ancient Celts and Saxons believed if anyone found themselves in the very depths of the underworld, the cross would be waiting for them, offering hope and salvation even there.

In the final book of the Christian scriptures, the Book of Revelation, Christ comes to John on the Island of Patmos; Jesus no longer appears as a suffering mortal but as glorified and risen, radiant and irresistible. He says to John, "Do not be afraid; I am the First and the Last and the Living One. I was dead, and see, I am alive forever and ever, and I have the keys of Death and of Hades."[350]

Apparently, when Jesus left Sheol, he took the keys with him. Now he has free access to the underworld—and can take from there whomever he wishes, whenever he wishes, for all eternity. As the psalmist says, "If I make my bed in Sheol, you [God] are there."[351]

These depictions of Christ as the strong warrior-hero we described in the last chapter, someone who triumphantly sets the captives free, are very different from the images of the crucifixion prevalent in Western art from the Late Middle Ages through to today. These later images portrayed the crucified Christ with his body twisted and tortured, his face contorted in agony, ribs pushing out of his emaciated chest, blood pouring from his wounds. From the fourteenth century until now, artists have sought to show us Christ as a sacrifice, a victim, rather than a champion.

Why did portrayals of Christ's crucifixion shift from conquering hero to tortured sacrifice? They changed because of a major theological shift, based on a different understanding of Christ's work of atonement.

The Meaning of Christ's Atonement

When we break down the parts of *atonement*, we can see its original meaning: *at-one-ment*. Atonement heals the divide between God and humanity; as the apostle Paul proclaimed, "God was in Christ reconciling the world to himself."[352]

But while the older meaning of *atonement* was "reconciliation, the creation of harmony and unity," in the early 1600s, a new definition replaced this understanding. Then, as today, *atonement* was understood as "the satisfaction or reparation for wrong or injury, propitiation to an offended party."[353] This changing definition reflected a change in Christians' understanding of Christ's work on the cross.

The Wideness of God's Mercy

From the second to the twelfth centuries, Christ's preaching to the dead was accepted Christian doctrine for most Christians in both the Eastern and Western churches. It was practically unquestioned, since it dovetailed so perfectly with what they knew about Divine mercy. In the centuries since then, however, many Christians lost their confidence in God's unconditional love.

Augustine of Hippo (354–430) was the one who changed the way Christians in the West thought about their faith. He limited the wideness of mercy expressed in the Harrowing of Hades, insisting that Christ delivered from Sheol only righteous Jews, the ones who had looked forward to Christ's prophesied coming. [354]

Differing Doctrines

This narrowing of the Harrowing was based on two new doctrines that Augustine formed: original sin and predestination. Unlike other thinkers of his time (most notably the Welsh theologian Pelagius), Augustine believed every person is born sinful and deserves to be damned. To show some measure of mercy, God "predestined" a small minority of humanity for salvation and caused them to repent and be baptized. Augustine's new theology fit well with the recent adoption of Christianity as the official Imperial religion; now, just as all people should be subject to Rome's Imperial decrees, they also had to submit to Rome's church and its creeds.

Meanwhile, the Eastern churches continued to teach that Christ's harrowing rescued *all* souls. The Celts in Britain and Ireland, geographically distanced from the ecclesiastical authorities in both Constantinople and Rome, heard both sides of the story. In Continental Europe, Augustine's influence stamped out the teaching of Pelagius, but in Ireland and throughout the other Celtic lands, his ideas remained popular. Celtic Christians did quote Augustine, but they quoted Pelagius even more. This meant that Celtic Christians' views varied considerably.

Pelagius taught that humans are born as they were created, in a state of original goodness,[355] and his Celtic followers affirmed that all souls in Hades could accept Christ's offer of forgiveness in the after-life.[356] Christ's Gaelic followers sought to emulate the Egyptian saints (as we discussed in an earlier chapter), and the wider salvation achieved in the Harrowing was one factor that drew them to Coptic theology.

John Scotus Eriugena (John the Irishman from Ireland), the most influential Christian theologian of the ninth century, wrote that "all of human nature will be called to return to its original angelic status into Paradise."[357] At the same time, Roman church authorities did exert their influence in Celtic lands, especially after the Synod of Whitby in 664 CE, so Augustine's more limited view of God's mercy had a Celtic following that grew larger over the centuries.

Still, the older perspective was never completely erased. Later in the Middle Ages, the mystic Julian of Norwich describes the Harrowing as something that's constantly ongoing. Jesus' life force, she writes,

> could not be contained by this world, and so it overflowed into Hell, where it burst Hell open and delivered all who were separated from God and brought them home to Heaven. . . . Those who have lived in the past, those who are living now, and those who will live in the future are all revitalized . . . ; not one from that number will miss out on the life it gives.[358]

In the nineteenth century, one Christ-follower reminded the church:

> *There's a wideness in God's mercy,*
> *like the wideness of the sea.*
> *There's a kindness in God's justice,*
> *which is more than liberty.*
>
> *But we make God's love too narrow*
> *by false limits of our own,*
> *and we magnify its strictness*
> *with a zeal God will not own.*
>
> *For the love of God is broader*
> *than the measures of the mind,*
> *and the heart of the Eternal*
> *is most wonderfully kind.*[359]

What the Devil?

For early Christians, the process of atonement may have been straight-forward: The devil caused all humanity's sin and suffering, but Christ came "to destroy the works of the devil."[360]

Throughout the Gospels, a being referred to in Greek as *satanas* (the adversary) or *diabolis* (the slanderer) seems to refer to a particular, individual being—the personification of evil—and that is how we usually think of the devil today. As second- and third-century Christians struggled to make sense of their faith, however, they added new interpretations; Origen, for example, believed God would ultimately redeem the individual being known as "the devil" (which Origen was the first to call "Lucifer"), since the principle of evil and death was separate from the devil's essential identity.[361]

These earlier Christians focused on a more abstract concept of evil—as the absence of all good—but by the Early Middle Ages, many theologians wanted a more concrete and exterior image for the enemy that breaks our unity with God and the Way of Christ. In Europe, Christian ideas combined with Pagan, creating a vivid folklore about the devil.[362] This was the context in which the Celts became Christ-followers.

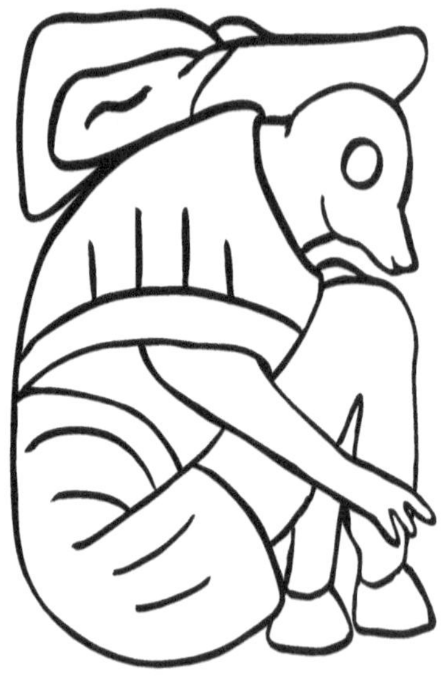

In the mid-twentieth century, when the stone was less worn, archeologists identified this image on the base of the North Cross at Castledermot in Ireland as the devil (based on its bird head and hooved feet, characteristic of other Celtic portrayals of the devil). If that's the case, it portrays the devil dead, bound with grave bands, and buried in the crouched position of Pagan burials, "a profound spiritual story, symbolic of the triumph of Christ over Satan."[363]

However, with only a few exceptions, they seldom portrayed the devil on their high crosses.[364] Instead, the ancient Celts and Saxons more often focused on the strength required to smash the walls of hell, as described in another Old English poem:

> *Then the Master of Humanity hurried to the journey—*
> *the Helmet of Heaven wished to break down*
> *and humiliate the hell-walls, to hurl down*
> *the majesty of that capital, cruelest of all kings. . . .*
> *The locks fell down, . . . the king rode onwards.[365]*

Still, until the end of the eleventh century, most Christians believed Christ triumphed over a very real enemy when he harrowed hell. This idea held sway until Archbishop Anselm of Canterbury popularized the notion of *substitutionary atonement.*

Anselm's theology shifted the emphasis away from a battle between Christ and the devil. He argued that humanity had rebelled against their rightful overlord, and so all humans were born deserving damnation (which Anselm believed to be a state of everlasting conscious torture). God could not forgive sinners, according to Anselm, because the rules of universal justice are unwavering; God could only forgive someone if that person had lived a faultless life. To save humanity from their sins, God sent Jesus to live sinlessly; then, God tortured and killed Jesus so that justice would be satisfied. Christ was the *substitute* who was punished in the place of sinful humanity, redeeming the sin of Adam.

In a time when the emerging merchant economy threatened feudal power structures, the elite classes no doubt welcomed the concept of substitutionary atonement as a reminder to their "underlings" to remain in fealty to earthly lordship. This newer doctrine—which became integral to Protestantism, especially in its Evangelical form—emphasized a legal rather than relational understanding of Christ's achievement. Many Evangelicals today would probably be surprised to learn that the earlier understanding of atonement differed from their own.

As C. S. Lewis remarked, however, "Any theories we build up as to how Christ's death did all this are, in my view, quite secondary: mere plans or diagrams to be left alone if they do not help us, and even if they do help us, not to be confused with the thing itself."[366]

No Chance in Hell? (Or Is It Hades?)

The concept of rescuing souls from hell might puzzle many Christians today, at least those who think of hell as a place of unending torment. If God sent people to hell, why would Jesus rescue them? And where would this cosmic drama take place?

People often refer to the Harrowing of *Hell*, but a more accurate wording would be the Harrowing of *Sheol* (the Hebrew Bible's word for the abode of the dead) or *Hades* (the Greek word used to translate *Sheol*). Most English versions of the Bible translate *Hades* (and the related word *Gehenna*) as "hell," a word that entered the English language from an early Germanic word that meant "a concealed or hidden place; a cave or cavern; a place of safety" (definitely not what we connect with *hell* today!). The name of the Norse Goddess *Hel* (meaning "someone who covers up or hides something") may have reinforced the new English meaning,[367] since Hel ruled over the evil dead in the lowest underworld. Our modern-day understanding of *hell* as a place of eternal torment has come a long way from the ancient one!

This is one reason I prefer to use *Sheol* or *Hades* when speaking of Christ's liberating action on Holy Saturday. Our English word *hell* is hugely laden with preconceptions (and misconceptions). We *assume* hell is a bad place, we *assume* it is only for sinners, we *assume* it is a place of everlasting torture, and we *assume* there is no escape from it—yet none of these assumptions are explicit in either the biblical scriptures or the most ancient Christian teachings. Our views of hell are largely based on the writing and preaching of the High Middle Ages, popularized by Dante. But if our modern concept of hell is not biblical, what is?

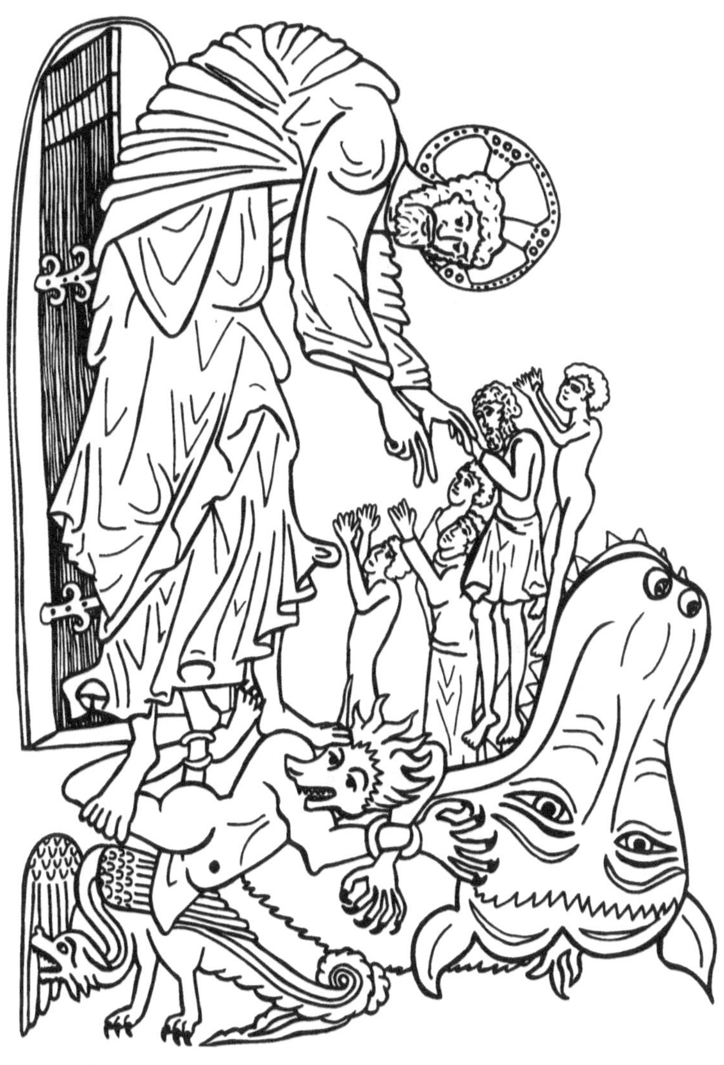

Another image of the Harrowing of Hades, this one from the 11th-century Tiberius Psalter, which was produced at an abbey in Winchester shortly after the Norman Conquest of England.

The concept of Sheol evolved throughout the time when the scriptures were written; in earlier portions of the Hebrew Bible, the word referred to the grave or the state of having passed away in death, and in later biblical texts, it took on the meaning of "the afterlife" of the "abode of the dead."

The Gospels' writers (and Jesus in his recorded teachings) assumed the understandings of their time. Sheol was *not* exclusively a place for sinful and unredeemed souls of the dead (as is presumed by our word *hell*). It was simply the Jewish way of saying the *afterlife*. Matt Arnold, a leading scholar on this topic, explains in his book *The Invisible Dimension*: "Sheol was where *all the dead, good or bad*, were believed to enter upon passing into the afterlife" (italics are mine).[368] The ancient writer of the Book of Ecclesiastes expresses this belief: "The same fate comes to all, to the righteous and the wicked, to the good and the evil, to the clean and the unclean, to those who sacrifice and those who do not sacrifice."[369]

In the scriptures' worldview, three large realms comprise the universe: The realm of Heaven is above the Earth and is the unseen realm of God and the Divine's servant-creatures, the angels; Earth is the familiar material realm of human habitation; and the afterlife is beneath the Earth, the unseen realm of all who have departed this life (both the righteous and the unrighteous). This three-tier cosmology can be thought of in spatial terms, as the ancients did, or in more current thinking, as overlapping dimensions.

According to first-century Jewish understanding, the inhabitants of Sheol dwell in differing subdivisions (or different circumstances) determined by their earthly decisions and actions. In the centuries before Christ, Jewish writings provided something like a tour book of the afterlife's differing neighborhoods of the afterlife (for example, 2 Enoch 7:75–101 details ten separate abodes for souls in the afterlife).

The books of the Christian scripture do not include elaborate explanations of Sheol's compartments, but they do refer to the underworld's regions in a way that's consistent with Jewish writings of their time. In Luke 16, for example, when Jesus describes the separate accommodations of Lazarus and the poor man, he's assuming the contemporary understanding that both souls are in Sheol but in separate compartments. Paradise (also known as "Abraham's Bosom") was a beautiful place for people who followed God's ways during their lives. Meanwhile, people who made poor choices in life were confined to Gehenna. This last name also refers to a specific earthly location, the valley of Gehenna, Jerusalem's garbage dump, as well as the place where ancient people were said to have sacrificed children; clearly, the background implications indicate this afterlife region was less than pleasant. Finally, when the word *Hades* is used in the Greek Christian scriptures, it refers broadly to *all* of Sheol—encompassing both Gehenna and Paradise (as well as any other regions of the afterlife).

Even at its best, though, life in Sheol lacked joy's full-bodied completion. Sheol was figuratively and literally beneath the pleasures of earthly life. Some Hebrew scriptures indicate that inhabitants of Sheol—even the departed righteous—could not experience the union with God that is every soul's ultimate satisfaction (although Psalm 139 tells us the Divine is present even in Sheol).

We all have "Sheol moments" (or longer periods) in our lives, times when life seems dim and flat, when we feel apathetic and weak. But the light of Christ burst open Sheol. "The people who . . . lived in a land of deep darkness—on them light has shined."[370]

APPLICATIONS FOR TODAY

The Powers of Evil

Does the story of Christ's Harrowing still have value in a worldview uncertain of supernatural beings? Although I personally believe in the spirit world, you don't need to believe in a literal devil to gain spiritual insight and comfort from this chapter's focus. We certainly don't need to imagine Old Nick with red leotards and pitchfork (which is as ridiculous as picturing God wearing a long robe and white beard)!

Late-twentieth-century theologians suggested we think of the Bible's "powers and principalities" not as horned-and-tailed fiery figures but as systemic powers of oppression—corporations, legal codes, authoritarian governments, misleading media—forces bigger than any person and more damaging than the actions of any single individual. If you think of "the devil" as the "forces of oppression," the imagery of Christ defeating the arch-enemy retains a liberating power.

Still, even in our day, evil often takes an anthropomorphic shape in our stories and conversations; Thanos destroys half of the Marvel Universe, the Balrog casts Gandalf into the abyss, the Sith seek to take control of a galaxy far away, and politicians make clear that their opponents are the epicenter of evil. The names change but the monomyth remains the same.

The ancient belief in Christ's Harrowing is a way of saying, "The way to God's heart through faith is always open—in mortal life and beyond." Christ's descent into the death-realm extends the proclamation and invitation of God's boundless love to every member of Adam and Eve's race. No one is forced to migrate from Sheol to God's presence against their will, but the glorious and transforming beatific vision is revealed in all its enticing wonder to every human.

Praying for the Dead

If the dead are still conscious, "alive" and aware in some form we cannot yet fully imagine, then it makes sense we should continue to pray for them. The ancient Celts, living in an everyday world that contained what we call the "supernatural" as well as the natural, did not feel separated from their loved ones who had passed through the membrane of death; they continued to feel their love and support, and they extended that same love and support through prayer.

An early Celtic Christian story tells of a spirit from hell who visits a "holy elder" and asks for prayer. The elder agrees and prays for the lost soul for twenty days. At the end of that time, the soul reappears, this time gleaming with light. He recounts the terror and suffering he experienced in hell, and then he tells the elder, "Your prayer has freed me from the land of curses." Full of gratitude, he blesses the elder, and "after that he departed with the angels, radiant as the sun."[371]

C. S. Lewis was also a believer in praying for the dead. He writes:

> Of course I pray for the dead. The action is so spontaneous, so all but inevitable, that only the most compulsive theological case against it would deter me. And I hardly know how the rest of my prayers would survive if those for the dead were forbidden. At our age the majority of those we love best are dead. What sort of intercourse with God would I have if what I love best were unmentionable to Him?[372]

If you're Catholic, you will feel quite comfortable praying for the dead; it's an established part of your tradition. Many Protestants, however, believe that once a person is dead, there's no point praying for them: If we leave this world in a state of union with God, says this theology, then we are in Heaven and have no more need of prayer—and by the same token, if we die while turning our backs on God, then we will spend all eternity in "hell," where prayer can no longer reach us.

Lewis, however, believed "the fires of hell" were not punishment but a part of the soul's restoration. He writes:

> I assume that the process of purification will normally involve suffering. Partly from tradition; partly because most real good that has been done me in this life has involved

[suffering]. I can well believe that . . . [t]he treatment given will be the one required, whether it hurts little or much.

He then goes on to liken the afterlife purification process to the experience of being worked on by a dentist—something intended entirely for one's healing despite the possibility of being unpleasant.[373]

As Lewis points out, if we pray that people will be healed (physically and spiritually) in this life, should we not pray just as much for their growth in the life beyond?

PRAYER FOR THE DEAD

If you're not familiar with the concept of praying for the dead, but you'd like to add it to your spiritual practice, you may find the following prayer helpful:

O Living One,

Your power brings us to birth,

Your providence guides our lives,

and by Your command, we return to dust.

And yet, Gracious Majesty,

those who die still live in Your presence.

Their lives change but do not end.

I pray in hope for my family,

relatives, and friends,

and for all the dead known to You alone.

In company with Christ,

who died and now lives,

may they rejoice in Your kingdom,

Freedom

God's gonna bust you out.

That's the central message of this chapter. If you're feeling trapped by some aspect of yourself or your life, Christ is planning a jailbreak. If you're scared about death, Jesus has taken care of that too; his standard, the cross, is planted firmly in death's realm, offering an eternal way out.

As the Christian scripture says: "For freedom Christ has set us free. Stand firm, therefore, and do not submit again to a yoke of slavery." Wherever Spirit is, there is freedom.[375]

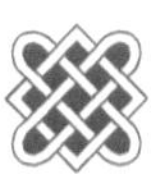

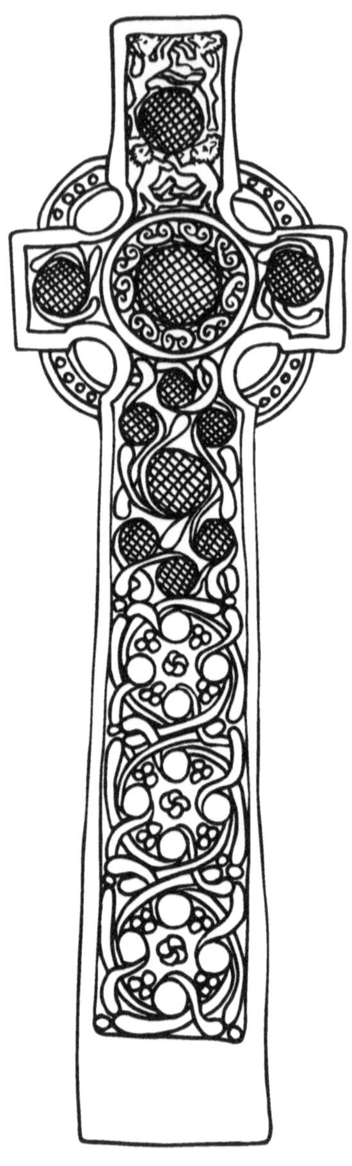

*St. Martin's Cross on the Isle of Iona, standing more than 4 meters tall,
is dedicated to Martin of Tours, who was much venerated in the Celtic lands.
It is thought to date from the end of the 8th or beginning of the 9th century.*

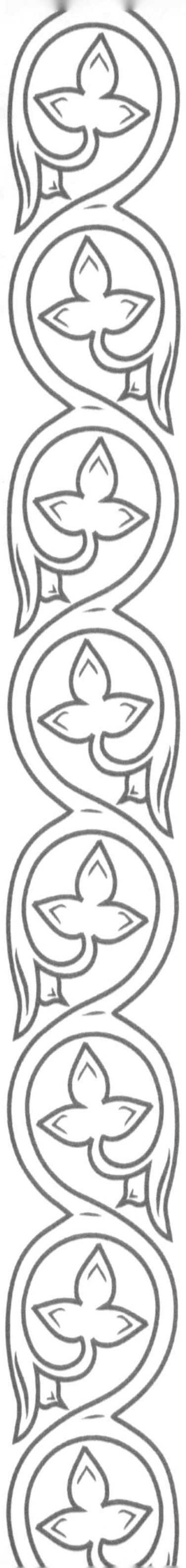

CHAPTER 12

Cosmic Wholeness Embraces a Threatened World

*With all wisdom and insight God
has made known to us
the mystery of the Divine mind,
finding pleasure in the work of Christ,
a plan for the fullness of time,
to gather up all things in Christ,
things in heaven and things on earth.*

EPHESIANS 1:8–10[377]

*Behold the orb that shines with the rays of the sun,
which the cross of salvation
spreads from its height,
embracing the earth, the sea, the
winds and the sky
and everything else believed to exist far away.*

JOHN SCOTUS ERIUGENA (NINTH CENTURY)[378]

ENCOUNTER

May of 2009: Iona, Scotland

When I stepped off a ferry onto an island, it was one small step. But my emotions reacted almost as if this were humankind's great leap onto the Moon.

For a very long time, I had dreamed of treading on the Holy Isle of Iona, the ancient home of druids and Saint Columba, and the burial place of medieval kings and saints. Now that I was finally here, the colors seemed brighter; the air seemed fresher. My heightened senses told me, "This is a thin place indeed."

Not long after disembarking onto the fabled island, I stood gazing up at Saint Martin's Cross in front of the abbey. It stood tall and proud, fourteen feet above the hallowed ground, twelve hundred years old, its sculptured images rounded by time.

Peter Stanford, author of the book *If These Stones Could Talk*, tells us:

> When we stand before fittings and furnishings that have
> stood there for a thousand years . . . there is an invitation to
> join the long chain that links us to those who were once in
> exactly the same spot. This is where we come from.[380]

Gazing at Saint Martin's Cross that bright, crisp morning on Iona, I thought about the people who had stood in this same spot for more than a thousand years and how the world has changed from their time to ours.

When this cross was erected, the global population was around 220 million; now it is more than thirty-six times that amount. If a medieval pilgrim decided to travel from Iona to Jerusalem, it would take months; nowadays, it can be done in less than twenty-four hours. The Northern Hemisphere was merely a fable in the Early Middle Ages, and knowledge of Asia and Sub-Saharan Africa mostly consisted of far-fetched rumors. Today, we have nearly instant access to information from around the globe.

The world now is connected in ways that would seem like the mightiest magic to the people who inhabited Iona in its monastic heyday. Long-distance exchange of funds, knowledge, and correspondence was virtually impossible in the Middle Ages. The combined knowledge of all the medieval libraries wouldn't hold a candle to the vast range of information most people in the twenty-first century can access on their phones. Even impoverished people in the twenty-first century's developed world enjoy luxuries of lighting, heating, communications, entertainment, plumbing, and transportation exceeding that of the ancient past's elite classes.

Yet the promethean advances of the last thousand years have not made our world into a paradise. In fact, a sense of global anxiety is growing, due to the threats of climate crisis, warfare, nuclear arms, and changes wrought by rapidly changing technology. As the Reverend Dr. Martin Luther King Jr. said, "Our scientific power has outrun our spiritual power. We have guided missiles and misguided men."[381] A 2022 report to the United Nations warns bluntly: "Humankind is making the world an increasingly insecure and precarious place."[382]

Two thousand years ago, the apostle Paul wrote to fellow Christ-followers in the Greek city of Corinth:

When I came to you, brothers and sisters, I did not come proclaiming the testimony of God to you with superior speech or wisdom. For I decided to know nothing among you except Jesus Christ and him crucified.

In Paul's reckoning, he went on to say, the message of the cross was "the power of God" adequate for all human need.[383] Could he still say that today, were he living in the twenty-first century with all its danger and stress?

In this final chapter, I want to answer a daunting question: *Do these ancient stone monuments hold a message pertinent to the global and existential challenges facing humanity in our time?*

DEEPENING

A Belief Adequate for Our Time?

Paul Dirac, an expert in quantum mechanics, explains a contemporary view of reality: "Pick a flower on Earth and you move the farthest star."[384] Not only is everything interrelated, but all things may also share consciousness. Current scientific speculation affirms that the universe is composed not of discrete material substances, as we previously supposed, but of inseparably entangled energy fields. Some physicists go so far to say that the universe's building blocks are consciousness, rather than physical matter.[385] A scientific universe of melded mind and matter: Who would have thought of such a thing?

Well, actually, similar ideas have been around for a very long time. The pre-Socratic Greek philosopher Heraclitus recognized a Being whose consciousness held all things together; he called this unitive Being the Logos.[386] Centuries after Heraclitus' time, the brilliant Jewish mystic-teacher John the Evangelist riffed off Heraclitus' philosophy when he explained Christ's Divine-and-human nature:

"In the beginning was the Word [in Greek, *Logos*], and the Word was with God, and the Word was God. . . . All things came into being through him."[387]

An early expression of the unitive, conscious universe is the classical concept of panentheism, the belief that all things (*pan*) are in (*en*) God (*theos*). The apostle Paul affirmed this reality: "In [God] we live and move and have our being."[388] Celtic Christians of the Early Middle Ages also expressed this view; Saint Ninian's eighth-century catechism, for example, says, "Perceive the eternal Word of God [*Logos*] reflected in every plant and insect, every bird and animal, and every man and woman."[389] John Scotus Eriugena, the most influential Christian theologian of the ninth century, taught panentheism as well; he believed the whole of reality is God.[390]

Our pre-modern spiritual ancestors achieved insight into the real nature of things not through scientific experiments and mathematical formulas but through contemplative practices. Mystics, realizing the human intellect's shortfalls, sought to experience God directly—and when they did so, they found God in the material fabric of all things around them. As medieval mystic Angela of Foligno wrote, "The world is pregnant with God!"[391]

Ilia Delio, an exceptional thinker who combines the wisdom of Christian mysticism with the expertise of a scientist, tells us: "In the future the only religion possible is the religion which will teach us to recognize, love, and serve with passion the universe (i.e. the Whole) of which we form a part."[392] In other words, the religion that will adequately serve humanity's future is one that not only recognizes connection and widespread consciousness but that also teaches us to *love and serve* our interwoven reality.

In light of this growing awareness about the nature of reality, is the symbolism of the Celtic crosses, as we have discussed throughout this book, outdated? Do ancient Celtic crosses hold only historical and anthropological information, rather than any timeless truth? Or do the sacred stones impart meaning that's adequate to anchor our faith through the twenty-first century? Can they "teach us to recognize, love, and serve with passion the universe"? I believe when we turn to scripture, looking for the original meanings hidden in our English translations, we can find the answer to these questions; after all, the artists who created the Celtic crosses shaped them to reflect scripture's deepest meanings.

The most famous Bible verse in modern Christianity, John 3:16, says, "God so loved the world that he gave his only Son." The word translated "world" is the Greek word *cosmos*, which is still used in the English language in its wider meaning of "the universe." The Greek word denotes something that is "orderly," or "arranged," a reminder of the ancient philosophers who intuited the existence of a universal consciousness ordering the universe. The word "loved" is a form of the Greek word *agape*, denoting love that is unconditional and unselfish. John the Evangelist saw the universe in its entirety enfolded in loving Divine consciousness.

Likewise, Paul affirms: "In Christ God was reconciling the world to himself."[393] Again, the Greek word translated "world" is *cosmos*, with the same meaning of expansiveness and conscious connectedness as in John 3:16. Paul says that in Christ, God connected again (Greek, *katalasso*) the cosmos. This acknowledges the forces of dis-harmony in God's creation, while affirming that Divine consciousness seeks harmony, beauty, and mutual well-being (*shalom* in the Hebrew language). On the cross, God worked to restore Creation's original wholeness.

The Christian scriptures point to the cross as the embodiment of a theology adequate for our troubled times' planet-wide challenges. The cross affirms that Divine love unites all beings within the vast matrix of our world. The creators of the Celtic crosses recognized this universal message and expressed it in their work. As a result, these ancient monuments of Ireland and the British Isles convey a life-affirming message for our imperiled and ideologically fractured twenty-first century.

Embracing *All* Creation

Many writers have sought to summarize the symbolic meaning of the wheel cross, offering a great variety of interpretations. Most of these theories lack a primary source that's contemporaneous with the time and place of the ancient Celtic crosses, one that explicitly states the meaning of the symbol. Lacking such evidence, we should consider all these theories with a healthy skepticism.

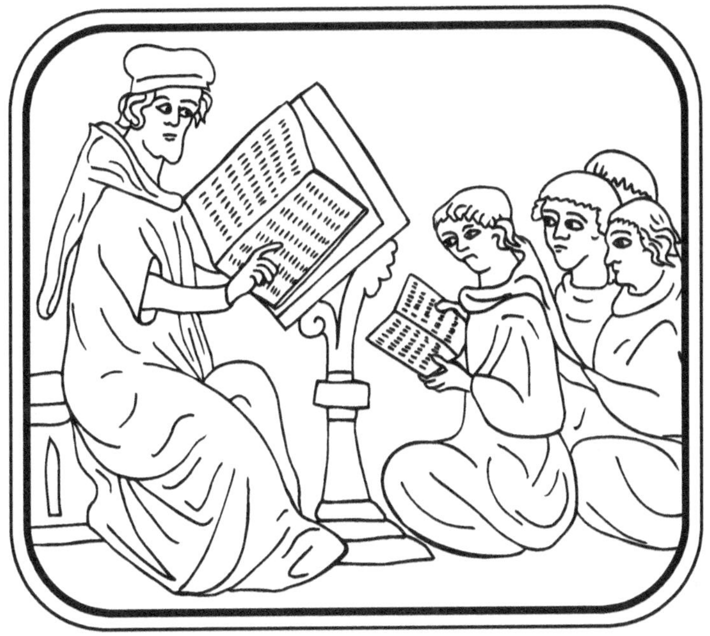

A medieval illumination shows a monk teaching, demonstrating the importance of scholarly study during the Early Middle Ages.

As far as I have been able to ascertain, only one source from the early medieval Celtic world explicitly tells what the encircled cross signifies. And while it is only one voice, it is authoritative, since it comes from the great ninth-century theologian, John Scotus Eriugena.

Eriugena was an intellectual tour de force. Twentieth-century philosopher Bertrand Russell describes Eriugena as "the most astonishing person of the ninth century."[394] Later medieval mystics Meister Eckhart and Nicholas of Cusa noted Eriugena's influence on their spiritual development.[395] He was influential in the history of Christian thought as (in Russell's words) "a mystic who emphasizes the ultimate unity . . . of the entire creation with God."[396]

We could not ask for a better interpreter of the early medieval Irish crosses than Eriugena. Not only was he a genius, an individual born and shaped in the heart of Irish Christian thought and practice, but he lived at the time when the most spectacular of the Irish high crosses were erected.

In a poem written in the mid-ninth century, Eriugena wrote,

> *Behold the orb that shines with the rays of the sun,*
> *Which the cross of salvation spreads from its height,*
> *Embracing the earth, the sea, the winds and the sky*
> *And everything else believed to exist far away.*[397]

To the best of my knowledge, this is the only primary document from the time of Celtic saints and scholars that describes the shape of a Celtic wheel cross: "the orb . . . which the cross of salvation spreads from its height." As Eriugena indicates, the cross's circle embraces "the earth, the sea, the winds and the sky / And everything else believed to exist far away." The first time I read this, the words set my heart alight. What beauty and magnificence! *The Celtic cross expresses the whole of God's universe.*

Eriugena wasn't the first person to speak of a cosmic cross. In the fourth century, Gregory of Nyssa writes that the symbol of the cross expresses the presence of Christ throughout "the quadripartite cosmos."[398] Two centuries earlier, Irenaeus of Lyons believed the cross symbolized six spatial dimensions, comprising Heaven and Earth and encompassed by Christ: height and depth, length from east to west, and breadth from north to south.[399] Two Anglo-Saxon scholars of Northern England, Bede and Alcuin of York, likewise wrote that the arms of the cross symbolically encompassed the visible and invisible worlds.[400]

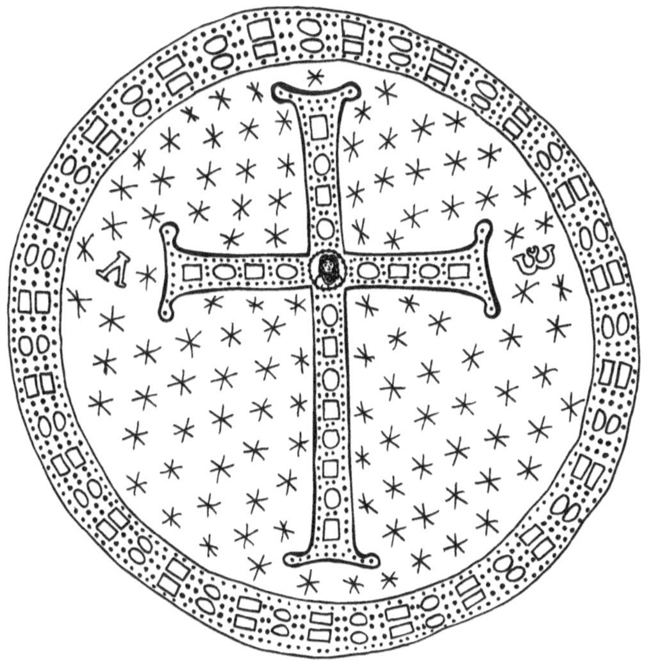

The 6th-century mosaic in the Basilica of Sant'Apollinare is a profound affirmation of the cross's cosmic embrace. This drawing shows the central image, the encircled cross with Christ's face at the center, while the cross's arms point to the Greek letters Alpha and Omega, the beginning and the end. Beneath the cross (not shown in this drawing), the mosaic presents a verdant, fertile world of trees and stones, birds and flowers, scattered with snowy white sheep. The Divine hand reaches down from the golden sky above the cross.

An outstanding artistic expression of the cosmic cross is found in the Basilica of Sant'Apollinare in Ravenna, Italy. The apse is completely encased in a stunning mosaic that depicts Christ's transfiguration—and a cross within a circle hovers in the sky. In the dark sky surrounding the cross are ninety-nine stars, representing both the angels of Heaven and the ninety-nine sheep whom Christ left to find the one missing; these stars signify the completeness of Christ's work on the cross, encompassing all the universe as well as all people.

The mosaic's larger composition has copious depictions of plants, animals, and geological features—all the elements of the physical world. The arms of the cross also indicate that Christ spans all of time. The cross of Christ contains both time and Creation, all of which is depicted as good. Like the Sun in the sky, the encircled cross illumines the whole world.

Embracing All Creation

Notice, in Eriugena's poetic description of the orbed cross, God's attitude toward the cosmos. Eriugena does not emphasize either Divine rule over Creation or Divine causality, ideas common in his time. Instead, he expresses the lovely idea that the cross *embraces* Creation.

An embrace is the universal way humans express deep connection, closeness, trust. A hug can say "I'm glad to see you" or "I'm going to miss you." It brings human beings close together, both physically and emotionally. According to Eriugena, the cross is equivalent to a Divine hug.

I had an experience of this at the Ermita Carceri in Assisi, outside the city's medieval walls, a good walk up a steep hill. This is where Saint Francis and his brothers regularly retreated from the world to seek communion with God.

Marsha and I had woken early on a warm summer morning in order to beat the tour busses to our intended destination, and our diligence was rewarded. When we reached the hermitage, only a few tourists were there already. We walked through the hallowed stone halls all by ourselves.

I stepped through a doorway into a room with a sign noting that this was Francis's sleeping space. The room also held an altar, and I realized this was the saint's private prayer cell, the "holy of holies" for followers of the humble saint of Assisi. On the altar was a small copy of the cross of San Damiano set on a pedestal. (See chapter 1 for more about the cross that spoke to Saint Francis.)

Alone in this sacred space, as I knelt before the cross to pray, my eyes happened to focus on Christ's arms and chest. I was vividly struck by the wide stretch of those outspread arms, their hands wide open. I saw the gentlest expression on Christ's face.

As I knelt there, a memory hit me: Alone in my church office a few weeks earlier, I had been in a state of emotional crisis. When a wise and kindly man stopped in and asked how I was, my answer was a blurt of hurt. He simply walked over and gave me a bear hug; I cried, releasing the pain as I remembered I was loved. That hug was like a life preserver tossed to a drowning man.

Now, gazing at the crucifix on Francis's prayer altar, seeing the arms of the ancient Byzantine likeness of Christ spread out to embrace me, I remembered other hugs as well—from my wife, our children, my granddaughter, and other dear ones. The memories formed a healing compound that merged into the singular reality of Christ's deep and strong affection. I knew I was loved, never alone.

Later that day, back in Assisi, I stopped into one of the many gift shops and bought a wooden facsimile of the San Damiano cross, about the size of the crucifix in Francis's cell. It now resides on the desktop in my home office, and when I am feeling down, I gaze at Christ's welcoming embrace. I feel again the Divine connection strengthening me.

Since then, I've noticed that the widespread, welcoming arms are a common feature on Byzantine-style crosses. Byzantine art influenced the early medieval stone carvers of Ireland and the British Isles, and portrayals of Christ on Irish high crosses often have unnaturally elongated arms and oversized hands. Francoise Henry, the first scholar to extensively study the high crosses, noted "the offering gesture of the two large open hands" typical on these Irish monuments.[401]

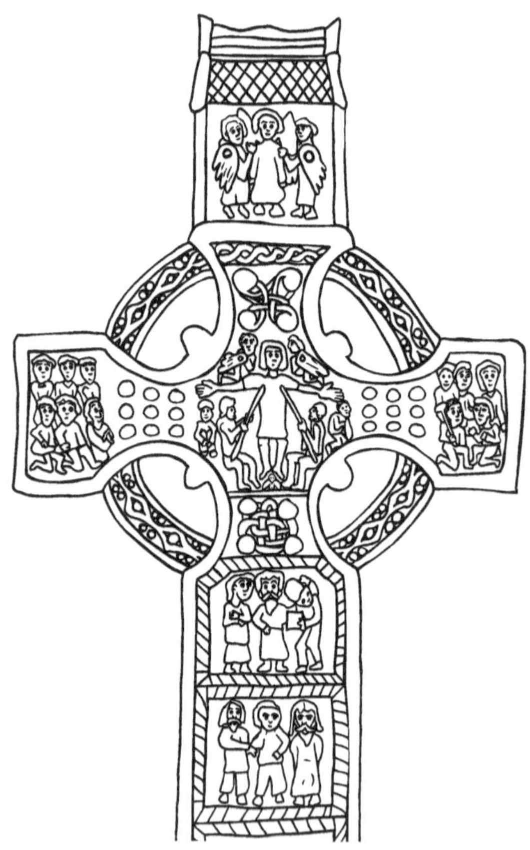

Notice Christ's large, open hands in this drawing of Muiredach's Cross.

United by Love, United by Suffering

Theories of contemporary physics indicate connections between the subatomic and energetic levels of reality. Meanwhile, biological research increasingly reveals how the flora, fauna, and even minerals of our planet are thoroughly intermeshed in a symbiotic web of life. And yet we humans have tragically lost the script of our interconnectedness. As Mother Teresa reflected, "Today, if we have no peace, it is because we have forgotten that we belong to each other—that man, that woman, that child is my brother or my sister. . . . Let us . . . become one heart full of love in the heart of God."[402]

The cross reminds us that all beings in the universe are not only connected by fields of energy but also by experiences of suffering. The cross—inherently a symbol of suffering—speaks of the universal fellowship of adversity. "Unfortunately," James Cone writes in *The Cross and the Lynching Tree,* "during the course of 2,000 years of Christian history, this symbol of salvation has been detached from any reference to the ongoing suffering and oppression of human beings." Cone goes on to say that the cross "is not a rational concept to be explained in a theory of salvation, but a story about God's presence in Jesus' solidarity with the oppressed," the suffering, the sorrowful.[403] In Franciscan teacher Richard Rohr's book *The Universal Christ,* he says mystics have experienced "that individual suffering doesn't exist at all . . . there is only one suffering, it is all the same, and it is all the suffering of God."[404]

In a world torn apart by human hatred, division, and aggression, the universality of all suffering is a necessary and profound theological insight. Once we each realize that our portion of pain is only part of a vast whole, it ironically becomes more bearable. We can seek then to resolve our pain by moving *toward* other beings rather than *against* them.

This awareness also calls us to see and respond to the suffering of others; your pain is mine and vice versa. Those of us living on the other side of the globe are nonetheless connected to the starving baby and her mother in Sudan, the frightened family in Ukraine, and the husband mourning his wife in Palestine; the separation we assume protects us is a false one. Nor can those of us who are white hold ourselves distant from the agony the Black community suffers each time police officers gun down a Black person in the streets; in the spiritual realm, *our* bodies are also beaten and tasered. We are the LGBTQ+ teenager facing intolerance and hatred, the Indigenous woman beaten and murdered by a white man, the prisoner on death row, and the man who huddles in a cardboard house in an alleyway. As Paul wrote to the church at Corinth, "God has so arranged the body . . . that there may be no dissension within the body, but the members may have the same care for one another. If one member suffers, all suffer together with it."[405]

Ancient Celtic crosses proclaim to us this message: Our suffering is connected to the suffering of the whole cosmos, and it is all incorporated in the suffering of the God-Human on the cross. But suffering is not the last word! If there is one suffering, there also is, as Bob Marley reminds us in song, *one love*.

The ancient Celtic crosses proclaim to us, in the image of Christ crucified, the universal, all-in-one nature of suffering, of humanity, Creation, and God. And with the same voice, they proclaim our liberation from the powers of death (the Harrowing) and our eventual restoration to Shalom (the universal healing of the world). The conscious universe shares one experience of suffering, but the entirety of Creation is also caught up in the liberating work of the cross.

The Divine Purpose

The Epistle to the Ephesians proclaims God's endgame:

> With all wisdom and insight God has made known to us the mystery of the Divine mind, finding pleasure in the work of

Christ, a plan for the fullness of time, to gather up all things
in Christ, things in heaven and things on earth.[406]

Modern Christians often reduce the gospel to an insurance plan,
a "get out of jail free card" for individual transit from eternal damnation to a state of bliss. This is a massive reduction of the far grander
promise that scripture offers: *God's ultimate goal is for the elements of
the interconnected universe to experience together the delight of their unity
in God's very essence.*

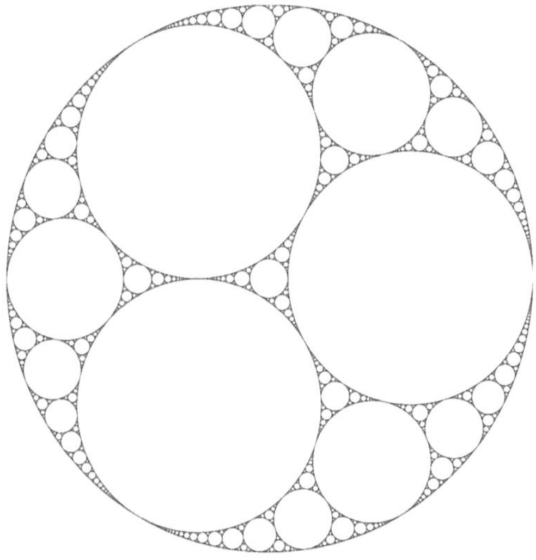

*This image is an example of a fractal pattern, containing similar patterns
at increasingly smaller scales in what is known as expanding or unfolding
symmetry. This particular one was first described in 1706, but it dates back
to a problem proposed by Apollonius of Perga in the 3rd century BCE.*

Consider the fractal nature of reality. Fractals are infinitely complex patterns; they reproduce similar elements on enlarging or dimin-
ishing scales, repeating over and over to create a constantly changing
and fascinating effect. Our individual bodies can be seen as a fractal
phenomenon: Patterns repeat in our cells and atoms to produce the

phenomenon we describe as "myself." Human society contains other repeating patterns, changing constantly into new forms, yet at the same time repeating common forms. In the entire realm of Nature, forms oscillate, replicate, and create the whole—the shape of a nautilus in the ocean, leaves on a lawn swirled by the wind, and the patterns of thousands of stars in a spiral galaxy.

When God's purpose is achieved and all is Shalom, we shall still be ourselves—yet we shall see ourselves as one unique detail of the entirely holy and unspeakably beautiful fractal consciousness of God. We need not fear loss of our individual selves as we gather into the unitive mind of God. Instead, we shall each experience our truest, most complete identity, even as we are fully one with God and with each other.

The Celtic crosses, with their cosmological circle and arms outstretched to embrace, still speak today. They affirm the most vital spiritual lessons for our time: We are all united in the One—and the One embraces us all in universal love.

APPLICATIONS FOR TODAY

Life Interwoven

A great many people today are deconstructing their inherited religious beliefs. They may identify as "spiritual but not religious" and check the "none" boxes on surveys when they're polled regarding their religious affiliations. Fewer and fewer people attend church; more and more are disillusioned with organized religion.

In part, this is because the institutional church has failed to produce deep and meaningful transformation. All the rock-band worship and glitzy preachers put together couldn't put shattered interior lives back together again. Christianity had forgotten how to connect people experientially with the Oneness that scripture and ancient

Christian wisdom affirms. Think of the "religious" people you know: Do they seem to be growing inwardly? Are they well-adjusted, loving folks who have an ever-deepening experience of God? Or are they obsessed with the letter of the law, with religious texts, with political partisanship, with harsh judgements of others who don't live up to their moral standards?

It might seem that the answer to this shortfall of transformation is more laxity: Don't make any demands, do away altogether with codes and structures. I would argue, though, that healthy modern spirituality *does* require discipline and structure to deliver the promise of inner transformation. Formative disciplines have always been part of Christianity, starting with the teachings of its founder.

Jesus used the image of a yoke to speak of spiritual exercise. It's a common Asian metaphor too; the Sanskrit word *yoga* means "yoke" and refers to any form of spiritual discipline. Jesus assured his followers, "My yoke is easy and my burden is light"—but he never suggested that there was no yoke. He knew his followers would need to practice Jesus yoga. He told his followers, "If you want to follow me, you're going to have to take up your cross," indicating that we cannot grow spiritually without letting go of our need to put ourselves exclusively at the center of the world.

Of course, in another sense, we *are* each the center—but only in the same way that all created things from pigeons to porpoises are also at the center of the world. As the ancients proclaimed, God is a circle whose center is everywhere. So how do we shift to seeing the Divine center in all beings, while simultaneously seeing the center within each of ourselves?

Such both-and thinking requires mental training. Some of the spiritual disciplines that characterized Celtic Christianity in its golden age may offer us the mental and spiritual exercises we need to grasp the deeper meanings of scripture.

THE MANDELBROT SET

For this exercise, you'll need to search online for a video that demonstrates the Mandelbrot set. (You can find a number of these on YouTube.) This set is a mathematical formula that's been made visual, revealing an intricate fractal world.[407] The video version allows you to zoom in, over and over, so that what at first seemed to be a tiny aspect of the background becomes the focal point of the foreground. Watch the video in a state of contemplation, allowing the pattern to swirl and expand, again and again and again.

Do any thoughts occur to you as watch? For example: Does anything happen to your ideas about "small" and "big"? Can you see that size is merely a comparison with no true reality in light of the Mandelbrot's ever-unfolding lacework?

Now consider the hierarchy humanity has imagined for reality, a structure that places humans at the top of a descending ladder of complexity and importance. According to this model, a human is more important than an octopus, and a person has very little connection with an earthworm. But does this structure make sense as you watch the Mandelbrot fractals?

The spiraling pattern indicates a different sort of reality. This one does not consist of a succession of ever-smaller, ever-simpler items. Instead, it reveals a "continuum of complexity . . . in which the human no longer occupies the privileged position"[408] that determines the value of everything else. Both scale and complexity are relative, depending on the viewer's position, rather than absolute values.

Green Martyrdom

The saints and scholars of the Celtic nations in the Early Middle Ages
were noted for their martyrdom, a word that holds little appeal to most
of us today. We often connect martyrdom with either an unhealthy
masochism or a selfish desire for attention. But that's not how Celtic
saints saw it.

A document that might be the earliest surviving Irish sermon, the
Cambrai Homily, describes three colors of martyrdom: *White martyrdom* is voluntary exile from one's homeland; *red martyrdom* is literal
martyrdom—death for Christ's sake; and *green martyrdom* is "when
through fasting and hard work they control their desires." (In some
translations, it is blue rather than green martyrdom; the colors were
the same for the ancient Irish.) None of these martyrdom variations
were built on self-hatred. They sprang instead from the self-giving
love that puts the needs of God and others ahead of our egos' needs
for pleasure, admiration, and power.

The homily says this green martyrdom has two purposes. The first
is self-control: "We afflict abstinence upon the body." And the second is
"when we believe that the need of our neighbor is our own need." Both
these purposes bring to mind a more recent expression: "Live simply
that others may simply live."[409] We give up our "right" to some of our
own pleasures, not to punish ourselves but so that the planet and all its
inhabitants can experience the health and peace God wants. Green martyrdom was the lived expression of the truth expressed in the Celtic cross.

The Process of Integration

Throughout this book, we've focused on private spiritual exercises. Most of these have involved you and a cross you chose; they were intended to help you form deep interior connections with Christ and merge "the mind of Christ" with your own. Now, however, I invite you to let the cross draw you into awareness of your cosmic connections.

FINDING YOURSELF WITHIN THE CIRCLE OF THE CROSS

This exercise will take a while; you'll need your cross, a journal, and some hours of uninterrupted time. I recommend for this exercise an encircled Celtic-style cross, ideally one that has some knotwork patterns on its surface.

Gaze at the cross's circle, letting it settle into your mind. Try to envision all the things Eriugena mentioned in his explanation of his beloved Irish crosses: *"embracing the earth, the sea, the winds and the sky and everything else believed to exist far away."* Can you see the great knotwork of reality, the all-in-one and one-in-all connection of the cosmos?

If you can, imagine the subatomic particles in your body dancing in choreography with particles on the far side of a distant galaxy. Picture an intricate reality like the one you saw in the previous exercise involving the Mandelbrot fractals. Affirm God's high destiny: *"a plan for the fullness of time, to gather up all things in Christ, things in heaven and things on earth."*

Now ask yourself: *As I see myself as a valuable part of an inseparable whole, how can I best live the "green martyrdom" of a balanced life?*

You might begin by considering your money, your financial resources. Like your physical and spiritual self, your finances are entangled in an interlinked system (we call that system "economics"). Ask yourself: *Am I positioned in the right place in the financial flow? Do I have what I need? If not, what actions might I take to change that? Is enough of my wealth flowing from me to others? Do my economic decisions allow others to thrive? Or do they, inadvertently, exploit my global neighbors?*

Free your thinking from simple stereotypes and assumptions. Pray:

> *O Christ, who gathers all into yourself,*
> *show me the interweave and the flow of resources.*
> *Reveal to me how I can craft the use of my resources*
> *in harmony with your beauty.*

Now shift your attention to your time and ask yourself these questions: *Am I channeling the mind of Christ as I act and think? Does the pattern of my time—waking, sleeping, eating, moving, transacting, giving, taking, love-making, scrolling, worrying, hugging—form a delightful knotwork pattern?*

Finally, think about the precious gift of yourself: your personality, your body, your psyche, your spirituality, your unique skills and talents. Ask yourself: *How do I receive energy, joy, and wisdom from others? How do I send forth energy, joy, and wisdom to others?*

Spend some time prayerfully journalling your answers to all these questions.

Like the knotwork patterns on the ancient sacred stones, each person's life is interwoven with others. When we spend our time, talent, and treasures thinking only of ourselves—as if the entirety of the cosmos resided within the flask of our individual skin—we live out of sync with reality. Conversely, if we think ourselves unimportant and irrelevant, we likewise fall short of the universe's overarching reality.

As we see ourselves within reality's interconnections, however, that awareness will shape our attitudes, actions, and decisions. We are each of great worth, we each contain God, and we each experience health and true happiness only in balanced relationships with others. We are each a precious part of the great interwoven whole.

O Wonder,
Beauty within all things,
Weaver and Riven One,
you who are at the center
of all vertical and horizontal planes,
the Conjunction of Love
reaching wide to embrace all,
make known to me
today and always
how my life may express
the all-one pattern
of your Cross.

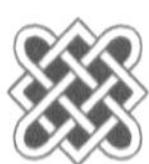

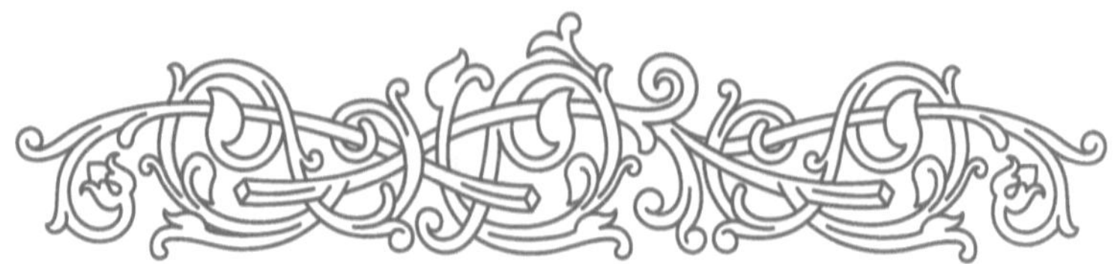

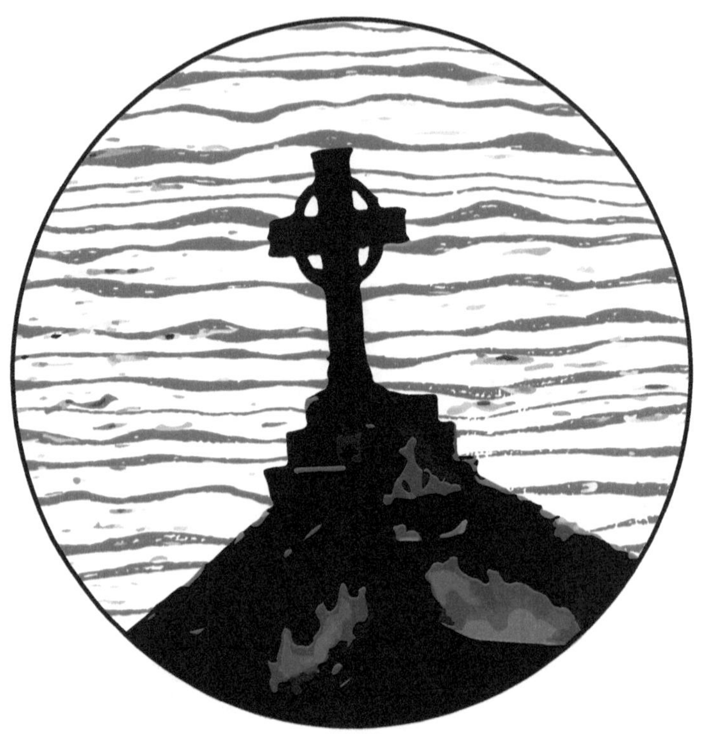

The wheel cross at the church of the Virxen de Barca, Muxia, Spain.

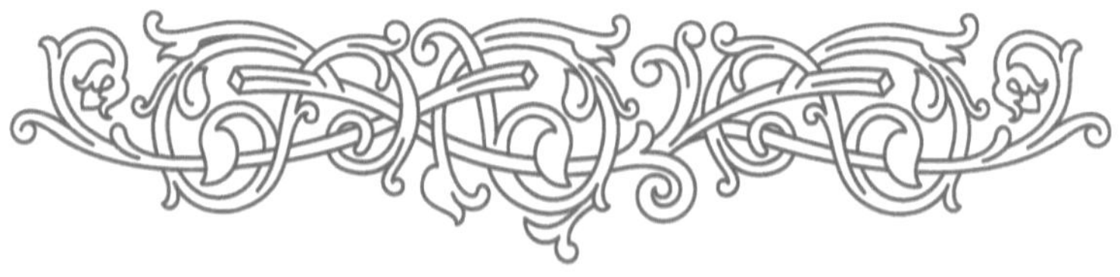

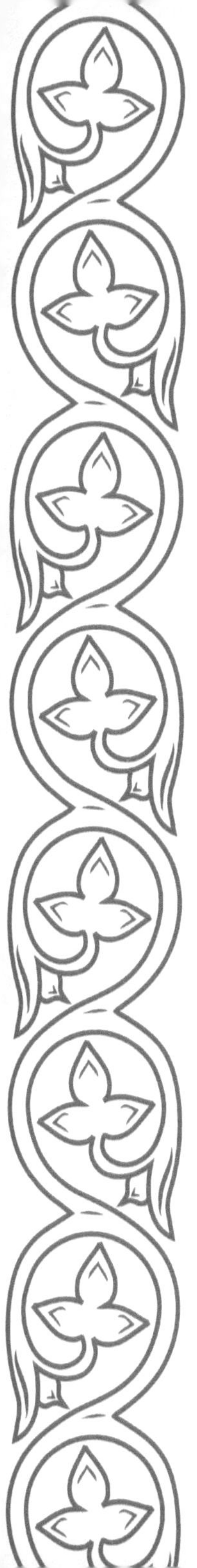

The Celtic Cross at the End of the World

n a Wednesday evening—June 22, 2023, to be precise—Marsha and I took the very last steps of our two-month pilgrimage on the Camino de Santiago. We had already reached the Camino's primary goal, the Cathedral of Santiago de Compostela, where we hugged the effigy of Saint James (Santiago). But our hearts still yearned for something more.

I had blistered soles—but a fire still burned in my soul. So we walked further westward, along a pre-Christian pilgrim trail, to the seaside town of Finisterre, a name that literally means "the end of the world." Still, something called us to keep walking. We trekked north for another two days, through eucalyptus forests and along delightful beaches, to another far-westward peninsula and the town of Muxia. Finally, as the Sun dipped toward the horizon, we crossed a walkway atop a rounded stone ridge. The ridge pointed directly toward the setting Sun.

As the Sun turned the ocean to liquid gold, the solid stone form of the Church of the Virxen de Barca (Virgin of the Boat) rose before us. Atop the church's roof, silhouetted against the blazing sunset, was a Celtic wheel cross.

What could possibly have been more appropriate at the end of our journey than this encircled cross? After all, a pilgrimage is a microcosm of life: We journey from Christ at our conception, travel with the Spirit through life's ups and downs, and then we return to Christ at the end our lives.

Framed by the setting Sun, marking the furthermost point of land known to the ancient world, we had come to . . .

the orb that shines with the rays of the Sun,
the cross of salvation
that embraces the Earth, the sea, the winds, and the sky
—and everything else, both near and far away.

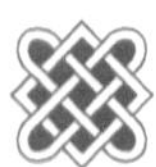

Endnotes

Beginning and Welcome

1. Wendy A. Stein, *How to Read Medieval Art* (New York: Metropolitan Museum of Art, 2016), 17. (Italics are mine.)
2. *The Icon Cross: The Monastic Church of St. Augustine* (Holy Cross Monastery, West Park, New York, acquired from the Monastic Church of St. Augustine October 6, 2023), 1. (Italics are mine.)
3. 2 Peter 1:4.
4. Alexander Carmichael, *Carmina Gadelica, Volume 1 & II, Hymns and Incantations* (London: Forgotten Books, 2007), 47. Between 1860 and 1909, Carmichael collected, recorded, and translated these prayers and sayings from ordinary people in Scotland.

Chapter 1

5. Robert Boenig, *Anglo-Saxon Spirituality: Selected Writings* (Mahwah, NJ: Paulist Press, 2000), 260. All quotes from "The Dream of the Rood" are from this source.
6. "The Ruthwell Cross," *Historic Environment Scotland* (November 13, 2021), https://www.historicenvironment.scot/visit-a-place/places/ruthwell-cross/history/.
7. Luke 19:39–40.
8. Oliver Crilly, *The Great Irish High Crosses: Meaning and Mystery* (Dublin: Columba, 2013) 64.
9. 1 Peter 4:10.
10. John Scotus Eriugena, *Periphyseon on the Division of Nature*, I. P. Sheldon-Williams, trans. (Washington, DC: Dumbarton-Oaks, 1987), 390.
11. 2 Corinthians 5:19.

12. Judith Couchman, *The Mystery of the Cross* (Downers Grove, IL: Intervarsity, 2009), 92–93.

13. Eamonn O Carragain, "High Crosses, the Sun's Course, and Local Theologies at Kells and Monasterboice," in *Insular & Anglo-Saxon Art & Thought in the Early Medieval Period*, Colum Hourihane, ed. (University Park: Penn State University Press, 2011), 156.

14. Fr. George Corrigan, "San Damiano Cross: Telling the History of Christ's Passion," Franciscan Mission Service (October 5, 2012), https:// franciscanmissionservice.org/2012/10/san-damiano-cross-telling-the-history-of-christs-passion/. (Accessed September 10, 2024.)

15. Stein, 16.

16. Quoted in ibid., 41.

17. Richard Rohr, *The Universal Christ: How a Forgotten Reality Can Change Everything We See, Hope For, and Believe* (New York: Convergent Books, 2019), 13.

18. Psalm 19:3–4.

19. 1 Corinthians 8:1.

20. Galatians 5:6.

21. Quoted in Paul C. Stratman, *Prayers from the Ancient Celtic Church* (Lexington, KY: CreateSpace, 2018), 5. This particular prayer is Irish, from approximately the tenth century.

Chapter 2

22. Aubrey Burl, *Prehistoric Astronomy and Ritual* (Oxford, UK: Shire Publications, 2005), 18. (Italics mine.)

23. C. G. Jung, *Dream Analysis* (Milton Park, UK: Taylor & Francis, 2013), 358.

24. Ibid., *The Archetypes and the Collective Unconsciousness* (New York: Bollingen Foundation, 1969), 388.

25. Genesis 28:10–22.

26. 1 Samuel 7:12.

27. Exodus 20:25.

28. English Heritage, "History of Avebury Henge and Stone Circles," https:// www.english-heritage.org.uk/visit/places/avebury/history/. (Accessed September 11, 2024.)

29. Julian Richards, *Stonehenge* (London: English Heritage, 2007), 9.

30. Sarah Steele, "The Myths, Legends and Controversy Behind Ancient Preseli Bluestone," *The Gemological Association of Great Britain* (April 2016), https://gem-a.com/gem-hub/gem-knowledge/stonehenge-preseli-

bluestone-ancient-stone.

31. Pierre Teilhard de Chardin, *Writings in Time of War* (New York: Harper & Row, 1968), 14.

32. Ibid.

33. Thomas Erskine, quoted in Robin A. Parry's *A Larger Hope?* (Eugene, OR: Cascade, 2019), 201.

34. Romans 1:25.

35. 1 Samuel 2:2, Psalm 18:2.

36. Exodus 28:7.

37. Exodus 28:15–21.

38. Exodus 28:30.

39. Job 5:23.

40. Mark 12:10.

41. Luke 19:40.

42. 1 Corinthians 10:4.

43. Revelation 2:18.

44. Revelation 21:11.

45. Revelation 21:19–21.

46. John 14:6.

47. 1 Corinthians 10:4.

48. Hermes Trismegistus, *Aureus: The Golden Tractate* (Rome: Volume Edizioni, 2013), Section 1. Hermes Trismegistus was a legendary figure from the Hellenistic period who was seen as the combination of the Greek god Hermes and the Egyptian god Thoth. Up until the Renaissance, people believed he had been alive at the time of Moses, and many church fathers believed him to have contributed to what they called *Prisca Theologia,* a thread of true theology that weaves through all religions, given by God in antiquity and passed down through a series of prophets that included Zoroaster and Plato. From the seventeenth century on, however, the work attributed to Trismegistrus was now believed to have been written by various unknown authors, all probably Greek, at various times during the four centuries before the Common Era.

49. Thomas Traherne, quoted in Tessie Prakas, *Poetic Priesthood in the Seventeenth Century* (Oxford, UK: Oxford University Press, 2022), 200.

50. Gustav Mahler, quoted in Hal A. Lingerman, *Life Streams: Journeys into Meditation and Music* (Chennai, India: Theosophical Publishing, 1988), 171.

51. Nicola Tesla, "The Problem of Creating Human Energy," *My Inventions and Other Writings* (Mineola, NY: Dover, 2016), 72–73.

52. Carl G. Jung, *Man and His Symbols* (New York: Doubleday, 1964), 207.

53. Eckhart Tolle, *A New Earth: Awakening to Your Life's Purpose* (New York:

Penguin, 2008), 26.

54. Steven Charleston, *The Four Vision Quests of Jesus* (New York: Morehouse Publishing, 2015), 104.

55. Barbara Taylor Brown, *When God Is Silent* (Cambridge, MA: Cowley, 1998), 46–47.

56. Richard Rohr, *What the Mystics Know: Seven Pathways to Your Deeper Self* (New York: Crossroad, 2015), 87.

57. M. Scott Peck, *In Search of Stones: A Pilgrimage of Faith, Reason, and Discovery* (New York: Hyperion, 1995), 415–416.

58. Rachel Armstrong, *Soft Living Architecture: An Alternative View of Bio-Informed Practice* (New York: Bloomsbury, 2018), 8.

59. Gary Zukav, *The Dancing Wu Li Masters: An Overview of the New Physics* (New York: Morrow, 1979), 71.

60. Ilia Delio, *A Hunger for Wholeness: Soul, Space, and Transcendence* (Mahwah, NY: Paulist Press, 2017), 27.

61. Robby Berman, There's Gold in Your Brain—We Now Know Where It Came From," Big Think (May 8, 2019), https://bigthink.com/hard-science/gold-neutron-stars/#.

62. The following story illustrates two very different perspectives on stones: Where a tributary meets the Missouri River, the churning waters create smooth, spherical stones. The Lakota people believe these are sacred stones, which they regard as kinfolk; they also use the stones as prayer tokens. When European colonizers and explorers encountered these stones, however, they saw them quite differently: as potential weapons. They named the tributary the Cannonball River, and used the stones in their cannons as agents of destruction. Still today, Westerners tend to look at the Earth's elements as either tools or weapons, resources for human use; from this perspective, stones are the epitome of dead matter, since, many people believe, they can't move on their own, they can't speak, they have no soul, no consciousness. But Indigenous people (including not only North American First Nations people but also Indigenous groups around the globe) see each aspect of the Earth as sacred and alive, capable of relationship with human beings.

63. Christ is referred to as the "living Stone" in 1 Peter 2:5. Other scriptures that refer to Divinity as a stone include 1 Corinthians 10:4; 1 Samuel 2:2; Deuteronomy 32:4; and Psalms 18:2, 31, 46; 28:1; 62:2, 6; 71:3; 89:26; 95:1; 144:1 (and many others).

Chapter 3

64. Danaan, Sacred Nature–Druids in North America, "Summer Solstice," https://www.danaan.net/druidry/wheel-of-the-year/summer-solstice/. (Accessed September 13, 2024.)

65. Richard Cavendish, "Newgrange: Neolithic Tomb, Ireland," *Encyclopaedia Britannica,* https://www.britannica.com/topic/Newgrange. (Accessed September 13, 2024.)

66. Sharon Weadick, *The Winter Solstice at Newgrange*, National Museum of Ireland, https://www.museum.ie/en-IE/Collections-Research/Irish-Antiquities-Division-Collections/Irish-Antiquities-Articles/The-Winter-solstice-at-Newgrange. (Accessed September 13, 2024.)

67. Ibid.

68. Jakob Streit, *Sun and Cross: From Megalithic Culture to Early Christianity in Ireland* (Edinburgh: Floris Books, 1984), 30.

69. Ibid., 31.

70. Jarett A Lobell, "The Nebra Sky Disc," *Archaeology* (May 2019), https://www.archaeology.org/issues/337-1905/features/7543-maps-germany-nebra-sky-disc.

71. Genesis 1:16

72. Psalm 19:1–6.

73. Isaiah 58:8.

74. See, for example, John 8:12.

75. Matthew 5:45.

76. Hippolytus of Rome, *Easter Homily:* SC 27, 116–118.

77. Archelaus, *The Acts of the Disputation with the Heresiarch Manes*, available online at https://ccel.org/ccel/archelaus/manes_disputation/anf06.vii.ii.html.

78. Cyprian of Carthage in *Ante-Nicene Fathers, Vol. 5.,* Alexander Roberts, James Donaldson, and A. Cleveland Coxe, eds., Robert Ernest Wallis, trans. (Buffalo, NY: Christian Literature Publishing Co., 1886).

79. Ambrose of Milan, "Exposition on Psalm 118" in *The Office of Readings According to the Roman Rite* (Boston: Daughters of St. Paul, 1983), 866. (Italics are in the original.)

80. Desiderius Erasmus, in *Prayers Ancient and Modern,* Mary Wilder Tileston, ed. (Boston: Little, Brown, 1921), 180. Available online at http://assets.newscriptorium.com/collects-and-prayers/prancmod.htm.

81. Charles Francois Dupuis, *The Origin of All Religious Worship* (Whitefish, MT: Kessinger, 2010), 243

82. D. M. Murdock, "Jesus as the Sun throughout History," Stellar House Publishing, https://stellarhousepublishing.com/jesussunexcerpt/.

(Accessed September 17, 2024.)

83. Paracelsus, in *Life and the Doctrines of Philippus Theophrastus, Bombast of Hohenheim, Known by the Name of Paracelsus,* Franz Hartmann, ed. (London: Creative Media, 2019), 334.

84. William Blake, *The Poetry and Prose of William Blake*, David V. Erdman, ed. (Garden City, NJ: Doubleday, 1965), 555.

85. Northrup Frye, *Fearful Symmetry: A Study of William Blake* (Toronto: Toronto University Press, 2004), 21.

86. Beebe Bahrami, *Moon Camino de Santiago: Sacred Sites, Historic Villages, Local Food & Wine* (New York: Hatchette, 2022), 485.

87. Quoted in Streit, 91.

88. Quoted in Thomas O'Loughlin's *Discovering Saint Patrick* (Mahwah, NJ: Paulist, 2005), 152.

89. Sion Mowddwy, "Detholiad o Englynion," *Bulletin of the Board of Celtic Studies*, Part III (1953), 187.

90. Geoffrey Moorhouse, *Sun Dancing* (New York: Harcourt Brace, 1997), 246.

91. Michael W. Herren and Shirley Ann Brown, *Christ in Celtic Christianity: Britain and Ireland from the Fifth to the Tenth Century* (Woodbridge, VA: Boydell, 2012), 201. (Italics are mine.)

92. Eamonn Ó Carragain, "High Crosses, The Sun's Course, and Local Theologies at Kells and Monasterboice," in *Insular & Anglo-Saxon Art & Thought in the Early Medieval Period*, Colum Hourihane, ed. (Princeton, NJ: Princeton University, 2011), 149.

93. Ibid., 151.

94. Lawrence Parmly Brown, "The Cosmic Eyes," *The Open Court* (1918: 11), 8. Available online at https://opensiuc.lib.siu.edu.

95. Matthew 3:12 and Luke 3:17.

96. Shawn Tribe, "The Flabellum of Tornus—a Rare Example of the Liturgical Fan in the West," *Liturgical Arts Journal* (August 2, 2022), https://www.liturgicalartsjournal.com/2022/08/the-flabellum-of-tournus-rare-surviving.html.

97. Shane Angland, "Oriental Influences in the Early Irish Church," *Anglandicus* (April 11, 2012), http://anglandicus.blogspot.com/2012/04/oriental-influences-in-early-irish.html.

98. Aidan Breen, "Colum Cille (Columba)," *Dictionary of Irish Biography* (Dublin: Royal Irish Academy, 2009). Available online at https://doi.org/10.3318/dib.001890.v1.

99. Mark Kurlansky, *The Basque History of the World* (New York: Penguin Books, 1999,) 81.

100. Rabbi Julie Hilton Danan, "From Our Sages: The Story of

Honi," *Wellsprings of Wisdom: The Nature Rabbi* (2017), https://
wellspringsofwisdom.com/sages-story-honi/. (Accessed September 26,
2024.)

101. Based on the vocabulary, linguists have determined the lorica was actually
composed sometime during the eighth century, some three hundred years
after Patrick's time. Fragments of the prayers are in a ninth-century *Life of
Saint Patrick,* and the full prayer, as we know it today, is part an eleventh-
century collection of hymns.

102. Carmichael, 53.

Chapter 4

103. Saint Patrick, *On the Great Works of God,* in Oliver Davies, *Celtic
Spirituality: the Classics of Western Spirituality* (Mahwah, NJ: Paulist Press,
1999), 78.

104. Woodrow Michael Kroll, *Roman Crucifixion and the Death of Jesus*
(Eugene, OR: Wipf and Stock, 2023), 3.

105. Kroll, 11.

106. Ibid., 59–60.

107. Ibid., 14.

108. Ibid., 181.

109. Derek Bryce, *Symbolism of the Celtic Cross* (San Francisco, CA: Barnes &
Noble, 2009), 48.

110. Bryce, 50.

111. See Acts 5:30, 10:39, 13:29.

112. Miranda J. Green, *Dictionary of Celtic Myth and Legend* (London: Thames
and Hudson, 1992), 212–213.

113. See Genesis 2:9.

114. Pseudo-Chrysostom, "The Cross as the Cosmic Tree," Crossroads
Initiative, https://www.crossroadsinitiative.com/media/articles/cosmic-
tree-pseudo-chrysostom/.

115. Herren and Brown, 211.

116. Bede, *The Ecclesiastical History of the English People* (Oxford, UK: Oxford
University Press, 1994), 57.

117. Adrián Maldonado, "Kirkmadrine Stones: Statement of Significance
PIC199" (Edinburgh: Historic Environment Scotland, 2016), https://
www.academia.edu/33765244/Kirkmadrine_Stones_Statement_of_
Significance_PIC199.

118. Nigel Pennick, *The Celtic Cross: An Illustrated History and Celebration*
(London: Blandford, 1997), 64–65.

119. M. Scott Peck, *In Search of Stones: A Pilgrimage of Faith, Reason, and Discovery* (New York: Hyperion, 1995), 366.

120. This entire section is inspired by a display of stone cross remnants and accompany artwork illustrating the purpose for each of these artifacts, seen in 2019, at the Lindisfarne Priory Museum, Church Lane, Holy Island, Berwick-upon-Tweed, United Kingdom.

121. Neil Prior, *What Do Medieval Carved Stones and Celtic Crosses in Wales Symbolise?* (18 July 2020), https://www.bbc.com/news/uk-wales-53435217.

122. Finola Finlay and Robert Harris, "Lady Mary Carbery's High Cross," *Roaringwater Journal* (April 21, 2019), https://roaringwaterjournal.com/tag/lady-mary-carbery/.

123. Fernando Alonso Romero, *Devociones y creencias sobre el agua: Galicia y otros pueblos europeos* (Santiago De Compostela, Galicia: Andavira, 2016).

124. Beebe Bahrami, *Moon Camino de Santiago: Sacred Sites, Historic Villages, Local Food & Wine* (New York: Hatchette, 2022), 475.

125. Ralph Merrifield, *The Archeology of Ritual and Magic* (New York: New Amsterdam Books, 1987), 38.

126. Gilbert Markus, trans., *The Life of St Cainnech of Aghaboe* (October 2018), 25, https://uistsaints.co.uk/wp-content/uploads/2018/10/Vita-Sancti-Cainnechi-with-GM-translation-and-notes.pdf.

127. Cuthbert was a seventh-century Celtic Christ-follower. He entered the monastery at Melrose when he was still a teenager; from there, he went on to become the prior and then bishop at Lindisfarne. His life followed an ongoing cycle between active service to his community—and a solitary life in his hermitage, where he spent his time in contemplation and prayer. After Cuthbert's death, numerous miracles were attributed to his intercession.

128. Nigel Marns, *A Cornish Celtic Way* (Penryn, Wales: Booths Print, 2016), 58.

129. Revelation 2:4.

130. Thomas Andrew Bennett, *Labor of God: The Agony of the Cross as the Birth of the Church* (Waco, TX: Baylor University Press, 2017), 1.

131. This paragraph is paraphrased from the writing of Iolo Morganwg, an eighteenth-century Welsh bard who helped resurrect interest in ancient Welsh literature, as well as druidism. (Unfortunately, he also forged some of the manuscripts he collected.) This particular quotation is from a section of his writing that scholars believe may have been genuinely an ancient description of Jesus. See *The Barddas of Iolo Morganwg, Vol. I.*, J. Williams Ab Ithel, ed. (1862), available online at Sacred Texts, https://archive.sacred-texts.com/neu/celt/bim1/bim1099.htm.

132. The woman's "homily" has so far been taken directly from a letter written by Pelagius, the fourth-century Celtic theologian. See Robert van de Weyer, *The Letters of Pelagius: Celtic Soul Friend* (New Alresford, UK: Arthur James, 1995), 71.

133. This portion of the woman's sermon is adapted from other letters written by Pelagius. See Brinley Roderick Rees, *Pelagius: Life and Letters* (Martlesham, UK: Boydell, 1998), 113, 117.

134. "Jesus was a good druid," is an old Outer Hebridean saying, and Columba (or Columcille, one of the great Celtic saints) said, "Christ is my druid." There is some scholarly evidence that in the early years of Christianity in the Isles, druid centers organically turned into teaching centers for Christ-followers, with little controversy on either side. An example of this may be Saint Brigid, who is said to have been taught by a druid. Her abbey at Kildare (which means "church of the oak") became a Christian center of learning and spirituality, but some scholars have hypothesized that prior to Brigid's conversion, it could have been a druid center—and that in fact, it continued to be a druid center during the first century after Christianity came to the Isles, with no sense of conflict between the old and new faiths. The Gaelic word for "nun" is even the same word that was used for "druidess."

Chapter 5

135. William Dalrymple, "The Egyptian Connection," *New York Review* (October 23, 2008). https://www.nybooks.com/articles/2008/10/23/the-egyptian-connection/.

136. Thomas C. Oden, *How Africa Shaped the Christian Mind: Rediscovering the African Seedbed of Western Christianity* (Downers Grove, IL: IVP Books, 2010), 9. See also my chapter in *Lorica: Celtic Voices Against Racism* (Vestal, NY: Anamchara Books, 2025), "Shamrock and Papyrus: Celtic Christianity's Debt to Africa," where I write about this in greater detail.

137. H. R. Hall, "Egyptian Beads in Britain," *The Journal of Egyptian Archeology* 1 (1:1914), 19.

138. R. Darcy and William Flynn, "Ptolemy's Map of Ireland: A Modern Decoding," *Irish Geography* 41 (1: 2008), 46–69.

139. Andrew Butterworth, "African Christianity Thrived, Long Before White Men Arrived," *Christian History* (November 16, 2022), https://africa. thegospelcoalition.org/article/african-christianity-thrived-long-before-white-men-arrived/. Butterworth mentions that many of the church

fathers were African, including Tertullian, Origen, and Augustine, and second-century Christian writings refer to Ethiopians who are preaching the gospel in their homelands.

140. Abba Seraphim, "On the Trail of the Seven Coptic Monks in Ireland," British Orthodox Church (2019), https://britishorthodox.org/miscellaneous/on-the-trail-of-seven-coptic-monks-in-ireland/. (Accessed September 26, 2024.)

141. Madeleine Stewart, *The San Damiano Cross: An Icon of the Crucifixion* (Coney Island, Northern Ireland: Conard Press, 2019), 19.

142. Stewart, 29.

143. Bryce, 52–53.

144. Christian Cannuyer, *Coptic Egypt: The Christians of the Nile* (New York: Harry N. Abrams, 2001), 10–11.

145. Cannuyer, 46–47.

146. Walter Horn, "Appendix—On the Origin of the Celtic Cross: A New Interpretation," in *The Forgotten Hermitage of Skellig Michael* (Berkeley: University of California Press, 1990), 92, 96–97.

147. This paragraph up to this point is drawn from Robert K. Ritner Jr's "Egyptians in Ireland: A Question of Coptic Peregrinations," *Rice Institute Pamphlet, Rice University Studies* 62 (2: 1976), https://hdl.handle.net/1911/63225.

148. Kees Veelenturf, "Osiris Once Again: A Pharaonic Motif on Irish High Crosses" in Conor Newman, Mags Mannion, & Fiona Gavin, eds., *Islands in a Global Context: Proceedings of the Seventh International Conference on Insular Art* (Dublin/Portland: Four Courts, 2017), 222–232.

149. For more on this, see my chapter in *Lorica: Celtic Voices Against Racism,* "Prejudice Disguised as Pride: Celtic Does Not Equal White" (Vestal, NY: Anamchara Books, 2025).

150. See Matthew 25:31–46.

Chapter 6

151. Adomnan of Iona, *Life of St Columba* (London: Penguin Books, 1995), 175.

152. Howard Fisher, "The Surgeon's Photograph of the Loch Ness Monster," *Hektoen International: A Journal of Medical Humanities* (Summer 2022), https://hekint.org/2022/08/10/the-surgeons-photograph-of-the-loch-ness-monster/. For another perspective on this, see Roland Watson's *The Water Horses of Loch Ness* (self-published, 2011), which is a scholarly account of the many Nessie sightings previous to the famous 1934

photograph.

153. Bella Isaacs-Thomas, "Loch Ness Monster Search Party Uses New Tools to Look for an Old Cryptid," PBS News (August 31, 2023), https://www.pbs.org/newshour/world/loch-ness-monster-search-party-uses-new-tools-to-look-for-an-old-cryptid.

154. Helen Scales, *Poseidon's Steed: The Story of Seahorses, From Myth to Reality* (New York: Gotham Books, 2009), chapt. 1.

155. Ibid.

156. Elizabeth Sunderland, *In Search of the Picts: A Celtic Dark Age Nation* (London: Constable, 1995), 87.

157. Ibid., 88.

158. Alistair Mack, *A Field Guide to the Pictish Symbols* (Edinburgh: Pinkfoot, 1997).

159. Colin D MacLeod and Ben Wilson, "Did a Beaked Whale Inspire the 'Pictish Beast'?" *Tayside and Fife Archeological Journal* 7 (2001), 45–47.

160. Martin B. Sweatman, *Athens Journal of History* 6 (3: 2020), 192–222.

161. Scottish Archeological Research Framework, "Carved Stones," ScARF, https://scarf.scot/regional/pkarf/early-medieval/6-7-religion-and-ritual/6-7-3-carved-stones/. (Accessed October 22, 2024.) See also, K. Forsyth, "Some Thoughts on Pictish Symbols as a Formal Writing System," in David Henry, ed., *The Worm, the Germ and the Thorn: Pictish and Related Studies Presented to Isabel Henderson* (Brechin, UK: Pinkfoot Press, 1997), 85–98.

162. Gordon Noble, Martin Goldberg, and Derek Hamilton, "The Development of the Pictish Symbol System: Inscribing Identity Beyond the Edges of Empire," *Antiquity* 92 (365: 2018), 1329–1348.

163. Bryce, 81.

164. Bryce, 83–84.

165. George Bain, *Celtic Art: The Methods of Construction* (Glasgow: Dover, 1973), 71.

166. M. Ruth Megaw and J. V. S. Megaw, *Celtic Art: From Its Beginnings to the Book of Kells* (London: Thames & Hudson, 2001), 21.

167. Bain, 81.

168. M. Mitchell Waldrop, "The Universe as a Coat of Chain Mail," *Science* 250 (December 14, 1990), 1510–1511.

169. Brent Doran, "Mathematical Sophistication of the Insular Celts: Spirals, Symmetries, and Knots as a Window onto Their World View," *Proceedings of the Harvard Celtic Colloquium* 15 (1995), 258–289.

170. Barney R. McLaughlin, *An Introduction to Irish High Crosses*, 51, Irishhighcrosses.com.

171. George Henderson and Isabel Henderson, *The Art of the Picts: Sculpture*

and Metalwork in Early Medieval Ireland (New York: Thames & Hudson, 2004), 77.

172. Gregory Mobley, *The Return of the Chaos Monsters—and Other Backstories of the Bible* (Grand Rapids, MI: Eerdmans, 2012), 125–126.

173. John 1:1.

174. Romans 8:38–39.

175. This quote, consistently attributed to Bohr, is impossible to trace back to its source; it is sometimes cited as a 1952 conversation Bohr had with Einstein.

176. Steven D. Boyer, "The Logic of Mystery," *Religious Studies* 43 (2007), 89–102.

177. Ecclesiastes 3:11.

Chapter 7

178. Crilly, 56.

179. Charita Goshay, "God Is Still Speaking, Says UCC President," *The Repository* (June 21, 2014), https://www.cantonrep.com/story/news/local/north-canton/2014/06/21/god-is-still-speaking-says/36980937007/.

180. Martin McNamar, "Love For and Study of the Bible, God's Word, in Early Irish Tradition," in Salvador Ryan and Brendan Leahy, eds., *Treasures of Irish Christianity: Volume II: A People of the Word* (Dublin: Veritas, 2013), 57.

181. Leslie Hardinge, *The Celtic Church in Britain* (New York: Teach Services, 2005), 29.

182. Joseph Falaky Nagy, *Conversing with Angels & Ancients: Literary Myths of Medieval Ireland* (Ithaca, NY: Cornel University Press, 1997), 237.

183. Benjamin C. Tilgham, "Writing in Tongues: Mixed Scripts and Style in Insular Art," in Colum Hourihane, *Insular & Anglo-Saxon Art & Thought in the Early Medieval Period* (Princeton, NJ: Princeton University Press, 2011), 93.

184. George Otto Sims, *Exploring the Book of Kells* (Dublin: O' Brien Press, 2008), 65.

185. Giraldis Cambrensis (Gerald of Wales), *The History and Topography of Ireland*, John O' Meara, ed. and trans. (New York: Penguin Books, 1982), 84.

186. John Scottus Eriugena, *Periphyseon on the Division of Nature*, I. P. Sheldon-Williams, trans. (Washington, DC: Dumbarton-Oaks, 1987), 390.

187. Harding, 18.

188. Karlfried Froehlich, *Biblical Interpretation in the Early Church* (Philadelphia, PA: Fortress Press, 1984), 17.

189. I discuss these ideas more deeply and at length in my book *The Peacock's Tail Feathers (Reading the Bible the Celtic Way)* (Vestal, NY: Anamchara Books, 2020).

190. Crilly, 57.

191. McLaughlin, 67.

192. McLaughlin, 70.

193. Ibid.

194. Crilly, 88–99.

195. Roger Stalley, *Early Irish Sculpture and the Art of the High Crosses* (London: Paul Mellon Centre for Studies in British Art, 2020), 130.

196. Heather Pulliam, "Between the Embodied Eye and Living World: Clonmacnoise's Cross of the Scriptures," *Art Bulletin* 102 (2: 2020), 12.

197. Ibid.

198. Crilly, 71.

199. Francoise Henry, *Irish High Crosses* (Dublin: Three Candles Limited, 1964), 37.

200. Herren and Brown, 203.

201. John 15:1–6.

202. Herren and Brown, 209.

203. Ian Bradley, *Following the Celtic Way: A New Assessment of Celtic Christianity* (London: Darton, Longman and Todd, 2018), 50.

Chapter 8

204. Robert Van Der Wyer, *Celtic Fire* (London: Darton, Longman, Todd, 1990), 96. Ninian's Catechism is an eighth-century document that explained the rudiments of faith to new Pictish believers.

205. For more on this topic, see my book, *Water from an Ancient Well* (Anamchara Books), chapter 8.

206. Quoted and translated by Robert Graves in *The White Goddess* (London: Faber, 1948), 10–12.

207. These lines are attributed to Taliesin the bard. Quoted in Tom Cowan's *Fire in the Head: Shamanism and the Celtic Spirit* (New York: HarperCollins, 1993),

208. Jocelinus, *Saint Mungo: Also Known as Kentigern,* Iain MacDonald, ed. (Edinburgh: Floris Books, 1993), 17.

209. Ibid., 33.

210. Ibid., 50–51.

211. Wisdom 13:5, New American Bible.

212. Job 12:7.

213. Romans 1:20.

214. Sarah Kay, *Animal Skins and the Reading Self in Medieval Latin Bestiaries* (Chicago: University of Chicago Press, 2017), 11.

215. Marina Smyth, "Isidorian Texts in Seventh-Century Ireland" in Andrew Fear and Jamie Wood, eds., *Isidore of Seville and His Reception in the Early Middle Ages: Transmitting and Transforming Knowledge* (Amsterdam: Amsterdam University Press, 2016), 131–158.

216. Gregory the Great, epistle XIII, quoted by Debra Hassig in "Beauty in the Beasts," *RES: Anthropology and Aesthetics* 19/20 (1991), 141.

217. Phyllis G. Jestice, *Encyclopedia of Irish Spirituality* (Santa Barbara, CA: 2000), 59.

218. Stalley, 80.

219. Kathleen Walker-Meikle, *Medieval Pets* (Woodbridge, UK: Boydell, 2012), 10–11.

220. Anonymous, translated from the Old Irish by Robin Flower, quoted in Bob Blaisdell, ed., *Irish Verse: An Anthology* (Mineola, NY: 2002), 4.

221. AKC Staff, "Scottish Deerhound History: A Hound Praised by the Kings," American Kennel Club (August 3, 2022), https://www.akc.org/expert-advice/dog-breeds/scottish-deerhound-history/.

222. Quoted from *The Letters of Symmachus* (1598) in Eleanor Hull's "Observations of Classical Writers on the Habits of the Celtic Nations, as Illustrated from Irish Records," *Celtic Review* 3 (10: 1906), 152.

223. Ibid., 153.

224. Jestice, 11.

225. Ibid.

226. Ibid.

227. Laura D. Gelfand, *Our Dogs, Our Selves: Dogs in Medieval and Early Modern Art, Literature, and Society* (Leiden: Brill, 2016), 151.

228. Alexander Neckham, *De naturis rerum librum duo,* quoted in Walker-Meikle, 10.

229. Elizabeth Sunderland, *In Search of the Picts: A Celtic Dark Age Nation* (London: Constable, 1994), 100.

230. Adomnan of Iona, *The Life of St Columba,* Richard Sharpe, trans. (London: Penguin, 1991), 227.

231. "Horses Saving Human Lives?! Horse Heroes," *Horse & Man: Exploring the Bonds Between Equines and Their People* (October 4, 2011), https://www.horseandman.com/.

232. Sunderland, 102.

233. Phyllis Fray Bober, "Cernunnos: Origin and Transformation of a Celtic

Divinity," *American Journal of Archaeology* 55 (1: 1951), 26.

234. David Flickett-Wilbar, "Cernunnos: Looking a Different Way," *Proceedings of the Harvard Celtic Colloquium* 23 (2003), 97–98.

235. Anthony Weir, "Enigmas of the Irish Crosses," Irish Megaliths, http://www.irishmegaliths.org.uk/crosses2.htm. (Accessed October 30, 2024.)

236. C. S. Lewis used the imagery of the white deer at both the beginning and the end of *The Lion, the Witch, and the Wardrobe*. A white stag pulls the White Witch's sleigh (a connection to evil), but at the end of the book, a white stag leads the children back to England. This may express Lewis's belief that even the things we perceive as evil may serve God's purposes and be redeemed, a perspective certainly reflected in the Celts' nondualism.

237. The Christian Celts considered their "place of resurrection" to be a particular place, unique to each individual, where God would lead them to settle—both physically and spiritually—to find the fullness of life and to prepare for death as the gateway to the next life.

238. J. G. McKay, "The Deer-Cult and the Deer-Goddess Cult of the Ancient Caledonians," *Folklore* 43 (2: 1932), 144–174. Like Brigid, who was both goddess and Christian saint, Gobnait and Ita may have been historical women whose stories were combined with earlier Pagan mythology about the goddess of the deer.

239. Number 21:9.

240. John 3:13–15.

241. David Voprada, "Good Serpent and Deer: Two Symbols of Christ in the Preaching of St Ambrose," *Studia Theologica* 15 (2: 2013), 238–252.

242. Only later in the Middle Ages did the snake become exclusively associated with evil. A later bestiary says, "The stag is the enemy of the snake. When the stag discovers a snake, it spits water into the hole where the snake hides, draws the snake out with its breath, and tramples it to death." In this case, the stag is a symbol of Christ who tramples the devil.

243. Weir.

244. Ibid.

245. Sutherland, 90.

246. Ibid.

247. Muirchu, *The Life of Saint Patrick by Muirchu*, in Oliver Davies, *Celtic Spirituality: The Classics of Western Spirituality* (Mahwah, NJ: Paulist Press, 1999), 102.

248. The first mention of this story occurs in the late twelfth century, in the writings of Jocelyn of Furness, a medieval chronicler.

249. J. Borsje, "Druids, Deer, and 'Words of Power': Coming to Terms with Evil in Medieval Ireland," in Katja Ritari and Alexandra Bergholm, eds.,

Approaches to Religion and Mythology in Celtic Studies (Newcastle, UK: Cambridge Scholars, 2008), 126.

250. For more on this, see Maxim Fomin, "Hunting the Deer in Celtic and Indo-European Mythological Contexts," in *Celtic Myth in the 21st Century: The Gods and Their Stories in a Global Perspective,* Emily Lyle, ed. (Cardiff: University of Wales, 2018), 73–87.

251. Sharon Begley, "Brainiacs, Not Birdbrains: Crows Possess Higher Intelligence Long Thought a Primarily Human Attribute, *STAT: Reporting from the Frontiers of Science and Medicine* (September 24, 2020), https://www.statnews.com/2020/09/24/crows-possess-higher-intelligence-long-thought-primarily-human/.

252. Luke 12:24.

253. Jestice, 293.

254. Badke, "Raven."

255. 1 Peter 5: 8–10

256. Revelation 5:5.

257. Badke, "Lion."

258. Badke, "Griffin."

259. Richard Stracke, *The Griffin: The Iconography, Christian Iconography* (April 15, 2022), https://www.christianiconography.info/griffin.html.

260. Kenneth McIntosh, *Water from an Ancient Well: Celtic Spirituality for Modern Life: Pilgrimage Study Edition* (Vestal, NY: Anamchara, 2023), 250.

Chapter 9

261. Ellyn Sanna, in Kenneth McIntosh, *Celtic Nature Prayers: Prayers from an Ancient Well* (Vestal, NY, Anamchara Books, 2015), 44–45.

262. Henning Kure, "Hanging on the World Tree: Man and Cosmos in Old Norse Mythic Poetry," in Anders Andrén, Kristina Jennbert, and Catharina Raudvere, eds., *Old Norse Religion in Long-term Perspectives: Origins, Changes, and Interactions* (Lund: Nordic Academic Press, 2006), 68–71.

263. Martyn Whittock and Hannah Whittock, *The Viking Blitzkrieg: AD 789–1098* (Stroud, UK: History Press, 2013), 20.

264. Psalm 120.

265. Whittock and Whittock, 18–19.

266. Jeremiah 1:14, quoted in ibid., 20.

267. In 2019, I walked with a group of church people the length of the Cuthbert Pilgrimage Trail, 62 miles from Melrose Scotland to Holy Island.

268. A more controversial theory is that Vikings targeted Christian places of worship as payback for the violent tactics of forced conversion the Frankish Empire had imposed on Saxony (Whittock and Whittock, 28–29).

269. Signage at the Church of Saint Mary's, Holy Island, Berwick-upon-Tweed, UK.

270. Whittock and Whittock, 217.

271. Ibid., 204–205. This incident is of dubious historical veracity, but the tale shows how biographers esteemed Canute's Christian faith.

272. Ibid., 22.

273. Ibid., 125.

274. J. R. Christianson, "Denmark: Planting the Seed," *Christian History Magazine* 63 (1999).

275. James W. Marchand, "Iceland: Althings Work to the Good," *Christian History Magazine* 63 (1999).

276. Whittock and Whittock, 206.

277. Máire de Paor, "The Viking Impact" in *Treasures of Irish Art 1500 B.C. to 1500 A.D.* (New York: Metropolitan Museum of Art, 1977), 152.

278. "The Gosforth Cross," Viking Archaeology, http://viking.archeurope.com/art/sculpture/gosforth-cross/. (Accessed November 5, 2024.)

279. Mark Redknap, *Vikings in Wales: An Archeological Quest* (Cardiff: National Museum Wales Books, 2000).

280. Nancy Edwards, *A Corpus of Early Medieval Inscribed Stones and Stone Sculptures in Wales, Vol. III* (Cardiff: University of Wales Press, 2013).

281. Revelation 12:9.

282. 1 John 3:8.

283. Elias Owen, *The Old Stone Crosses of the Vale of Clwyd* (Cardiff: Clwyd County Council Library & Information Service, 1995), 142–143.

284. Pennick, 114.

285. W. A. Chaney, "Paganism to Christianity in Anglo-Saxon England," *Harvard Theological Review* liii (1960), 209.

286. Quoted in ibid., 200.

287. G. K. Chesterton, *The Collected Works* (San Francisco, CA: Ignatius, 1986), 23

288. Luke 6:32, 35; editor's translation.

289. Luke 23:34.

290. John 19:34.

291. Mark 15:36.

292. Noel Muscat, "The Episode of San Damiano in the Sources for the Life of St. Francis," *Franciscan Studies* 10 (2018), 5.

293. Clare of Assisi, *Epistola Ad Sanctam Agnetem de Praga* IV, 15–18.

294. Marcus Borg, *Jesus and Buddha: The Parallel Sayings* (Berkeley, CA: Seastone, 1999), i–ii.

295. "Metta Meditation: A Complete Guide to Loving-Kindness," Lion's Roar: Buddhist Wisdom for Our Time, https://www.lionsroar.com/metta-meditation-guide/. (Accessed November 8, 2024.)

296. I recommend the resources you can find here: https://www.lionsroar.com/metta-meditation-guide/.

297. Philippians 4:8.

298. Calvin Miller, *The Path of Celtic Prayer* (Downers Grove, IL: IVP, 2007), 30.

Chapter 10

299. This "Encounter" is drawn from J. R. R. Tolken's *The Return of the King* (New York: Houghton Mifflin, 1955), 344ff.

300. Joseph Campbell, *The Hero with a Thousand Faces* (New York: Pantheon, 1949), 2.

301. Jean Shinoda Bolen, *Goddesses in Everywoman: Powerful Archetypes in Women's Lives* (New York: HarperCollins, 2004), 289.

302. John Micheal Porter, *He Descended into Hell* (Denison, TX: Porter Publishing, 2021), 38–39.

303. Porter, 43.

304. T. W. Rolleston, *Celtic Myths and Legends* (New York: Dover, 1990), 332.

305. Green, 30.

306. C. S. Lewis, *Miracles* (New York: Touchstone, 1996), 176.

307. Lewis, "Myth Became Fact" in *God in the Dock* (Grand Rapids, MI: Eerdmanns, 1998), 66–67.

308. Herren and Brown, 212.

309. Carol Jean Wolf, "Christ as Hero in 'The Dream of the Rood,'" *Neuphilogische Mitteilungen* 71 (2: 1970), 204.

310. Ibid., 203–207.

311. Psalm 24:8–9.

312. Psalm 107:17.

313. Ian Bradley, *Following the Celtic Way: A New Assessment of Celtic Christianity* (London: Dalton, Longman and Todd, 2018), 50.

314. Ibid.

315. In *The End and Beyond: Medieval Irish Eschatology*, John Carey, Emma Nic Cárthaigh, and Caitríona Ó Dochartaigh, eds. (Aberystwyth, Wales: Celtic Studies Publications, 2014), 449.

316. David H. Higgins, "'Christ Preaching in Limbo' Otherwise 'The

Harrowing of Hell' Bas-Relief in Bristol Cathedral," *Transactions of the Bristol and Gloucestershire Archaeological Society* 127 (2009), 213–231.

317. Morton W. Bloomfield and Charles W. Dunn, *The Role of the Poet in Early Societies* (Rochester, NY: D. S. Brewer, 1992), 82.

318. Ibid.

319. 1 Samuel 2:6.

320. Psalm 139:8.

321. John 5:25.

322. Acts 2:27.

323. Quoted in Porter, 77.

324. Luke 6:35–36.

325. Matthew 7:9.

326. Peter Burfeind, "The Harrowing of Hell: Filling in the Blanks," *Logia* 18 (2009), 7. (Italics are mine.)

327. Robert B. Burlin, "The Ruthwell Cross, 'The Dream of the Rood' and the Vita Contemplativa," *Studies in Philogyny* 65 (1: 1968), 40.

328. Ibid., 24.

329. Ibid., 33.

330. Carl Jung, *Psychology and Religion: West and East* (Princeton, NJ: Princeton University Press, 2014), 339.

331. Quoted in Michael Elgamal and Reda Fayek, *Anastasis: The Harrowing of Hades* (Guelph, ON: Creative Orthodox, 2017), 40.

332. Joseph Campbell with Bill Moyers, *Jospeh Campbell and the Power of Myth*, PBS (June 21, 1988).

Chapter 11

333. J. K. Elliott, *The Apocryphal Jesus: Legends of the Early Church* (Oxford, UK: Oxford University Press, 1996), 101.

334. Bahrami, 326.

335. Ibid.

336. "'Hate Put Me in Prison. Love's Gonna' Bust Me Out'—RIP Rubin 'Hurricane' Carter," CBC (April 20, 2014), https://www.cbc.ca/strombo/news/rip-rubin-hurricane-carter. (Accessed November 12, 2024.)

337. Herren and Brown, 213.

338. Ophelia Eryn Hostetter, trans., "The Descent into Hell," Old English Poetry Project, https://oldenglishpoetry.camden.rutgers.edu/. (Accessed November 13, 2024.)

339. Peter 3:18–20.

340. Luke 5:32.

341. 1 Peter 4:6.

342. 2 Esdras 4:40.

343. Archbishop Hilarion Alfeyev, *Christ the Conqueror of Hell: The Descent into Hades from an Orthodox Perspective* (Crestwood, NY: St. Vladimir's Seminary Press, 2009), 20–21.

344. Quoted in ibid., 32.

345. Quoted in ibid., 33

346. Quoted in Brown and Herren, 157.

347. Quoted in John Dominic Crossan and Sarah Sexton Crossan, *Resurrecting Easter: How the West Lost and the East Kept the Original Easter Vision* (New York: HarperCollins, 2018), 71.

348. Julian of Norwich, *All Shall Be Well: A Modern-Language Version of the Revelation of Julian of Norwich*, Ellyn Sanna, trans. (Vestal, NY: Anamchara Books, 2016), 64

349. Gospel of Nicodemus, Part II, available online at *Early Christian Writings*, https://www.earlychristianwritings.com/text/gospelnicodemus-roberts2.html.

350. Revelation 1:17–18.

351. Psalm 139:8.

352. 2 Corinthians 5:19.

353. "Atonement," *The Oxford English Dictionary (OED)*, second edition (Oxford, UK: Oxford University Press, 1989).

354. Porter, 91.

355. Genesis 1:31.

356. Brown and Herren, 156.

357. Dierdre Carabine, *John Scottus Eriugena* (Oxford, UK: Oxford University Press, 2000), 101.

358. Julian of Norwich, 64.

359. Frederick William Faber, "There's a Wideness in God's Mercy" (1862), available online at https://hymnary.org/text/theres_a_wideness_in_gods_mercy.

360. 1 John 3:8.

361. Ilaria L. E. Ramelli, "Origen in Augustine: A Paradoxical Reception," *Numen* 60 (2–3: 2013), 285.

362. Peter Dendle, *Satan Unbound: The Devil in Old English Narrative Literature* (Toronto: University of Toronto Press, 2001), 10.

363. Ibid., 134.

364. T. H. Mason, "The Devil as Depicted on Irish High Crosses," *The Journal of the Royal Society of Antiquaries of Ireland* 12 (4: 1942), 131. Most depictions of the devil on these crosses refer to two stories, either the temptation of Saint Anthony or the Last Judgement.

365. Hostetter. The publisher changed this translation only slightly, replacing "mankind" with "humanity."

366. C. S. Lewis, *Mere Christianity* (New York: Macmillan, 1952), 58–59.

367. "Hell," *OED*.

368. Matthew D. Arnold, *The Invisible Dimension: Spirits-Beings, Ghosts, and the Afterlife: A Biblical Perspective Based on Historical Context and the Original Languages* (Vestal, NY: Anamchara Books, 2024), 112.

369. Ecclesiastes 9:2–3.

370. Isaiah 9:2.

371. In *The End and Beyond*, 455–459.

372. C.S. Lewis, *Letters to Malcolm: Chiefly on Prayer* (New York, Harcourt, Brace & World, 1964), 107.

373. Ibid., 109.

374. Adapted from Judy Ponio's "10+ Catholic Prayers for the Departed" Lay Cistercians of South Florida (October 14, 2023), https://laycistercians. com/catholic-prayer-for-the-dead/.

375. Galatians 5:1; 2 Corinthians 3:17.

376. Fr. Peter Orfanakas, "Holy Saturday," Orthodox Christianity (April 14, 2014), https://orthochristian.com/69895.html.

Chapter 12

377. Author's gender-neutral translation.

378. Brown and Herren, 201.

379. Ilia Delio, *The Not-Yet God: Carl Jung, Teilhard de Chardin, and the Relational Whole* (New York: Orbis, 2023), 190.

380. Peter Stanford, *If These Stones Could Talk: The History of Christianity in Britain and Ireland Through Twenty Buildings* (London: Hodder & Stoughton, 2021), 4.

381. Martin Luther King Jr., *Strength to Love* (Boston: Beacon, 1963), 73.

382. António Guterres, *New Threats to Human Security in the Anthropocene: Demanding Greater Solidarity* (New York: United Nations Development Programme, 2022), iii, https://hs.hdr.undp.org/pdf/srhs2022.pdf.

383. 1 Corinthians 2:1–2, 4.

384. First quoted in Paul G. Hewitt's *Conceptual Physics* (Boston: Little, Brown, 1981), 51.

385. See Amit Goswami's *The Self-Aware Universe: How Consciousness Creates the Material World* (New York: TarcherPerigee, 1995).

386. Richard Geldard, *Remembering Heraclitus* (Great Barrington, MA: Lindisfarne Books, 2000), 156.

387. John 1:1, 3.

388. Acts 17:26.

389. Quoted in Robert Van Der Wyer, *Celtic Fire* (London: Darton, Longman, Todd, 1990), 96.

390. Carabine, 33.

391. Angela of Foligno, *The Book of the Visions and Instructions of Blessed Angela of Foligno* (London: Art & Book, 1903), 71.

392. Quoted by Ed Bacon in "Reconstructing Wholeness," Center for Christogenesis (September 14, 2018), https://christogenesis.org/reconstructing-wholeness/.

393. 2 Corinthians 5:19.

394. Bertrand Russell, *A History of Western Philosophy* (London: Routledge, 1946/1996), 400.

395. Ibid., 397.

396. Ibid.

397. Quoted in Brown and Herren, 201.

398. Ibid., 200.

399. Ibid.

400. Ibid., 201.

401. Francoise Henry, *Irish Art During the Viking Invasions* (Ithaca, NY: Cornell University Press, 1967), 162.

402. Mother Teresa, *Where There Is Love, There Is God: A Path to Closer Union with God and Greater Love for Others* (New York: Crown, 2010), 329–330.

403. James H. Cone, *The Cross and the Lynching Tree* (Maryknoll, NY: Orbis, 2011), xiv, 150.

404. Richard Rohr, *The Universal Christ: How a Forgotten Reality Can Change Everything We See, Hope For, and Believe* (New York: Random House, 2021), 162.

405. 1 Corinthians 12:24–26.

406. Ephesians 1:8–10 (author's gender-neutral translation).

407. If you're interested in finding out more about the mathematics behind the Mandelbrot set, as well as the history and implications of its discovery, see: Jordana Cepelwicz, "The Quest to Decode the Mandelbrot Set, Math's Famed Fractal," *Quanta Magazine* (January 26, 2024), https://www.quantamagazine.org/.

408. Peggy Reynolds, "The Mandelbrot Set: Mapping a Posthuman Ontology" (2013), http://www.peggyereynolds.com/mandelbrot_meditation.html.

409. This saying is often attributed to Gandhi, but it more likely derived from a popular bumper sticker in the 1970s.

Index

art 135–139, 143, 145, 153, 155–159, 161–164, 166–170, 172, 187, 203–204, 222–226, 255, 262
Arthur 248, 263
Artis, John 274
Asclepius, Rod of 197
Asia 132, 185, 299, 313
Athelston, King 221
Athlone Crucifix 251, 252
atonement 275, 283, 286–288
Augustine, Saint 67, 90, 283–285, 334
Avebury 39, 50, 62
Awen 255–256

Baldr 224
Balmacaan 195
barbarian 132, 203
bards 102, 158, 252
Basque 71–73
Bede 90, 305
Bennett, Andrew 100
bestiaries 185, 187, 191, 195, 201, 203
Beth El 39
Bible *See* scripture; also, individual books.
Blake, William 67
Blathmac 279
Bolen, Jean Shinoda 246
Bohr, Niels 150, 336
Boondock Saints 7
Bosch, Heironymus 135
boars 134, 183–184, 189
Bober, Phyllis Fray 193
Borg, Marcus 236
Boyer, Stephen 150
Boyne Valley 62

Brendan, Saint 253
Brigid
    Goddess 198, 339
    Saint 158, 162, 176–181, 190–191, 263, 333, 339
    Day 198
Bristol 255
    Cathedral 254
Brittany 10
Bronze Age 50, 117, 193, 263
Brown, Barbara Taylor 46
Brown, Lawrence Parmly 70
Brown, Shirley Anna 90
Bryce, Derek 88, 137
Buddha 37, 236
Burl, Aubrey 36
Burlin, Robert B. 260, 262
Byzantine
    art 25
    crosses 118, 307, 308
    Empire 88

Cadboll (cross) 136, 139, 143, 144, 191
caim 75–76
Cainnech, Saint 97
Calf of Man 230
Callanish stone circle 32, 36–37, 62
Camino de Santiago 67, 71, 95, 97, 98, 140, 272, 321
Campbell, Joseph 243, 245–246, 260, 263, 268
Canada 42, 275
Canute 220
Carbery, Mary 94
Carew Cross 136
Ceridwen 255
Carmichael, Andrew 69, 198

Ó Carragain, Eamonn 70

Oden, Thomas C. 116

Odin 200, 201, 210

Oengus the Culdee 117

Offaly, County 196

Ogham 159

Olaf, Saint 219

Old English 20, 260, 276, 287

Origen 160, 286, 334

Orkney 60–62, 215–217, 219

Orpheus 247

Osiris 71, 120, 167, 249

Otherworld 101, 102, 105, 193, 198,

Orthodox Church 25, 26, 71, 92,

118, 261, 295

Outer Hebrides 33–36

Paganism 60, 68, 89, 95, 133, 156,

181, 182, 184, 185, 193, 199, 200, 201,

222, 225, 227, 249, 251, 255, 286, 339

"Pangur Bán" 188–189

Paracelsus 67

Paradise 165, 248, 284, 291

Patrick, Saint 33, 68, 74, 76, 81, 89,

101, 157, 158, 162, 198–199, 331

Paul (apostle) 27, 43, 44, 149, 165,

239, 283, 299–302, 310

Paul (Egyptian saint) 20, 110,

112–116, 201

Peck, M. Scott 46–47, 91–92

Pelagius 284, 333

Pembrokeshire 136

Pennick, Nigel 227

Perth 141

Peter

    Epistles of 10, 21–22, 55, 202,

    274, 277–278

    Gospel of 22

Saint 165, 257

pharaohs 71, 117

Philippians, Epistle of 239

Physiologus 185

Picard, Jean Luc 264

Pictish beast 130–132, 134, 142, 145

Pict(ish) 52, 97, 116, 126–134, 136,

138–146, 157, 159, 168 ,169, 180,

181, 189–191, 194–196, 198–199,

201, 203, 204, 252

Pilgrim's Progress 274

Pliny 197

Portage, Michigan 154

Portuguese Way 140

prayers 75–78, 106, 107, 108, 123,

150–151

    for the dead 292–295

predestination 284

Presbyterian Church 7

Preseli 40

Protestantism 26, 92, 278, 287–

288, 293

Psalms, Book of 27, 43, 55, 65, 158,

159, 167, 214, 236, 251, 257, 271,

282, 291

Pseudo-Epiphanius 280

Pulliam, Heather 167–168

Pye, Patrick 26

Pyrenees 71

quantum physics 47, 138, 149, 300

Ravenna 306

ravens 114, 199–201, 206

Reask 91

resurrection (of Christ) 22, 66, 69,

154, 167–169, 261, 275, 276, 278

Water from an Ancient Well

Celtic Spirituality for Modern Life:
Pilgrimage Study Edition

This new version has more than 150 pages of previously unpublished material, including illustrated guides to Celtic pilgrimage sites, study questions, and updated research.

Using story, scripture, reflection, and prayer, Kenneth McIntosh offers us a taste of the living water that refreshed the ancient Celts, allowing them to perceive God as a living Presence in everybody and everything. This Earth-based and inclusive perspective suggests life-giving alternatives to modern faith practices, opening the door to a Christianity big enough to embrace the entire world.

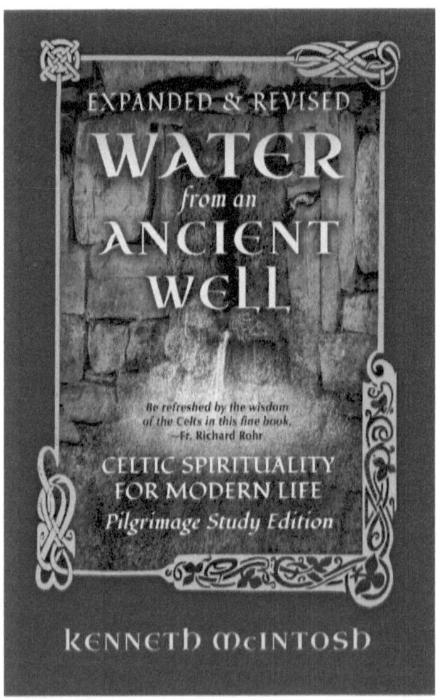

"If you want to run away to paradise for a couple of days, and drink living water from a source unlike any other, read Kenneth McIntosh's deeply satisfying book."

— Leonard Sweet,
best-selling author of *Nudge: Awakening Each Other to the God Who's Already There* and *So Beautiful: Divine Design for Life and the Church*

The Secret of the Green Man's Soul

I have a hidden meaning.
I was portrayed in a thousand different ways in the past,
and I keep sprouting again and again down through the centuries.
Don't you want to know who I am?

The Green Man is an ancient symbol that has gained new popularity, and yet his origins and meaning remain a mystery. Kenneth McIntosh, author of *Water from an Ancient Well: Celtic Spirituality for Modern Life*, offers a seldom-heard theory on the original significance of this leafy visage. With a wealth of drawings, the author traces the Green Man's family tree, revealing the deep spirituality embedded in this archetypal image, and concludes with the hope the Green Man offers us today in the twenty-first century.

"A joyful romp through the Celtic countryside, playing hide and seek with the illusive Green Man in all his forms. Part history, part spiritual journey, part memoir, Ken takes us face to face with the soul of Nature expressed through ancient carvings hidden in the architecture of the Celtic landscape. For anyone with a love of Celtic history, nature, and spirituality, whether it be Christian or Pagan, this book is a must read!"

— Lilly Weichberger, co-author of *Brigid's Mantle: A Celtic Dialogue Between Pagan and Christian*

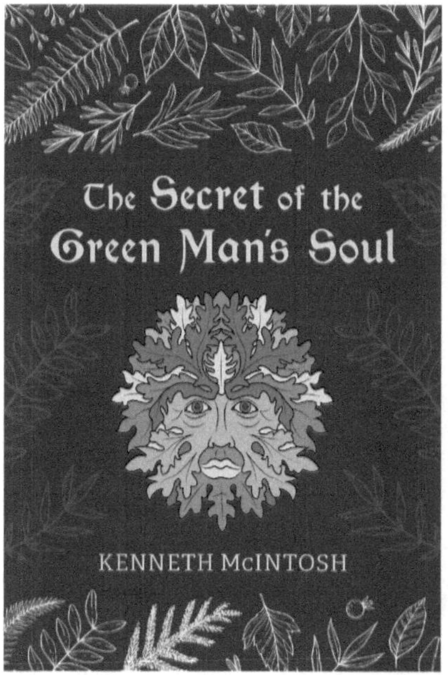

Brigid's Mantle

A Celtic Dialogue Between Pagan and Christian

Pagan and Christian Join Hands within Celtic Spirituality

Long ago, the story goes, Brigid flung out her mantle over the world. Beneath its shelter, the Earth and its people could find healing, insight, and growth. This legend, shared by both Celtic Pagans and Celtic Christians, makes the point that a mantle is not a box, a small rigid container meant to keep some things inside while excluding others. Instead, a mantle is wide, flexible, inclusive. Using this as their central metaphor, the authors—one a Pagan healer and the other a Christian minister—engage in a dialogue that is ultimately about what it means to be spiritual, to be a person of faith. While the authors agree that very real differences separate Paganism and Christianity, they affirm that shared points of understanding can be found under "Brigid's Mantle." They build on a concept of Celtic spirituality that embraces the arts, Nature, the supernatural world, compassion for those in need, and gender equality. Their

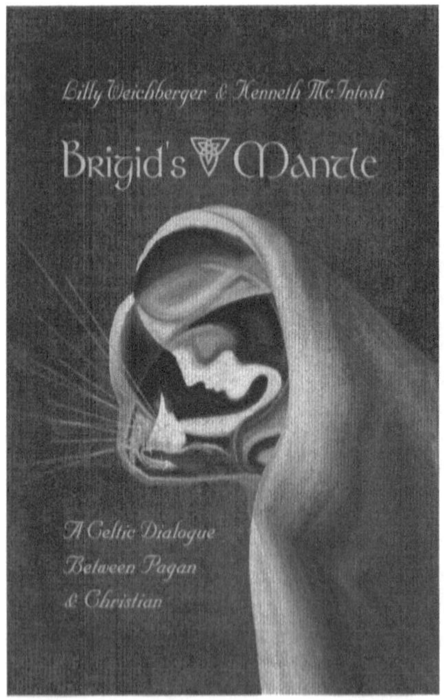

dialogue with one another allows us to see the ways in which this rich cultural heritage has deepened the authors' personal spiritual beliefs and practices in ways that are surprisingly similar. Readers—Christian, Pagan, and neither—will find here not only a fascinating example of comparative religion but also a rich source of personal inspiration and insight. With its emphasis on the natural environment, justice, and creativity, Celtic spirituality has much to say to the modern world.

Celtic Miracles and Wonders
Tales from the Ancient Saints

There are other accounts of these saints' lives, many that are far more historically accurate, but those contained here tell us as much about the people who told the stories as they do about the ancient saints. They show us those saints' legacy lived out in people's lives and imaginations more than a thousand years later. The power and vitality of that legacy is impressive. These stories reveal an ongoing conviction that the invisible world is as real as the visible one. They show us human beings living in constant, tangible friendship with God, with the supernatural, and with animals. They lead us into a world where holiness and the imagination have joined hands, a world where we can truly catch glimpses of miracles and wonders.

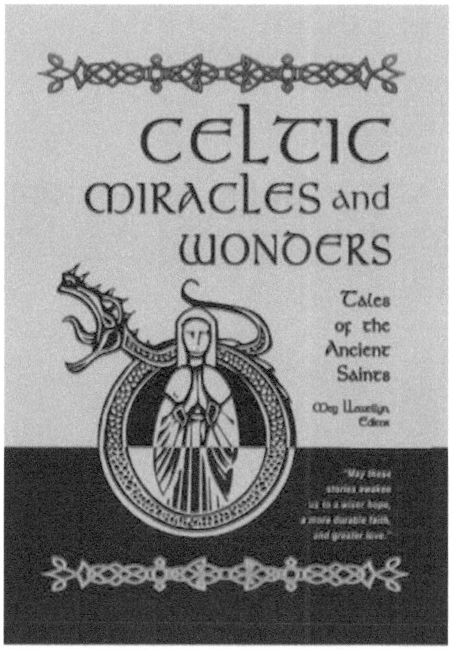

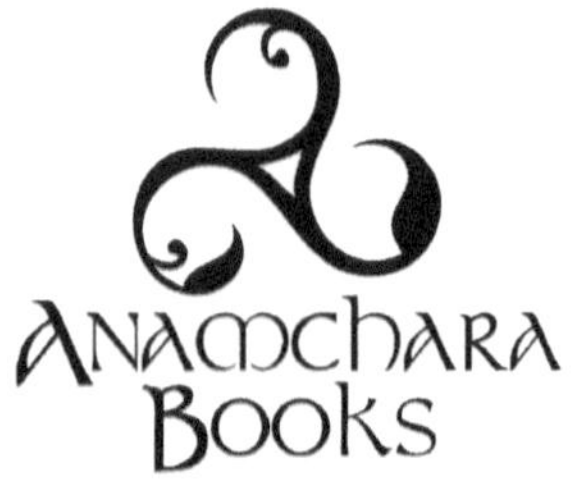

Anamchara
Books

AnamcharaBooks.com